Realism and Sociology

D0548106

Can philosophy guide empirical research in the social sciences?

In recent years methodological debates in the social sciences have increasingly focused on issues relating to epistemology. *Realism and Sociology* makes an original contribution to the debate, charting a middle ground between post-modernism and positivism.

Critics often hold that realism tries to assume some definitive account of reality. Against this it is argued throughout the book that realism can combine a strong definition of social reality with an anti-foundational approach to knowledge. The position of realist anti-foundationalism that is argued for is developed and defended via the use of immanent critiques. These deal primarily with post-Wittgensteinian positions that seek to define knowledge and social reality in terms of 'rule-following practices' within different 'forms of life' and 'language games'. Specifically, the argument engages with Rorty's neo-pragmatism and the structuration theory of Giddens. The philosophy of Popper is also drawn upon in a critically appreciative way.

While the positions of Rorty and Giddens seek to deflate the claims of 'grand theory', albeit in different ways, they both end up with definitive claims about knowledge and reality that preclude social research. By avoiding the general deflationary approach that relies on reference to 'practices', realism is able to combine a strong social ontology with an anti-foundational epistemology, and thus act as an underlabourer for empirical research.

Justin Cruickshank is a lecturer in Methodology and the Philosophy of Social Science in the Nottingham Graduate School for Social Research, at Nottingham Trent University. He is the Deputy Editor of the *Journal of Critical Realism*.

Routledge Studies in Critical Realism

Edited by Margaret Archer, Roy Bhaskar, Andrew Collier, Tony Lawson and Alan Norrie

Critical realism is one of the most influential new developments in the philosophy of science and in the social sciences, providing a powerful alternative to positivism and postmodernism. This series will explore the critical realist position in philosophy and across the social sciences.

1. Marxism and Realism
A materialistic application of realism in the social sciences
Sean Creaven

2. Beyond Relativism
Raymond Boudon, cognitive rationality and critical realism
Cynthia Lins Hamlin

3. Education Policy and Realist Social Theory
Primary teachers, child-centred philosophy and the new managerialism
Robert Wilmott

4. Hegemony
A realist analysis
Jonathan Joseph

5. Realism and Sociology
Anti-foundationalism, ontology and social research
Justin Cruickshank

Also published by Routledge:

Critical Realism: Interventions
Edited by Margaret Archer, Roy Bhaskar, Andrew Collier, Tony Lawson and Alan Norrie

Critical Realism
Essential readings
Edited by Margaret Archer, Roy Bhaskar, Andrew Collier, Tony Lawson and Alan Norrie

The Possibility of Naturalism 3rd edition
A philosophical critique of the contemporary human sciences
Roy Bhaskar

Being and Worth
Andrew Collier

Quantum Theory and the Flight from Realism
Philosophical responses to quantum mechanics
Christopher Norris

From East to West
Odyssey of a soul
Roy Bhaskar

Realism and Racism
Concepts of race in sociological research
Bob Carter

Rational Choice Theory
Resisting colonisation
Edited by Margaret Archer and Jonathan Q. Tritter

Explaining Society
Critical realism in the social sciences
Berth Danermark, Mats Ekström, Jan C. Karlsson and Liselotte Jakobsen

Critical Realism and Marxism
Edited by Andrew Brown, Steve Fleetwood and John Michael Roberts

Critical Realism in Economics
Edited by Steve Fleetwood

Realist Perspectives on Management and Organisations
Edited by Stephen Ackroyd and Steve Fleetwood

After International Relations
Critical realism and the (re)construction of world politics
Heikki Patomaki

Realism and Sociology

Anti-foundationalism, ontology
and social research

Justin Cruickshank

London and New York

First published 2003 by Routledge
11 New Fetter Lane, London EC4P 4EE

Simultaneously published in the USA and Canada
by Routledge
29 West 35th Street, New York NY 10001

Routledge is an imprint of the Taylor & Francis Group

© 2003 Justin Cruickshank

Typeset in Baskerville by Keyword Publishing Services
Printed and bound in Great Britain by Antony Rowe Ltd,
Chippenham, Wiltshire

British Library Cataloguing in Publication Data
a catalogue record for this book is available
from the British Library

Library of Congress Cataloging in Publication Data
Cruickshank, Justin, 1969–
   Realism and sociology: anti-foundationalism, ontology, and social
   research / Justin Cruickshank.
     p. cm.
   Includes bibliographical references and index.
   ISBN 0-415-26190-2
    1. Sociology – Methodology. 2. Sociology – Philosophy. 3. Realism.
    4. Ontology. I. Title.

HM511.C78 2002
301'.01–dc21   2002069961

ISBN 0–415–26190–2

Contents

Figures

Acknowledgements

The research undertaken for the writing of this book was made possible by a four-year research and teaching grant I received from the Sociology Department at the University of Warwick. I would like to thank Margaret Archer for encouraging me to apply for this, and for giving me critical input and support during the writing of this book. I would also like to thank Roger Trigg for his helpful comments on the draft chapters. Thanks are also due to Andrew Collier, Tony Elger, Richard Lampard, William Outhwaite, Ian Procter, and Andrew Sayer, for their comments, advice and help. When it came to finishing the text, Sandra Odell provided valuable editorial assistance, for which I am very grateful.

Introduction

Contemporary sociology is in something of a state of flux. Debates about the compatibility of quantitative and qualitative methods have followed on from years when quantitative methods and qualitative methods were thought by many to be antithetical; whilst in the realms of theory, debates turn on what role (if any) 'grand theory' may play, how theory may relate to methods, and what sort of truth claims may be advanced by theory in an age that views knowledge claims with suspicion. Whilst sociology has (ultimately) always been a discipline that has tended to avoid the development of a rigid canonical orthodoxy with regard to methods and theory, the contemporary debates mark a heightened degree of reflexivity concerning the intellectual character of the discipline. The present time is therefore a time that is quite conducive to the posing of meta-level questions, concerning the relationship between theory and methods, and the status of truth claims furnished by philosophy, social theory and research.

What I seek to do in this book is argue for a link between realist philosophy, realist theory and empirical research, in a way that gives theory (and philosophy) a strong role to play, but without assuming that theory supplies a privileged path to reality-in-itself. In Chapter 1 I begin this task by discussing the philosophies of Popper and Putnam. After describing Popper's critique of logical positivism, I argue that Popper has a post-Kantian approach to knowledge, which replaces a foundational epistemology, based on the notion of a manifest truth, with an anti-foundational epistemology, based on the notion that our knowledge of the world is mediated through conceptual schemes. This is post-Kantian because, with Kant, Popper agrees that our knowledge of the world is interpreted through 'categories', but against Kant, Popper holds that our categories change, because they are open to critical revision following empirical testing.

Turning from epistemology to ontology, Popper accepts the metaphysical realist claim that there is a reality beyond our perspectives, interpretations, beliefs, ideas, propositions, etc., and rejects the converse metaphysical claim, viz. idealism, that what is real is reducible to our ideas, or perspectives. Three points need to be made here. The first is that such a metaphysical claim simply holds that reality is irreducible down to our knowledge of it, or our ideas of it. Metaphysical realism has no specific claims about reality, such as the claim that 'superstrings' exist, for instance. The second point is that Popper does not claim that we can *prove* idealism wrong and realism right. He simply thinks that realism is a more *useful* thesis, as science is pointless if reality becomes that which we construct through our ideas. So metaphysical realism is psychologically useful, because without assuming it correct, scientists would lack the motivation to continue producing scientific knowledge. The third point is that as realism cannot be proved, because it is a metaphysical thesis and not an empirical claim, then for Popper it follows that metaphysical realism is not a necessary presupposition for science. Unlike the logical positivists of the Vienna Circle who held that any metaphysical claim was meaningless, Popper thinks that (some) metaphysical arguments can be meaningful but, as such arguments are metaphysical, they cannot be scientific (as, for Popper, science is defined exclusively in terms of empirical conjectures).

Consequently we end up with an argument for an anti-foundational epistemology that is not underpinned by a metaphysical realist ontology. The result is that reality (or being) becomes reducible to knowing, because *what* exists ends up being defined in epistemological terms of reference concerning *how* we may know the world. This reduction of questions about being into terms of reference concerning epistemological questions is referred to, following Bhaskar (1997: 16), as the 'epistemic fallacy'.

Putnam, unlike Popper, does take issue with metaphysical realism, because he maintains that metaphysical realism implies some sort of absolute knowledge. Against metaphysical realism Putnam argues for 'internal realism', whereby what we know is derived from a perspective and not by knowledge mirroring (all of) reality. Putnam is mistaken though because, as noted above, metaphysical realism is not a substantive ontology that makes claims about specific aspects of being and, further to this, a metaphysical realist ontology makes no claims about how we may know what exists.

Conversely, Putnam's internal realism is a position that is concerned with substantive claims about being, but this internal realism is predicated upon the epistemic fallacy and the genetic fallacy. Internal realism is predicated upon the epistemic fallacy because the ontological question concerning what exists is answered using (anti-foundational) epistemological terms of reference which hold that what exists is what we can know via our perspective. The epistemic fallacy leads on to the genetic fallacy because as reality becomes defined in terms of the perspective, it follows that the truth of a concept is not derived from its relation to an extra-discursive reality, but from its *origin within a conceptual scheme*. The real becomes what we know, and what we know is determined by perspectives, and so truth is reduced to perspectives that end up constructing their own (putative) reality. In other words, the emphasis on perspectives and denial of metaphysical realism leads to truth-relativism whereby all perspectives are equally 'true' as all perspectives are self-referential (given the lack of reference to an external reality).

From this I conclude that an anti-foundational epistemology needs to be complemented by a metaphysical realist ontology. This leads me to argue for a philosophical position that I refer to as 'realist anti-foundationalism', and to argue against what I refer to as the 'philosophical logic of immediacy'. Whereas the main claim of realist anti-foundationalism is that we can have a fallible access to a reality that is irreducible to our interpretations of it, the main tenet of philosophical logic of immediacy is that we have an unmediated and direct access to the truth. This can be a direct access to a material realm with the foundationalist philosophical logic of immediacy, or it can be in the form of having a direct access to social norms or concepts within a perspective *qua* truths, with the relativist philosophical logic of immediacy. So with the foundationalist philosophical logic of immediacy it is held that the mind can mirror discrete facts (or that propositions can correspond to discrete facts), and with the relativist philosophical logic of immediacy, to know the prevailing norms or concepts is to know the truth as truth is reduced to such norms or concepts. Against this, realist anti-foundationalism accepts that we know the world through perspectives but qualifies this by saying that truth is irreducible to perspectives because truth concerns an interpretation of a world that is irreducible to our interpretations of it, and such interpretations are fallible given the lack of direct access.

Whilst the relativist philosophical logic of immediacy underpins postmodernism, which therefore makes postmodern social science untenable, because the relativist claims are unable to give us any truth about social reality, the foundationalist philosophical logic of immediacy underpins the attempt to use social ontologies that furnish definitive accounts of social reality.[1] In the latter case a master-ontology would list all the facts that one needed to know to explain human behaviour. Such ontologies may list facts about individuals or social/holistic facts, giving us the individualist and structuralist sociological logic of immediacy, respectively. With the sociological logic of immediacy one may either explain all human behaviour by *reading it off* from the definitive ontology of, say, human nature or social structures; or one may *read it into* empirical work, verifying the ontology that one knew to be true already, and cutting the data to fit the theory. In neither case therefore could empirical research yield any knowledge of social reality.

With the sociological logic of immediacy, ontology assumes the role of what I refer to as a 'master-builder', meaning that an ontology is used as an exhaustive account of being. This is not to say that any ontological scheme that contains some substantive claims about being (unlike the metaphysical realist ontology that makes no substantive claims about being) will assume the role of master-builder. One may have a substantive ontology that is more modest: one may have a substantive ontology that acts as an 'underlabourer' and not a master-builder. An underlabourer ontology would not supply a set of specific facts about being, let alone presume to supply all the facts about being but, instead, it would supply *some general precepts to guide empirical research*.

The methodological individualists, as discussed in Chapter 2, sought to avoid the use of a master-ontology. So the methodological individualists argued against psychologistic reductionism and holism determinism, whereby a master-ontology of mind or social structures, respectively, would provide a definitive account of human behaviour. This did avoid the use of a master-builder ontology, but the methodological individualists used a form of empiricist epistemology as an underlabourer. This empiricism led the methodological individualists to argue that what was real was that which could be observed, with the consequence that only individuals were held to be real (as structures could not be seen). Methodological individualists tried to talk of individuals interacting in 'situational logics', but this simply begged the question as to what the social context could be that enabled and constrained individuals' agency. The methodological collectivists made bolder claims about social reality but they too were influenced by a form of empiricism and so they ran into the same problems as the methodological individualists. In both cases a notion of social reality is invoked, and then left undefined, which means that such a definition may be used in an arbitrary way.

The next step in my argument is not to consider how some people have developed social ontologies to be used as guiding underlabourers, but to consider the neo-pragmatist position of Rorty. If Rorty's position were accepted then we would have to change the definition of philosophy that I am using (viz. that of philosophy as a second-order discipline, that enquires into the conditions of possibility of social science knowledge), to a definition that (ironically) interprets philosophy as 'literature' or poetry or rhetoric by regarding philosophical argument in terms of its aesthetic ability to influence our perceptions of people, politics, and science. Rorty seeks to 'deflate' philosophy, together with social and political theory, and to put the emphasis on the practices that help people to go on within various 'forms of life' or 'language games'. One consequence of this is that social science could no longer be regarded as giving us some form of truth about social reality (through either theory or empirical research) because the notions of truth and reality are rejected in favour of reference to practices. Therefore either social science would have to concern itself solely with policies that 'worked', or social scientists would have to leave the academy and enter into political activity. Unless, that is, they were prepared to accept the view that their work (that was not directly related to policy) was to be judged on its aesthetic ability to appeal to people and to get them to change their minds by 'seeing things differently' (thus replacing social science with political rhetoric, or 'poetics'). In which case, such an 'aesthetic' social 'science' would produce texts for private edification (for men and women of letters, 'at the weekend'), rather than produce practical answers to practical problems in the realm of public policy.

Rorty seeks to use a post-Wittgensteinian neo-pragmatism to underlabour in the sense that such a position is to be used to 'deflate' the claims of philosophy (and, we may add, social science), and make us change our perspective on such claims, from a perspective concerning truth, to a perspective concerning 'usefulness' (and aesthetic value too). This project cannot succeed because, I argue in Chapter 3, it breaks down into a number of problematic positions, premised on the philosophical and sociological logics of immediacy.

In Chapter 4 I turn my attention to Giddens' 'structuration theory'. Giddens tries to resolve the structure-agency problematic, by producing a social ontology that avoids the sociological logics of immediacy, by avoiding an individualist reductionism or an holistic determinism. In developing his structuration theory Giddens draws upon Wittgenstein's later philosophy (amongst other work) to define social reality in terms of rule-following practices. This ontology of rule-following practices though cannot serve as an underlabourer to guide research because it unfolds into the individualist and structuralist sociological logics of immediacy. Further, Giddens holds that his ontology can be applied in a piecemeal way to sociological research. We may call this a deflationary approach to methodology, because it removes the claim of an underlabouring ontology to inform *all* research, in order to argue for a piecemeal 'pragmatic' use of the theory. I argue that this confuses the issue of how to apply an ontology with how much of a ontology to apply. It is not the case that if one applies only parts of an ontology then one avoids the sociological logic of immediacy, because (a) if the ontology is predicated on the sociological logic of immediacy then only applying a part of this will not avoid the problem, and (b) if the ontology is applied in a piecemeal way then its application will be arbitrary because one will have conceded that an underlabouring ontology is not *necessary* for research, in which case it can have no reasoned application (as an underlabourer).

In the fifth chapter I discuss the work on social realism by Bhaskar and Archer. It is argued that the social realist ontology, that seeks to link structure and agency by using the notion of 'emergent properties', can provide a useable ontological underlabourer for sociological research. This means then that realist anti-foundationalism may be complemented by a social realist ontology, for sociological research. Whilst the fifth chapter deals with a description of social realism and a discussion of the Marxist and Wittgensteinian critiques of social realism, the sixth chapter deals with how social realism may be used as an underlabourer for research into chronic unemployment. In Chapter 6 it is argued that for a general ontology to guide empirical research and the formation of specific theories, it is necessary to develop a 'domain-specific meta-theory'. This domain-specific meta-theory is developed from an immanent critique of some of the existing explanations of chronic unemployment. These explanations are examined to see to what extent they are able to account for chronic unemployment and, in developing some new concepts to deal with the deficiencies, the general precepts from the general social realist ontology are drawn upon. This is not to imply that the conceptual contents of the domain-specific meta-theory are infallible or a definitive guide to social reality, as the precepts guide research (rather than describing a set of 'facts' known prior to research), and the conceptual contents of the domain-specific meta-theory are open to revision during the course of research.

So, if the praxis approaches of Rorty and Giddens, with their deflationary approach to philosophy/theory and emphasis on practices, are regarded as an alternative to the self-negating relativism of postmodernism, and realism is shown as a better alternative, then I may have gone some way to achieving my task of showing that realism provides the best way to link theory and methods within sociological research. Of course it may be objected that empirical research does not need a theoretical underlabourer to supply some guiding precepts. Against this it can be argued that all research is informed and influenced by some precepts (as there is no direct access to reality-in-itself) and so it is better to make these precepts explicit, in order to avoid arbitrariness. This is especially true with ontological precepts, because our approach to the world is influenced by presumptions about being. Therefore it is important to resolve the structure-agency problematic, and apply the social ontology that can link structure and agency because without this, accounts of social reality will not be able coherently to achieve a grounded explanation of how people's agency is socially mediated (i.e. enabled and constrained). Instead we would have accounts that were arbitrary or begged the question.

The realism as developed in this book may therefore act as an underlabourer in two senses. It may act as a negative underlabourer to remove positions that are predicated upon the philosophical and sociological logics of immediacy. It may also act as a positive underlabourer to inform empirical research, by supplying some ontological precepts. Before seeing how realism may be applied though, we need to see how a realist philosophical stance may be justified, which is the task of the next chapter.

1 The philosophical logic of immediacy

The epistemic fallacy and the genetic fallacy

Introduction

The philosophical logic of immediacy is a term that refers to positions that hold that truth is knowable with immediacy. The temporal aspect of this is that truth is known 'immediately', meaning that the truth can be recognised 'straight away': the manifest truth is immediately recognisable as such. The corollary of this is that the truth is known without any conceptual mediation: it is not that the truth is mediated via this or that perspective through which we (may) gain (some) access to a reality beyond perspectives, but that the manifest truth presents itself as such without any mediating – or interpreting – factors. The philosophical logic of immediacy may be thought to underpin foundationalist epistemologies, such as empiricism, especially in the guise of the Vienna Circle's logical positivism. This is true, but the philosophical logic of immediacy also underpins what we may refer to as truth-relativism. The reason for this is that in making truth *wholly* relative to perspectives, such relativism *reduces* truth to perspectives, and the consequence of this is that to know the norms of a community, or to know the concepts that constitute, say, a scientific perspective, or paradigm, is to know the truth. In this case 'truth' becomes a synonym for the contents of the perspective.

Both foundationalism and relativism are therefore anthropocentric in the sense that the world is 'made for us'. In the former case, the world is defined to fit a philosophy that explains how the mind will get knowledge, and in the latter case, the world becomes socially constructed through the norms or concepts that constitute perspectives. With foundationalism we therefore have the epistemic fallacy whereby ontological questions concerning the definition of reality are framed and answered according to epistemological terms of reference; and so ontology is reduced into epistemology. Once ontological questions have been posed in epistemological terms of reference, a possible next step is to alter the epistemological terms of reference, from foundational terms of reference concerning how the mind may know reality, to anti-foundational terms of reference, concerning the use of perspectives to know reality. Such an anti-foundationalism would answer ontological questions using the epistemological argument that knowledge was situated within a perspective.

The result would be that what was real was what we knew to be real, and what we knew to be real would be constituted by the norms or concepts of the perspective in which we were situated. Such a position commits the genetic fallacy because the truth of a concept, or belief, or norm, etc., is derived from its origin within a perspective and not from its relationship to reality. If reality is defined in terms of the contents of a perspective, then it follows that the concepts within the perspective must be self-referential, as there can be no way to refer to a reality external to those terms of reference.

It may be objected that no names (other than that of the Vienna Circle) have been linked to the positions outlined above, which may be referred to as the foundationalist philosophical logic of immediacy, and the relativist philosophical logic of immediacy. This (initial) omission is deliberate because my purpose is to show how positions end up being predicated upon the philosophical logic of immediacy, rather than to list positions under headings. That is to say, my concern is with developing an immanent critique of positions whose terms of reference appear to be tenable, in the sense that they appear to say how our knowledge is neither foundational nor relative. This immanent critique aims to see how the tensions and problems that arise with such terms of reference arise because the said terms of reference lack the philosophical resources to support the claims being made. As a consequence of this lack, the positions criticised end up being predicated upon the logic of immediacy. The logic of immediacy therefore pertains to philosophical systems whereby the underlying logic is one which compels the argument into a foundationalist and/or relativist view of truth, and the epistemic and genetic fallacies, even though the explicit argument, or rhetoric, runs counter to this. So, whilst some positions may be clear examples of the logic of immediacy (as with logical positivism, for instance), my main concern is with developing immanent critiques to show how some philosophical arguments are predicated upon the logic of immediacy due to an absence of conceptual resources, as opposed simply to rejecting positions that clearly argue for immediacy (such as the positivist adherence to foundational immediacy or, arguably, some postmodern arguments which hold that everything is a construct within discourse).

The above points are developed in relation to the philosophies of Popper and Putnam. Rather than focus on Popper's arguments about deductive methods, I focus on Popper's general post-Kantian approach to epistemology and argue that whilst this avoids the foundationalism associated with logical positivism, it still ends up committing the epistemic fallacy and, ultimately, the genetic fallacy. So, Popper 'opens the door', so to speak, to relativism, with his post-Kantian alternative to positivism. The issue of relativism is then pursued in a discussion of Putnam's internal realism. Putnam, like Popper, takes Kant as a starting point, but Putnam argues that Kant's transcendental idealism may lead to questions about 'reality-in-itself' that are to be rejected because they lead us back to the questions posed by, according to Putnam, metaphysical realists who, he contends, seek a master-ontology of being (or

God's-eye view). His alternative is to turn to the work of the later Wittgenstein, and to argue that truth about reality is always situated within a perspective that helps us 'go on' in the world.

Whereas Popper takes up a post-Kantian view and opens the door to relativism by failing to complement this anti-foundational epistemology with a metaphysical realist ontology, Putnam starts with Kant and then moves on to argue that the later Wittgenstein asked better questions than Kant, viz. practical questions concerning how we go on within a form of life, with meaning being connected to the activities within a form of life, rather than philosophical questions about the condition of possibility of knowledge. The upshot of Putnam's internal realism is relativism and the genetic fallacy as truth is reduced to the contents of a 'language game'. One conclusion to draw from this is that Popper asked the better questions, concerning how we may have knowledge without empiricist immediacy, but he failed to develop the right answers, because he remained concerned with epistemology (albeit in an anti-foundational form), and neglected ontology. Another, and directly related, conclusion to draw from this is that anti-foundationalism needs to be complemented by a metaphysical realist ontology, giving us realist anti-foundationalism.

Popper and the critique of positivism

Popper responded critically to the logical empiricism, or logical positivism, advocated by the Vienna Circle. According to such positivism, meaningful propositions and science were to be demarcated from meaningless propositions, pseudo-science and empty metaphysical speculation, by the verification principle. A proposition was meaningful if it could be verified by sense-data/empirical observation. So, the proposition that the faster an engine runs, *ceteris paribus*, the more fuel it will consume, is meaningful, whereas propositions about art being beautiful, or not, God existing, or not, etc., would be meaningless. In searching for causal laws in nature, the verification principle was operationalised via an inductivist methodology. A causal law was said to exist if there was a constant conjunction between two observed events. From observing one event following another, it was assumed that one could derive a relationship of natural necessity. Scientific knowledge was thus based on the certainty that in observing regularities, causal laws, or relations of necessity, were being observed; whilst any proposition which could not be grounded in certainty, by being empirically verifiable, was held to be meaningless.

One problem with trying to ground knowledge on empirical certainty, by arguing that meaningful propositions can be open to verification, is that the verification principle itself cannot be verified. As Trigg argues, '[t]he starting-point of logical-positivism cannot itself be justified and indeed by its own lights should be regarded as meaningless' (1993: 20). As Trigg notes though, Ayer argued that the verification principle should be treated as an axiom rather than a criterion of meaning. However, Trigg continues, this failed to explain why we should retain the failed criterion (1993: 20). If the verification principle failed to do its job, it seems rather arbitrary to redefine its job, so that it can do some limited 'guiding' work.

If we move from the verificationist criterion of meaningfulness, to the inductivist search for empirical regularities, we meet another problem. The logical problem with induction is that from a limited set of observations one cannot say that one has observed a relationship of natural necessity, whereby the observed regularity will necessarily obtain in the future. As Popper argues,

> it is far from obvious, from a logical point of view, that we are justified in inferring universal statements from singular ones, no matter how numerous; for any conclusion drawn in this way may always turn out to be false: no matter how many instances of white swans we may have observed, this does not justify the conclusion that *all* swans are white.
>
> (1972a: 27; emphasis in original)

Popper argues that this logical 'problem of induction' was first recognised by Hume, but that Hume drew the wrong conclusion (1975: 96). Hume argued that even though induction is logically wrong, we still use it in practice, with habit and repetition being used to locate 'causal' relations, or constant conjunctions. We may *only* locate constant conjunctions which habit and custom pick out, but *this is all we can do* according to Hume. Popper though rejects this view, on the grounds that as induction is based on a logical fallacy, an alternative methodology is required; as we will see.

In addition to criticising the logical-positivist conception of scientific methodology, Popper also criticised the empiricist philosophy of mind, upon which positivism was premised. For Popper, the very attempt to define knowledge in terms of the mind is a fallacious endeavour.[1] The problem is that reality ends up being defined in terms of the mind: what *exists* is defined as what can be *known*, and what can be known is defined by *how the mind knows* via sense experience. We have certainty in knowledge because *what* the mind can know, meaning what exists, is defined to fit the conception of *how* the mind can know the world. Popper argues that

> The empiricist philosopher's belief 'that all knowledge is derived from sense experience' leads with necessity to the view that all knowledge must be knowledge of either our present sense experience (Hume's 'ideas of impressions') or of our past sense experience (Hume's 'ideas of reflection'). Thus all knowledge becomes knowledge of what is going on in our minds. *On this subjective basis, no objective theory can be built*: the world becomes the totality of my ideas, of my dreams.
>
> (1996: 82; emphasis in original)

The problem with the empiricist philosophy of mind therefore is that what is known is what is experienced, and all we can experience are our *ideas* of sensation, and not a material realm beyond those ideas of sensation. Therefore

> we are never 'justified' or 'entitled' to claim the truth of a theory, or of a belief, by reason of the alleged immediacy or directness of the belief. This, in my view, is putting the cart before the horse: immediacy or directness may be the result of the biological fact that a theory is true and also (partly for this reason) very useful for us. But to argue that immediacy or directness establishes truth, or is a criterion of truth, is *the fundamental mistake of idealism.*
>
> (1975: 68; emphasis in original)

So, we may think that having burnt our hand on a fire we will avoid such contact again, and the belief that the fire caused the pain will be true. Nonetheless, we cannot infer from this the conclusion that a belief is true *because we immediately recognise the truth*, through sensation. Sensation refers to ideas of sensation and not to the mind seeing an external reality as it really is.

Against the view that we have an immediate access to a manifest truth via sense-data, Popper argues that our experience of the external world is mediated via concepts and beliefs. Popper argues that

> According to my view, observations (or 'sensations' or 'sense-data', etc.) are [...] not the raw material of knowledge. On the contrary, observations always presuppose previous dispositional knowledge. An observation is the result of a stimulus that *rings a bell.* What does this mean? The stimulus must be *significant*, relative to our system of expectations or anticipations, in order to ring a bell, and thus to be observed.
>
> (1996: 99; emphasis in original)

If knowledge came from sense-data alone then we would be overwhelmed by a constant barrage of data. This is avoided because the incoming data are interpreted and filtered by a set of interests and concepts which may be either unreflective or explicitly formulated. Access to the world is always via a 'prejudice', '[y]et we proceed perfectly rationally: we learn, we extend our knowledge, by *testing* our prejudices; by trial and error rather than by induction through repetition' (Popper 1996: 100; emphasis in original). All of which brings us to Popper's distinction between the bucket and the searchlight.

Popper on post-Kantian epistemology, falsifiability and metaphysical realism

Discussing the 'bucket theory of science', or the 'bucket theory of mind' (1975: 341), Popper states that

The starting point of this theory is the persuasive doctrine that before we can know or say anything about the world, we must first have had perceptions – sense experiences. It is supposed to follow from this doctrine that our knowledge, our experiences, consists either of accumulated perceptions (naive empiricism) or else of assimilated, sorted, and classified perceptions (a view held by Bacon and, in a more radical form, by Kant). [...] According to this view, then, our mind resembles a container – a kind of bucket – in which perceptions and knowledge accumulate.

(1975: 341)

Against this bucket theory of the mind, Popper thus argues that scientists have to construct theoretical searchlights which, if well constructed, will at best only illuminate a small proportion of reality, until a better searchlight is constructed. Popper argues that

In science it is observation rather than perception which plays the decisive part. But observation is a process in which we play an intensely *active* part. An observation is a perception, but one which is planned and prepared. We do not 'have' an observation [...] but we 'make' an observation [...]. An observation is always preceded by a particular interest, a question, or a problem – in short, by something theoretical.

(1975: 342)

What we know of the world is therefore dependent upon the searchlight that scientists construct, and so the 'facts' accumulated by science will be relative to this or that searchlight, as opposed to being akin to unchanging pebbles placed into a previously empty bucket (as *tabula rasa* mind).

The general epistemological position here is that of post-Kantianism. In Popper's words, 'Kant argued that knowledge is not a collection of gifts received by the senses and stored in the mind as if it were a museum, but that it is very largely the result of our own mental activity' (1962: 214). For Kant, knowledge was a matter of actively imposing our 'categories' upon the noumenal realm, with knowledge of reality being 'filtered' through the categories. Instead of the rationalist emphasis on a priori ideas, or the empiricist emphasis on a posteriori (immediate) experience, we have the synthetic a priori. Here, according to Kant's transcendental idealism, knowledge is possible because we have a fixed set of categories, with which the mind 'imposes its stamp' on the mass of raw sensations, stemming from an unknowable reality-in-itself, or noumenal realm.

For Popper, 'the creative is the a priori' (cited in Corvi 1997: 137), meaning that our concepts, 'prejudices', etc., exist prior to experience and interpret that experience. This is not to say that reality is reducible to the categories. Whilst we cannot step outside our searchlight to see reality-in-itself, we can recognise that some searchlights are better than others and that new searchlights will be needed as limitations become apparent. As Popper argues

> Kant was right that it is our intellect which imposes its laws – its ideas, its rules – upon the inarticulate mass of our 'sensations' and thereby brings order into them. Where he was wrong is that he did not see that we rarely succeed with our imposition, and that we try and err again and again, and that the result – our knowledge of the world – owes as much to the resisting reality as to our self-produced ideas.
>
> (1975: 68. n.31. See also 1972b: 26–7, 95–6)

Against Kant's transcendental idealism, Popper's post-Kantianism switches the emphasis from the categories *per se*, to an external reality, to which categories may or may not relate with different degrees of veracity, or 'verisimilitude'. Now, Popper does agree with the correspondence theory of truth, as put forward by Tarski. This theory holds that a statement is true if and only if (or 'iff') it corresponds with the facts. Such a view may seem to imply a version of the bucket theory, with reality being defined in such a way that language (i.e. propositions) can grasp it directly, so that one can see that a proposition corresponds to reality. In which case one could step outside language to see how language corresponded to non-linguistic facts. This however is not a view shared by Popper. He argues that the correspondence theory of truth provides us with an objectivist or absolutist notion of truth, whilst not providing us with certainty. The reason for this is that there is no *criterion* of truth. In Popper's words, 'the idea of truth is absolutist, but no claim can be made for absolute certainty: *we are the seekers for truth but we are not its possessors*' (1975: 46–7; emphasis in original). A statement is true if, and only if, it corresponds to the facts, but there can be no general a priori criterion of truth, with which to say how a theory may be judged against the facts. We cannot step outside perspectives to define how perspectives, or propositions, may directly mirror facts. Instead, theories have varying degrees of 'verisimilitude', meaning that they approximate to the truth to varying degrees (Popper 1975: 47).

This post-Kantian notion of scientific knowledge as fallible searchlights leads Popper to replace the verification criterion with the notion of falsifiability. Thus Popper argued that science can be *demarcated* from non-science by the principle of falsifiability (see 1972a, especially 78–2; 1972b: 253–92; 1996: xix–xxxix). To be classed as scientific, a proposition must be testable and open (in principle and actuality) to empirical refutation. In constructing a theory, it ought to be clear under what circumstances the theory could be refuted. The clearer and bolder the theory the better, for this will make testing easier. Science therefore turns on making bold empirical conjectures open to empirical refutation.[2] Applying this principle to social science, Popper argues that Marxism and psycho-analysis are unscientific because they are unfalsifiable. Popper argues that Marxism and psycho-analysis 'opened the eyes' of those initiated, who could find proof of the theories everywhere.

Once your eyes were thus opened you saw confirming instances everywhere: the world was full of *verifications* of the theory. Whatever happened
always confirmed it. Thus its truth appeared manifest; and unbelievers
were clearly people who did not want to see the manifest truth; who
refused to see it, either because it was against their class interest, or
because of their repressions which were still 'un-analysed' and crying
aloud for treatment.

(1972b: 35; emphasis in original)[3]

Any event could thus be used to prove that, for instance, the state served
capital, or that the conscious self was influenced by unconscious drives,
respectively. Therefore theories such as Marxism and psycho-analysis are
unscientific because they rely on propositions that cannot be refuted. The
propositions are general enough for any specific event to be interpreted as a
verification of the universal truth of the theory. The advocates of Marxism and
psycho-analysis may regard irrefutability as a virtue but for Popper this is
a vice, because it seeks to verify a theory by *fiat*: the theory is *absolutely* right
which is why any attempt to test the theory will *necessarily* prove it to be
correct. The propositions of the theory are exhaustive of their subject-matter,
which is why no revisions are necessary in the light of experience, which just
furnishes verifications. In contrast to this form of social science, Popper advocates methodological individualism, which puts forward empirical propositions about specific individuals in specific situations; and this individualism
will be discussed and criticised in the following chapter.

This emphasis on empirical testability did not lead Popper to dismiss
metaphysics, though. Consequently, rather than dismissing the idealist view
(that there is no material world) as meaningless, Popper considers plausible
reasons for not accepting idealism. I say 'not accepting' rather than 'disprov-
ing' or 'refuting', because as idealism is a metaphysical thesis it cannot be
empirically refuted and, as regards (deductive) logical consistency, idealism is
a coherent position. Popper considers idealism in relation to another metaphysical thesis, viz. metaphysical realism, which holds that there is a material
reality beyond our ideas of it. Popper begins by defining idealism as the
position that the world is just my dream. This, incidentally, implies (correctly
in my view) that idealism results in solipsism, because other minds would be
dependent upon my idea of them for their existence: what exists are the ideas
I have and nothing more. Popper then puts forward five arguments in favour
of realism (1975: 38–42). The first is that realism is acceptable common-sense
whereas idealism is 'philosophical' in the pejorative sense, meaning that it is
sophistry. Although, ironically, idealism, whilst being sophistical, draws upon
common-sense, in the form of the bucket theory of mind. It begins uncritically
with the view that mind sees reality as it really is, and then moves to the
conclusion that this reality is a posit of the mind. That is, what exists is what
we can know, and what we can know are our ideas, so what exist are our
ideas, and nothing more. The second argument is that science purports to

explain reality and so the success of scientific ideas suggests that there is a reality which is irreducible to ideas. The third argument moves from science to language, holding that language is used to describe reality, which suggests that there is a reality beyond our ideas of it. The fourth argument is that aesthetic appreciation is not reducible to my ideas, and to argue otherwise is to fall into megalomania, because beauty would be whatever I thought was beautiful because I thought it. Finally, Popper argues that if realism were true, then it would be impossible to prove. This is because our knowledge is fallible: we cannot see reality as it really is, because there is no manifest truth. Yet '[a]t the same time, the whole question of the truth and falsity of our opinions and theories clearly becomes pointless if there is no reality, only dreams or illusions' (1975: 41–2).

Metaphysical realism therefore should be favoured in place of idealism. We may not be able to disprove idealism and prove realism (or disprove realism and prove idealism), but we can say that realism is more *useful*. With idealism there is no point in doing science, as the total expanse of reality is set by the confines of the mind (i.e. my mind). Science is about acquiring knowledge, and if knowledge comes from within, there is little point in an activity that purports to gain knowledge of a reality beyond our opinions and dreams. Nevertheless, the usefulness of realism is circumscribed by its metaphysical nature. We can say that it makes more sense to be a realist than an idealist, if one wants to accept that science gives us knowledge of the world, but science, or rather scientific methodology, does *not need to presuppose* metaphysical realism, according to Popper.

Popper does argue that science 'can hardly be understood if we are not realists' (1996: 145). He continues though by saying, '[a]nd yet it seems to me that *within methodology we do not have to presuppose metaphysical realism*. Nor can we derive any help from it, except of an intuitive kind' (1996: 145; emphasis added). His point is that if science is about exploring the world, then in constructing a theory, the scientist will be seeking knowledge of that world. This does not mean however that scientific methodology requires a metaphysical realist philosophy. Metaphysical realism may be a useful *psychological* presupposition, but it is not a *methodological* presupposition (1996: 75). This view arises given the demarcation criterion, which demarcates science from non-science and metaphysics, by using the principle of empirical falsifiability. Given the demarcation criterion, we have a clear divide between science, which concerns empirical testability, and non-science, which includes metaphysical arguments for and against idealism. Therefore metaphysical realism cannot be used as a transcendental argument, to say that the condition of possibility for empirical science is a *necessary* commitment to the metaphysical presupposition that there is a reality beyond our concepts. Science is to be understood in terms of empirically testing different theoretical searchlights, seeking increased verisimilitude, and this does not *need* to be explained by reference to the bucket-mind, or *metaphysical conjectures* about a reality beyond ideas.[4]

Popper, the epistemic fallacy and the genetic fallacy

From positivism to an anti-foundationalist version of the epistemic fallacy

Popper's philosophy could be said to rest upon a positivist conception of natural laws. The reason for this is as follows. Popper not only replaces the verification criterion with the point about falsifiablity, but he also replaces the inductive method with a deductive method. With this deductive-nominological cal method, scientific method tests a theory by saying that general law X, under condition Y, will result in Z (with X and Y being the explanans, or premises, and Z being the explanandum or conclusion). This deductive model of scientific method, as Bhaskar (1997: 129–30) argues, is underpinned by a conception of natural laws that defines such laws in terms of empirical regularities; rather than making a distinction between causal mechanisms that were unobservable in themselves and separate from their contingent observable effects, which is the realist position argued for in Chapter 5. So, in seeking to test a theory, to see when and how it could be falsified, one would presume a model of causality that was essentially positivist, because it held that the laws of nature were observable as constant conjunctions: a theory could be falsified then if the expected constant conjunction failed to obtain.

Whilst it is certainly true that a deductive method may rely on a positivist model of causality as observed constant conjunctions, we should be wary about concluding that Popper's philosophy is best characterised as 'positivist'. The reason for this is that Popper's post-Kantianism leads him to qualify the view that a deductive approach to scientific method can allow us decisively to refute, or falsify, a theory, by comparing it against reality-in-itself (in the form of empirical constant conjunctions). Thus in place of falsification*ism*, or 'naive falsificationism', which seeks to make definitive claims, Popper talks of falsifi*ability* (1996: xxxiii). He argues that a falsification is not definitive, because there is no direct comparison, or immediate recognition, of a manifest truth. In observing regularities, we are not observing fixed laws in themselves, and so reference to an expected regularity failing to occur is not a definitive refutation of a theory. Therefore '[a]ll knowledge remains fallible, conjectural. *There is no justification, including, of course, no final justification of a refutation.* Nevertheless we learn by refutations, i.e., by the elimination of error, by feedback' (Popper 1996: xxxv, emphasis added). In short, the post-Kantian position allows us to change our categories, as some searchlights are seen as being better than others, but the deductive method does not by-pass categories to give us a direct access to reality.[5]

However, the problem is that we cannot make much sense of fallibilism. As Popper rejects metaphysical realism, there can be no reference to a reality that is external to our categories or perspectives, and so there can be no way to explain how we can change perspective after realising that an alternative perspective gave a better account of reality. Therefore it would be the case not just that the regularities we observed were to some extent constructed by our categories, but that all the regularities that we saw were constructed by our categories. What we knew of reality would be reduced to what we knew via our perspective. This may give us a post-Kantian version of the deductive method, but such an approach could only verify and not falsify perspectives, as there is no way to sustain the notion of fallibilism.

The upshot of all this is that we have moved from the foundationalist epistemic fallacy, whereby positivism would define being according to an empiricist epistemology, to a post-Kantian anti-foundational version of the epistemic fallacy. With this anti-foundational version of the epistemic fallacy, reality is defined in terms of how we know it via our 'categories'. These categories are meant to change over time because we can see their fallibility, but we cannot sustain the notion of fallibilism given the lack of a metaphysical realist ontology.

Popper, Kuhn and the genetic fallacy

Against the view that all we can know and refer to are our concepts, Popper argues that

> I do admit that we are prisoners caught in the framework of our theories; our expectations; our past experiences; our language. But we are prisoners in a Pickwickian sense: if we try, we can break out of our framework at any time. Admittedly, we shall find ourselves again in a framework, but it will be a better and roomier one; and we can at any moment break out of it again.
>
> (1993: 56)

Here Popper is arguing against what he calls the 'myth of the framework', which is the truth-relativist view that what we can know is *wholly* relative to our theoretical framework. With the myth of the framework, truth is wholly relative to the framework, as there is no external referent. If a concept is part of a theory it is necessarily 'true' for the relativist myth. In putting this view forward, Popper is criticising Kuhn's argument that what constitutes scientific knowledge is determined by the prevailing paradigm (or theoretical framework), to the extent that failures of a theory are misperceived as failures of the individual to apply the theory properly. Popper argues that whilst knowledge is relative to a framework, it is not wholly relative, because an external reality means that such frameworks are fallible and can be recognised as such. Thus we are able to break out of an old theory and enter a better theory (that has increased verisimilitude).

Such a conception of Kuhn is too narrow though, because Kuhn is rather ambivalent about the status of truth. On the one hand Kuhn appears to be a clear-cut relativist, arguing that paradigms determine knowledge. Here knowledge would be relative to a paradigm in that it would be reduced into a paradigm. In place of reference to external objects, truth would be definable in terms of a concept being part of a paradigm. Thus Kuhn famously argues, for instance, that 'in so far as [scientists'] only recourse to the world is through what they see and do, we may say that after a revolution [i.e. change of paradigm] scientists are responding to *a different world*' (1970: 111; emphasis added). On the other hand, though, Kuhn makes reference to a reality that is external to the paradigm, separating what is known and what exists. He argues that '[*w*]*hatever he may then see*, the scientist after a revolution is still *looking at the same world*' (1970: 129; emphasis added). Here then truth cannot be wholly reducible to a paradigm because there is a referent beyond the paradigm. A concept or theory may be false, as it may not approximate to the external object of knowledge to any degree.

To be sure, there is a strong aspect to Kuhn's work which does adhere to the myth of the framework, but Kuhn's argument is essentially a socio-historical study of scientific development, which says that scientists are heavily influenced by socio-cultural factors, meaning the norms of their (professional) community influence what 'normal science' is. It is not a clear-cut defence of the view that truth is relative to a paradigm, with every paradigm being equally true. Now, although Popper does not place so much emphasis on socio-cultural influences, his position is much closer to Kuhn's than either he or Kuhn thought.[6] The reason for this is that Popper, like Kuhn, put a lot of emphasis on the 'framework', with reference to a reality beyond this, but without being able to say how this external reality affected the framework.

It is all very well for Popper to say that we are Pickwickian prisoners who can break out of the framework we are in, and move into a better one, but there is no ontological support for this assertion. We cannot make a meaningful and useful reference to a reality that is external to our framework, and so we cannot make sense of the notion of having a *better* framework. Although we may be able to change frameworks, we cannot have a rational reason for doing so.[7] Without any notion of how an external reality can affect a framework, there is no way to say that one framework has more verisimilitude than another. Instead, every framework would be equally true. Devoid of any meaningful notion of an independent reality, concepts thus become self-referential, so every framework becomes equally true, as truth could only be relative to – i.e. reducible into – a framework.

This brings us to the notion of the genetic fallacy. The genetic fallacy occurs with truth-relativism, because as truth-relativism reduces truth into a framework, the *origin* of a belief (in such a framework), rather than its relationship to an external referent, is held to determine its truth. A logical fallacy therefore occurs because it is impossible for the origin of a belief to determine its truth or falsity. Reducing issues of truth to issues of the origin of a concept in a framework results in absurdity, as every framework is equally true, even if frameworks are mutually exclusive. In addition to this, it is of course impossible to state such a thesis without blatant self-contradiction: one cannot make a universal statement about truth being relative.

Putnam's critique of metaphysical realism[8]

Putnam, unlike Popper, will have no truck with metaphysical realism. Putnam defines metaphysical realism in terms of the following propositions: (1) the world consists of a fixed totality of objects, or essences; (2) there is one true and complete description of this world; (3) truth is based upon a correspondence between linguistic/thought signs and external objects (1981: 49; 1992a: 30). This realism is referred to by Putnam (1981: 49) as 'externalism', because of its belief that there is one true and complete description of the fixed set of objects that constitute the world, which is external to our particular perspectives. Such externalism thus favours the 'God's-eye point of view', whereby knowledge is absolute. Instead of knowledge being perspectival (which is, by definition, partial) and fallible, knowledge is knowledge because it maps all the existing and knowable facts. Knowledge can only exist if we can step outside our perspectives to achieve an absolute conception of reality; although the time required to attain such a view is unclear.

The metaphysical realist is described by Putnam as an 'evil seducer' of the 'Innocent Maiden' (1991: 4). The realist promises to protect the common-sense view that contrary to idealism (and relativism), the world does exist outside our ideas. However, such beguiling promises to the Innocent Maiden are empty. The seducer fails to deliver what was promised. As Putnam puts it, the Maiden chooses to travel with the realist,

> But when they have travelled together for a little while the 'Scientific Realist' breaks the news that what the Maiden is going to get *isn't* her ice cubes and tables and chairs. In fact, all there *really* is – the Scientific Realist tells her over breakfast – is what 'finished science' will say there is whatever that may be. She is left with a promissory note for She Knows Not What, and the assurance that even if there *aren't* tables and chairs, still there are some *dinge an sich* [i.e. noumenal 'things-in-themselves'] that her 'manifest image' [...] 'picture'. Some will say that the lady has been had.
>
> (1991: 4; emphasis in original)

If knowledge only exists with a finished science, which is the position taken up by the first two defining propositions of metaphysical realism, then metaphysical realism does nothing to support the notion that reality exists. We cannot *know* what exists until we know everything. So, given human fallibilism, we cannot say reality exists, i.e. *we cannot say anything exists, because we cannot know everything.*[9] In which case, to turn to metaphysical realism as a guarantor that reality 'really exists' is misguided, because it cannot deliver what it promises.

Putnam also attacks the correspondence theory of truth, which is the third defining proposition for metaphysical realism. For Putnam knowledge is not to be understood in terms of propositions corresponding to fixed, discrete external referents. The theory of truth or theory of reference which holds that propositions correspond to external referents is referred to by Putnam as the 'similitude theory of reference'. This theory 'holds that the relation between the representation in our minds and the external objects that they refer to is literally a *similarity*' (1981: 57; emphasis in original). In the seventeenth century, according to Putnam, this theory of reference became more restricted, with a distinction being made between primary qualities and secondary qualities; i.e. between 'real' properties of the object, such as size, and qualities such as colour, which are not intrinsic to the object as such (1981: 56–9; 1991: 4–8).

However, this distinction pointed to the Achilles' heel of the similitude theory of reference, because it led people, such as Berkeley, to argue that all sense-data are of secondary qualities. As Putnam puts it

> To state Berkeley's conclusion another way, *Nothing can be similar to a sensation or image except another sensation or image.* Given this, and given the (still unquestioned) assumption that the mechanism of reference is similitude between our 'ideas' [...] and what they represent, it at once follows that no 'idea' (mental image) can represent or refer to anything but another image or sensation.
>
> (1981: 59; emphasis in original)

So Putnam argues that to define knowledge in terms of mental images that have similarity to their referent results in idealism. Mental images are similar to mental images, not external material referents.

Internal realism: conceptual relativity and realism

The philosopher who first broke away from the similitude theory of reference was Kant, who argued that the object of knowledge was as much a product of our concepts as it was of the noumenal thing-in-itself, to which it pertained. Instead of having direct knowledge (of our ideas) we have, for Kant, a mediated access to reality. So 'the representation is never a mere copy; it is always a joint product of our interaction with the external world and the active powers of the mind. The world as we know it bears the stamp of our conceptual activity' (Putnam 1992a: 261). Concepts contribute to the object of knowledge, rather than having a relationship of immediacy to an external object.

Putnam (1991: 52) argues that Kant 'celebrates the loss of essences', meaning that Kant breaks from (what Putnam takes to be) the metaphysical realist conviction that there are a set number of fixed essences, which concepts mirror. However, to break fully from such essentialism, we need to break from the notion of unknowable things-in-themselves. We need to break from the concept of a noumenal realm. For to say that there is a world of things-in-themselves is to open the door to the metaphysical realist question, enquiring what these things are (Putnam 1995a: 29). This enquiry, for Putnam of course, would be to entail the externalist view that we can step outside our perspectives to know fixed essences. The notion of a noumenal realm leads one back to essentialism. Or rather, it would lead one back to essentialism, were it not for the fact that the concept of a noumenal realm did no work. As the things-in-themselves cannot be known, one may apply Ockham's razor, and remove the noumenal world, leaving concepts as the sole constituent of the putative object of knowledge. If concepts which are known contribute to the object of knowledge there is no need to make reference to an unknowable noumenal thing-in-itself also contributing to the object of knowledge.

What is needed, Putnam believes, is a way to retain the emphasis on concepts in constituting the object of knowledge, whilst avoiding reference to an unknowable reality. The answer lies in the philosophy of the later Wittgenstein, who Putnam (1995a: 39) describes as 'deflating' Kant. Putnam interprets Wittgenstein as a form of pragmatist, meaning that Wittgenstein rejected epistemology for practices. Instead of asking questions about how knowledge was possible or achieved, the focus should be on how people 'go on' within a 'form of life', i.e. on the practical basis of meaning. Instead of asking how beliefs copy non-beliefs, etc., we should see how people follow practical rules, in different forms of life. This means that we do not just drop the notion of a noumenal realm, but also drop the notion that the concepts – or categories – are fixed. We should drop Kant's transcendental idealism, which argues that the condition of possibility for knowledge is that we have a fixed set of categories, which impose their 'stamp' on the noumenal realm. Instead we ought to recognise there are different concepts, formed in different perspectives, that are relative to their location within a particular culture or form of life. In short, concepts pertain to *practical life* within a *community* rather than a fixed set of entities in the *mind*; and we should replace questions about concepts somehow connecting with mysterious unknowable things-in-themselves, in order to recognise that concepts are rooted in the social realm of a community's practical life.[10]

So, although Kant broke from the similitude theory of reference, his philosophy may entail either externalism, with a definition of the noumenal realm being required, or idealism (the outcome of the similitude theory of reference) if we remove reference to the noumenal realm. The way to continue Kant's argument about knowledge being conceptually mediated is to move from a metaphysical and transcendental argument about a fixed set of categories being the condition of possibility for knowledge, to an argument about practices. In the latter case, concepts would be contingent upon the different ways of going on within different forms of life. Such a position is realist, but it is realism with a small 'r', which accepts the common-sense view that reality really exists, rather than Realism with a big 'R', which seeks a direct access to a reality-in-itself beyond perspectives.

Putnam contrasts the external realism of metaphysical realism with what he refers to as 'internal realism'; a position which maintains that we can be both realists (with a small 'r') and conceptual relativists (1991: 17). This means replacing the metaphysical realist correspondence theory of truth, which is premised upon similitude, with a coherence theory of truth. As Putnam argues:

> 'Truth', in an internalist view, is some sort of (idealized) rational accept-ability – some sort of ideal coherence of our beliefs with each other and with our experiences *as those experiences are themselves represented in our belief system* – and not correspondence with mind-independent 'states of affairs'. There is no God's eye point of view that we can usefully imagine; there are only the various points of view of actual persons reflecting various interests and purposes that their descriptions and theories subserve.
>
> (1981: 49–50; emphasis in original)

Given this, Putnam (1981: 60; 1991: 43) can describe Kant as the 'first internal realist', because Kant broke from the similitude emphasis on truth as correspondence to a mind-independent reality, to emphasise the importance of concepts.[11] The next step was to argue for conceptual relativity, with concepts being contingent upon their location within a particular form of life.

Conceptual relativism does not mean truth-relativism for Putnam. What we know may be relative to some perspective, but this does not mean that there are as many truths as there are perspectives with every perspective being equally true. When Putnam talks of holding a coherence theory of truth, he does not want this to imply that truth can be reduced into the origin of a concept within a conceptual scheme. He wants to avoid the genetic fallacy. He does therefore say that concepts deal with reality, rather than just being self-referential components of an internally coherent framework. Putnam argues thus:

> Internalism does not deny that there are experiential *inputs* to knowledge; knowledge formation is not a story with no constraints except *internal* coherence; but it does deny that there are inputs *which are not themselves to some extent shaped by our concepts*, by the vocabulary we use to report and describe them, or any inputs *which admit of only one description, independent of all conceptual choices*.
>
> (1981: 54; emphasis in original)

We deal with reality, but our experience and knowledge of reality are always mediated through some conceptual scheme: there is no immediate access. As we deal with reality, it follows that some perspectives may be better than others; and it does not follow that we can adopt a God's-eye view, to say that from a God's-eye view there is no God's-eye view, meaning that we cannot step outside all perspectives to say that all perspectives are *necessarily* equal in truth (Putnam 1992a: 25).

For internal realism, knowledge is contingent upon a perspective, although relativism is avoided because knowledge is fallible. This emphasis on fallibilism is clear, when Putnam defines truth in terms of 'warranted assertability', rather than in terms of beliefs corresponding to external essences. What he does is set out five points to define warranted assertability, and these points may be classed under the heading of contingency and fallibilism. Under the heading of contingency he argues that our norms and standards always reflect our interests and values. Under the heading of fallibilism we may place the following propositions: (1) in ordinary circumstances there is usually a *fact of the matter* as to whether statements are warranted or not; (2) whether or not a statement is warranted or not is *independent of what one's cultural peers say is warranted or not*; (3) that our norms and standards are historical in that they evolve over time;[12] and (4) our norms and standards are capable of reform – there are *better and worse norms and standards* (1992a: 21). From this it seems clear that warranted assertability and conceptual relativity are defined more in terms of fallibilism (i.e. in relation to reality) than in terms of social contingency.

Putnam may seem to have a tenable theory of knowledge, with internal realism replacing metaphysical realism (as he defines it), because he is arguing that we have a conceptually mediated and fallible access to reality. However Putnam's internal realism is based on the relativist philosophical logic of immediacy, and this is because he misunderstands metaphysical realism. To show why this is, I will begin by discussing Searle's arguments about realism.

Searle on external realism and conceptual relativity

For Putnam metaphysical realism is fallacious because it is *metaphysical*. Metaphysics is regarded as trying to be a pure science of being, with metaphysical realism being based on the presumption that we can have a direct access to a reality that is beyond mere perspectives, via the correspondence theory of truth. In other words, the metaphysical realist ontology (that a reality exists beyond conceptual schemes) is taken to be a definitive *master-ontology*, whereby what exists is defined in terms of fixed, discrete essences, that the 'realist' ontology can, or will eventually, mirror *in toto*.

As Searle (1995) argues, though, Putnam's position is subject to confusion. Searle puts forward six propositions that define his realism, in contrast to Putnam's internal realism (1995: 150–1, paraphrased). These are:

1 The world and the universe exist independently of our representations of it. This view is called 'external realism'; and it is the same as the 'metaphysical realist' position, as defined by Popper, viz. that there is a reality independent of our conceptions of it.
2 Access to the world is via representations.
3 Representations are true if and only if they correspond to the facts in reality. This is a correspondence theory of truth.

4 The same reality can be represented in any number of ways. This is the thesis of 'conceptual relativity'.
5 Social, historical and psychological factors influence representations.
6 Knowledge consists of true representations, which can be justified and supported by evidence.

Searle argues that the first proposition concerning external realism is an ontological proposition because it asserts that reality exists independently of our representations of it: it is a statement about *being*, not a statement about *knowing*. As this is an *ontological* statement only, it has no necessarily *epistemological* implications. To assert that there is a reality which is independent of our representations of it, is not to assert that we can know this reality directly, or immediately. From the ontological premise that our representations which seek to be knowledge pertain to something external to the representations, one cannot necessarily conclude that we can know this external reality with immediacy. External realism says nothing about how we may come to have knowledge, for that concerns epistemology, and not ontology. In other words, external realism may be a metaphysical thesis, but *it does not follow that a metaphysical thesis is an epistemic thesis concerning how we know reality.* Metaphysical assertions concerning ontology, which say that reality is separate from representations of it, say nothing of how we can know reality, or even whether we can know reality. So metaphysics ought not to be regarded as a quasi-religious attempt to fashion a master-science of being, or a definitive master-ontology, which has absolute knowledge. Metaphysics *per se* does not imply a presumption of omnipotence; and it does not even maintain that knowledge is necessarily possible.

If external realism is an ontological thesis with no necessary epistemic corollary, then it follows that the fourth proposition concerning conceptual relativity does not contradict the first proposition concerning the external realism thesis. The representations of the world may be from different conceptual schemes, but these representations are still of the world or, to be more precise, they may be of the world (given that putative representations may be false). As Searle argues, 'if conceptual relativity is to be used as an argument against realism, it seems to presuppose realism, because it presupposes a language-independent reality that can be carved up or divided up in different ways, by different vocabularies' (1995: 165). The example Searle (1995: 165) gives is of describing his weight as being 160 pounds in one conceptual scheme, and 73 kilograms in another conceptual scheme. Similarly a room's temperature may be measured in either Centigrade or Fahrenheit. One cannot conclude that, given different conceptual schemes for measuring weight or temperature, there is no John Searle or room with a certain temperature, outside the conceptual schemes.

It may be objected that the third proposition concerning the correspondence theory of truth clashes with the fourth proposition concerning conceptual relativity. As Collier (1994: 239) argues though, the correspondence theory of truth is a *definition* of truth and not a *criterion* of truth. So, Kant held a correspondence theory of truth (*contra* Putnam), arguing that knowledge was in agreement with its object; which is not to attempt the meaningless task of defining a priori what truth is in specific instances (Collier 1994: 239). Thus a correspondence theory is not a resemblance – or similitude – theory (1994: 240). As Collier puts it '[e]veryone understands that if the inspector says "your inventory did not correspond to what was really in the warehouse", she is not complaining that a sheet of paper did not resemble a stack of tinned fruit' (1994: 240). The concepts within a conceptual scheme will be true if they correspond to reality but this is not to say that the concepts will 'picture' extra-discursive discrete facts.

Putnam and the philosophical logic of immediacy

Given that any reference to a reality that is external to our concepts implies 'metaphysical realism', all referents must be wholly internal to a conceptual framework. *What* we can know is defined by *how* we can know; which in this case pertains to conceptual schemes (rather than minds). Conceptual relativity without external realism results in the epistemic fallacy, therefore, because ontology has to be defined in terms of conceptual relativity, in order to avoid 'metaphysical realism'. Reality is definable only in terms that are wholly relative to a conceptual scheme. In other words, the thesis of conceptual relativity moves from the acceptable view that how we interpret the world is relative to a conceptual scheme, to the objectionable view *that the world we interpret is relative to our conceptual scheme*. As reference to anything beyond conceptual schemes implies, according to Putnam, an essentialist conception of knowledge, all referents – i.e. all objects of knowledge – are wholly definable in terms of their location within a conceptual scheme.

The genetic fallacy stems from this epistemic fallacy, because having defined the object of knowledge in terms of conceptual schemes, it follows that truth pertains to the origin of a concept within a conceptual scheme. Given the emphasis on conceptual relativity, and denial of external realism, correspondence must be replaced by coherence, as it would not make sense to say that propositions corresponded to something beyond conceptual schemes (whether such correspondence was defined in terms of similitude or verisimilitude). Putnam may say that his coherence theory does not mean that truth is definable wholly in terms of internal coherence, but as he has no way to support his common-sense realism (realism with a little 'r') without contradicting his denial of external realism, questions of truth are reduced into questions of coherence alone. One cannot simply presume that there is a reality beyond conceptual schemes, when one argues for the very denial of external realism, on the mistaken ground that such realism erroneously argues for epistemic immediacy and a God's-eye view. Without external realism, concepts become self-referential, as there is no external object of knowledge to act as a separate referent. Concepts correspond to nothing but themselves, and so truth turns on whether a concept forms part of an internally coherent conceptual framework and nothing more. Truth is made wholly relative to a conceptual framework. The result is the relativist philosophical logic of immediacy, because truth is manifest in the sense that in knowing a framework, we know the truth. The result is also idealism, because internal realism internalises reality to conceptual schemes, with such schemes being self-referential.

Having said this, though, it could be pointed out that when Putnam discussed warranted assertability, he put forward propositions that pertained to fallibilism. What are we to make of this? The propositions concerning a fact of the matter, warrant being independent of peer approval, norms evolving over time, and norms being reformed, all imply that an external reality is used to test the utility of beliefs. However, the appeal to such an external reality is explicitly denied. Putnam wants to assist the Innocent Maiden, by saying that there is a reality. However, by denying the thesis of external realism for an internal realism, which is an epistemic doctrine concerning conceptual relativity, devoid of any ontological reference to reality, the result is that the Innocent Maiden has, in Putnam's words, 'been had'. What this means is that Putnam is in the same position as Kant. As Searle argues (1995: 174), for both Kant and Putnam the notion of a reality beyond the concepts becomes redundant. Reference is just reference to our concepts.

To conclude, therefore, we may say that whilst it is necessary to move from a foundational approach to epistemology to an anti-foundational approach, this is not sufficient to avoid the epistemic fallacy. Indeed, an anti-foundational epistemology may move from the epistemic fallacy to relativism and the genetic fallacy. The way to avoid the foundationalist and relativist philosophical logics of immediacy, and the epistemic and genetic fallacies, is to complement an anti-foundational epistemology with a metaphysical realist ontology. This realist anti-foundationalism would overcome the problems concerning the impossibility of explaining how we acquired a mediated and fallible knowledge of a reality beyond our perspectives.

2 The influence of empiricism on social ontology

Methodological individualism and methodological collectivism

Introduction

As mentioned in the Introduction, the foundationalist philosophical logic of immediacy, which holds that we have a direct access to reality-in-itself, may underpin the sociological logic of immediacy. The sociological logic of immediacy, it may be remembered, pertained to the use of a definitive ontology, of either human being (with the individualist sociological logic of immediacy) or social structures (with the structuralist sociological logic of immediacy). Such ontologies were definitive in the sense that they explained all aspects of human behaviour, so that to know the ontology was to know all the causes of behaviour. Given this one may simply read off behaviour from the ontology, which would make research pointless as one would know why people acted as they did, or one may read the ontology into observed actions, and thus 'verify' the ontology that one knew to be true prior to research.

Obviously positions that end up entailing the sociological logic of immediacy would be antithetical to realist anti-foundationalism. Such positions were also antithetical to the methodological individualists, such as Popper and Watkins. When it came to social science Popper was more empiricist than post-Kantian. What this means is that from a basically empiricist starting point Popper, and the other methodological individualists such as Watkins, held that social reality was ultimately to be defined in terms of individuals rather than 'social structures', as individuals could be empirically observed (although this did not mean that a form of psychologistic reduction was advocated). This created problems though because the reference to social factors influencing individuals begged the question as to what these might be. Given the lack of a definition, the argument about social reality could be arbitrary: it could move from an over-emphasis on agency or free will to an over-emphasis on constraint. The same problem befell the methodological collectivists, for the same reason.

So, Popper and Watkins develop their argument for methodological individualism by rejecting psychologistic reductionism and holistic determinism. This means that they start by criticising positions that are clear examples of the sociological logic of immediacy, in order to show the strengths of methodological individualism. The problem though is that the empiricist epistemological underlabourer prevents them (and their methodological collectivist critics) of succeeding in their aim of linking structure and agency, by saying how individuals' agency is mediated and not determined by social factors.

Anticipating the sociological logic of immediacy

Methodological individualists anticipated what I refer to as the sociological logic of immediacy, arguing against the notion that social science can be based upon a definitive ontology of either human being or social structures. Against the notion that to understand human behaviour we can reduce the level of explanation down to the level of mental states, or human nature, Popper argues that

> It [psychologism] can hardly be seriously discussed, for we have every reason to believe that man or rather his ancestor was social prior to being human [...]. But this implies that social institutions, and with them, typical social regularities or sociological laws, must have existed prior to what some people are pleased to call 'human nature', and to human psychology. If a reduction is to be attempted at all, it would therefore be more helpful to attempt a reduction or interpretation of psychology in terms of sociology than the other way round.
>
> (1962: 93)

In other words, the social context pre-exists specific individual acts. So, to understand the actions of individuals, therefore, we need to understand how individuals are influenced by the prevailing social context and how, as this context is not determining, individuals may act back upon the context to effect social change.

This would obviously require empirical investigation, to see exactly how individuals interacted with the social context. If one had a definitive ontology of human being or social structures, though, then one would not have to engage in empirical research, as one could simply read-off from the ontology the categories which mirrored the essences that determined human behaviour. Or, if one did engage in empirical research, then it would be based upon verifying an ontology which was known to be 'correct'. As Watkins argues,

> There is a parallel between holism [the view that structures determine behaviour] and psychologism which explains their common failure to make surprising discoveries. A large-scale social characteristic should be explained, according to psychologism, as the manifestation of analogous small-scale psychological tendencies in individuals, and according to holism as the manifestation of a large-scale tendency in the social whole. In both cases, the *explicans* does little more than duplicate the *explanandum*.
>
> (1992a: 175–6)

With both psychologism and holism therefore, there can be no 'surprising discoveries' because the ontologies in both cases are taken to be definitive. Thus the *explicans* mirrors the *explanandum*, because the phenomena explained are identical with the theory which seeks to explain them, given that observed human behaviour mirrors the determining essence which causes that behaviour. Conversely, to make surprising discoveries is to discover how the social context interacts with individual agency in specific circumstances. Which brings us to the question of whether or not methodological individualism is able to achieve what it implies is the nature of social scientific explanation.

Methodological individualism defined

In his critique of psychologism, Popper argues that human actions are to a large extent explicable in terms of the situations in which they are located. He admits that psychological factors may have some role to play. However, 'this "psychological" part of the explanation is often very trivial, as compared with the detailed determination of [an agent's] action by what we may call *the logic of the situation*' (1962: 97; emphasis in original). So, one may refer to self-interest, for instance, but this would not go very far in explaining how capitalist economies actually worked. Rather than refer to some general notion such as self-interest, we would need to know the 'logic of the situation', to explain why, for instance, people withdrew money from the stockmarket and produced, unintentionally, an economic crash. Rather than read-off behaviour from a model of human being, social science should be concerned with 'the difficulties which stand in the way of social action – the study, as it were, of the unwieldiness, the resilience or the brittleness of the social stuff, of its resistance to our attempts to mould it and work with it' (Popper 1962: 94). What we need then is a study of individuals in relation to 'social stuff', or the logic of the situation, meaning a context which gives meaning to, enables and constrains individuals' actions.

How are we to study individuals *vis-à-vis* social stuff? Watkins argues that '[e]very complex social situation, institution, or event is the result of a particular configuration of individuals, their dispositions, situations, beliefs, and physical resources and environment' (1992a: 168). He goes on to draw a distinction between 'half-way explanations' of 'large-scale social phenomena', and 'rock-bottom explanations'. Watkins argues that we may explain one large-scale phenomenon (such as inflation) in terms of another large-scale phenomenon (such as full employment). To reach a rock-bottom explanation, though, we must 'deduce' an explanation in terms of the dispositions, beliefs, resources and interrelations of individuals (1992a: 168).[1] The methodology then is to be reductionist. One is to reduce explanations of large-scale phenomena down to the level of individuals and their beliefs and interrelations. Thus sociological explanations are derived from statements concerning '(a) principles governing the behaviour of participating individuals and (b) descriptions of their situations' (Watkins 1992b: 149).

The alternative to methodological individualism is sociological holism according to Watkins (1992a: 168; 1992b: 149–50). Such holism would maintain that social systems constitute 'organic wholes' which are controlled by macro-level laws. Therefore the level of analysis concerns *sui generis* laws, rather than individuals. Watkins argues that

> If methodological individualism means that human beings are supposed to be the only moving agents in history, and if sociological holism means that some superhuman agents or factors are supposed to be at work in history, then *these two alternatives are exhaustive.*
>
> (1992a: 168; emphasis added)

So unless one adopts methodological individualism one will have to adopt an holist position. If one ends up adopting an holist position then one will be holding a position which reifies social forces, by invoking some notion of 'superhuman' social structures. Such reference to structures beyond individuals will also be deterministic, because instead of dealing with individuals who can make decisions (within situations, i.e. a particular context), one would be referring to structures which controlled individuals. Individuals' behaviour would be epiphenomenal: individuals would be mere puppets controlled by some form of mysterious social structures.

Further, such holist determinism would also be 'well-nigh equivalent to historicism' (Watkins 1992a: 168). This is because if one moved from the synchronic issue of structures controlling society to the diachronic issue, of factors influencing historical development, then the emphasis would still be on superhuman structures. These structures would not only exert a causal deterministic influence over individuals in the present, but they would also determine the course of historical development. Consequently, if one argued for historicism then one would be presuming to know the laws which controlled human development, and this could be used by authoritarian regimes to legitimatise their rule by appeal to the 'laws of historical development' (Popper 1989).

In short, one can explain how individuals interact within a specific social situation, by reducing the explanation down to the level of individuals, or one can turn to a definitive ontology of human being or social structures. Such definitive ontologies fail as social scientific positions because they fail to make surprising discoveries and, in addition to this, an holist ontology may well have authoritarian political ramifications if applied to history.

Assessing methodological individualism: the need for a non-individualist ontology

With 'rock-bottom' explanations we would be dealing with facts about individuals but, as Lukes (1968) argues, it is not so clear what facts about individuals actually are. Lukes raises two questions, addressing the issues of what a fact about an individual is, and what an explanation about an individual is. As regards facts about individuals, Lukes lists four such facts ranging from the most non-social to the most social, such as brain states, stimulus response, co-operation and cashing cheques, respectively (1968: 123). Dealing with facts that pertain to the most social type of predicates about individuals, Lukes argues that '[h]ere the relevant features of the context are, so to speak, built into the individual' (1968: 125). So, for instance, when describing facts concerning such acts as cashing cheques, saluting and voting (the examples come from Lukes), one is describing individual acts by drawing upon a prior knowledge of the social context. One could not meaningfully describe an individual act of the type mentioned without drawing upon a social context that gives meaning to the act. Thus Army is more than the plural of soldier, because to understand why someone dresses in a particular type of uniform, and performs acts such as those called saluting, one must know what the social context is, which gives meaning and purpose to individual acts. One cannot understand the concept of an *individual* soldier, and the acts deemed appropriate to that role, without knowing what the *collective* Army is.

As regards the question concerning explanations about individuals, Lukes argues that '[i]t is important to see, and it is often forgotten, that to *identify* a piece of behaviour, a set of beliefs, etc., is sometimes to explain it' (1968: 125; emphasis in original). Lukes draws upon the apocryphal 'Martian' social scientist who is confused until being able to make sense of observed events by understanding their social contextual meaning, saying that an action such as cashing a cheque in a bank can be explained by being identified. In other words, by saying what the individual act is, by drawing upon the social context, one explains the act. Lukes goes on to say that if an individualist were to restrict him/herself to explanations concerning the first three types of individual predicates (such as brain states etc.), then the result would arbitrarily rule out what most people and (presumably) all social scientists find interesting, which is explanations about social action.

Alternatively, if reference is made to the fourth type of individual predicate, then the individualist is 'proposing nothing more than a futile linguistic purism. Why should we be compelled to talk about the tribesman but not the tribe, the bank-teller but not the bank?' (Lukes 1968: 125). Or the soldier but not the Army? Further, if the fourth type of individual predicate is accepted, then, whatever the use of language, one will have violated the criterion of reducing all reference down to individuals, in order to identify and explain just what it is that individuals are doing. Propositions about individuals often 'presuppose and/or entail other propositions about social phenomena. Thus the latter have not really been eliminated; they have merely been swept under the carpet' (Lukes 1968: 127). This, understandably, leads Lukes to say '[i]t is worth adding that since Popper and Watkins allow "situations" and "inter-relations between individuals" to enter into explanations, it is difficult to see why they insist on calling their doctrine "methodological individualism"' (1968: 127).

Given that, as Lukes noted above, to identify a piece of behaviour can be to explain it, because one is explaining the social context, a pure form of empiricist individualism would be prevented from explaining social phenomena because it could not proffer such identifications. Nonetheless, because some social reference is always necessary, the putative individualism of Popper and Watkins 'smuggles' social references in implicitly and, in doing this, the question is begged as to what social reality is. 'Sweeping it under the carpet' or 'building it into the individual' may avoid the impossibility of a purely atomistic view, but it tells us nothing about how the social context which gives meaning to individuals' actions enables and constrains individuals.

This is not just a logical problem, though. Any putative methodological individualist could subscribe to the ontology of 'individualism' and then put forward theories and explanations that make reference to non-individual factors. As these non-individual, or putatively social factors are not defined, they can be used in any way that suits the social scientist concerned. One could talk of a situational logic of employer–employee relations in a way that both prioritised individual agency and made the situational logic a determining constraint, without explaining how it might influence individuals in different ways at different times. One would confusingly adhere to a meta-theory of individuals, and then escape from empty descriptions to provide social explanations, by making reference to undefined social factors, that could be used in the most elastic fashion, to mean whatever one wanted to imply. One could not know how the social context acted as both a constraint and an enablement, because the question-begging reference to situational logics would do the work of an explanation concerning how individuals with free will had their agency affected by a social reality that was irreducible to individuals.

If the individualist was confronted with the accusation of begging the question then s/he would simply opt for a reduction to individuals, explaining the situational logic in terms of individuals' dispositions and beliefs. This however builds the social context into the individual. If one described the situational logic of employment relations, for instance, in terms of individuals' dispositions to act in certain ways, then one would be providing an explanation which defined individuals' dispositions in terms of the prevailing social context. In other words, reference to individuals' dispositions is not sufficient to warrant a reduction down to individuals, unless one were seeking to produce a psychologistic explanation, whereby 'social' relations were a direct expression of fixed mental states, and nothing else.

As Goldstein argues:

> The point here is that the kinds of dispositions to be found in people of any given type are socially induced dispositions. It seems odd to talk about widely occurring dispositions among Huguenot entrepreneurs and not to wonder about the coincidence of the recurrence in just this group. It was, to be sure, individual Huguenots who successfully

competed in the business world of the seventeenth century. But this was presumably because the Huguenot upbringing or enculturation produced people who could operate effectively within the socio-economic framework of the time.

(1992: 284)

To this Watkins replies that methodological individualism can sustain the notion of socially induced dispositions. Watkins argues that

I agree that methodological individualism allows for the formation, or 'cultural conditioning', of a widespread disposition to be explained only in terms of other human factors and not in terms of something *in*human, such as an alleged historicist law which impels people willy-nilly along some pre-determined course. But this is just the anti-historicist point of methodological individualism.

(1992a: 172; emphasis in original)

So, Watkins allows for cultural conditioning, but then holds that this must be reduced to individuals to avoid references to reified superhuman structures.

Given the adherence to an empiricist epistemology, Watkins retains the dichotomy between individuals and reified structures, and consequently he argues that dispositions are a product of cultural conditioning, which is to be explained in terms of other individuals, rather than sinister structural forces. Dispositions then are to be explained in terms of individuals creating and transmitting a set of ideas. Now whilst it would be erroneous to say that individuals did not create and transmit ideas, this is not sufficient to support Watkins' case. This is because Watkins cannot tell us where dispositions 'come from'. Individuals may transmit and change beliefs, but cultural systems pre-date and post-date particular individuals. Thus we can talk of Christianity separate from any particular individual's beliefs. People get socialised into pre-existing belief systems, and these belief systems are separate from the individuals who adhere to them. This is not to say that individuals are determined puppets, doomed to have a 'false consciousness' because of some structural determinism. Rather, it is just to say that cultures influence the beliefs and acts of individuals, and that cultures do not only exist in the present tense, when they are explicitly articulated or acted upon. Cultural systems are 'more than' the individuals who happen to adhere to the beliefs of a particular culture, because cultures have a continuity that far exceeds that of individuals; and such continuity could not be explained if cultures were reduced to the caprice of individual whim in the here and now. With Watkins' view, one is left with the impression that a culture could change at a minute's notice. This is not to deny that individuals can change their minds, but this cannot explain the longevity of cultures. How we are to conceptualise cultures as enabling and constraining factors upon agency will be discussed in Chapter 5, when it is argued that cultures exist as emergent properties.

So, the beguiling simplicity of methodological individualism is a siren call into unresolvable problems, whereby methodological individualists had to keep a 'double set of books', so to speak. On the one hand, they adhered to an empiricist epistemology as an underlabourer, arguing that one must reduce to individuals or reify social structures, whilst on the other hand they recognised the impossibility of realising this for actual *social* research, and made reference to situations and situational logics. This means that *methodological individualism had to violate its own epistemic underlabourer, and that in doing so, it produced a question-begging ontology of undefined social situations which could be interpreted in any way possible.* If pushed, individualists could turn to individual dispositions, but the danger here is of falling into psychologism, by explaining social relations as a manifestation of fixed mental states or a fixed human nature. Individualists may reject this, to try and give an account of cultural conditioning in individualist terms, but this fails to say why cultures exist as cohesive entities over very long periods of time.

Methodological collectivism: overcoming the problems?

Gellner rejects the 'reduce or reify' dichotomy by arguing that a reduction down to the level of individuals would result in psychologism. For Gellner (1969: 266) an individualist would have to reduce explanation down to the level of individuals, which means reducing explanation down to the level of individuals' dispositions (Gellner ignores the reference to situations). The result is psychologism, because what one is doing is explaining how individuals act by reference to psychological states. Here individuals' dispositions would be the independent variable and all 'social' actions would be the dependent variable, explainable wholly in terms of mental states. With such a reduction then, one could read-into any behaviour the categories used to define one's model of human nature or mental states, and verify one's ontology of human being.

Against this psychologistic reductionism, Gellner argues that dispositions should be regarded as the dependent variable. He argues that '[t]he real oddity of the reductionist case is that it seems to preclude a priori the possibility of human dispositions being the dependent variable in an historical explanation – when in fact they often or always are' (1969: 260). This is not to say that Gellner endorses the holistic notion that individuals are determined by social structures. Rather, it is just to say that individuals' dispositions are created within an irreducible social context that gives meaning to those dispositions. Gellner states that '[h]istory is *about* chaps. It does not follow that its explanations are always in terms of chaps. Societies are what people do, but social scientists are not biographers *en grande série*' (1969: 268; emphasis in original). Thus, to use Goldstein's example, we can explain the dispositions of individual Huguenots in terms of socially induced dispositions, meaning that we can talk about the actions of individuals (or 'chaps' in Gellner's parlance) in terms of their location within a specific social-cultural *milieu* which gave meaning to their actions.

Similarly, Mandelbaum argues that the concepts in 'sociological language "S"' are irreducible to concepts in 'psychological language "P"' *without remainder* (1992a: 226; emphasis added). Mandelbaum's point is that statements in the language S cannot be wholly reduced to the language P, as any discussion of individuals' actions would draw upon some form of social referent. Mandelbaum gives the example of the institution of marriage changing from monogamous to polygamous marriage within the Mormon community. He argues that this could be translated into statements about the actions of an aggregate of individuals. 'However, it is by no means certain that such translations could be effected without using the concepts which appear in the sociological language' (Mandelbaum 1992a: 227). To discuss the actions of individuals we need to make some reference to a social context. Thus instead of saying that individuals A, B, C, etc., decided to change the institution of marriage, and that this was a direct reflection of individual psychological features, we should say that individuals changed an institution because the socio-historical conditions had changed.[2]

As methodological collectivists recognise the need for reference to social factors, the next step is to enquire as to their definition of social ontology. Here we meet problems. Gellner says that '[w]e cannot even describe the state of mind of typical individual participants in the situation [military drill] without referring to the situation as a whole' (1969: 264). Yet he then goes straight on to say that the pattern of behaviour in different situations 'is not "merely abstracted" but is, as I am somewhat *sheepishly tempted to say*, "really there"' (1969: 264; emphasis added). So, having stressed the need for reference to a social context that is irreducible down to the level of individuals, Gellner feels rather guilty about accepting his conclusion, that social reality is 'more than' individuals.

Mandelbaum considers what he calls the 'ontological objection' to methodological collectivism, which is that without individuals there would be no society or social facts (1992a: 230). Against this he puts forward two arguments. The first is that social facts are not independent of the individuals existing in the present, but that they are independent of individuals in the past, meaning that the past acts of individuals affect actors in the future, because past forms of social organisation influence how people act now. The second argument is that social facts may depend upon individual facts without being identical. The argument here is a bit vague and Mandelbaum uses an analogy to make his point. He says that as the content of consciousness is dependent upon brain states whilst not being identical with brain states, so the 'component parts of a society' are irreducible to individuals (1992a: 231–2). Mandelbaum says that he prefers the second argument to the ontological objection. The reason for this seems to be that the second argument is more intuitive and relies on metaphor, whilst the first makes the issue of a literal definition more pertinent. Of course both raise the question of how to define social reality, but the first response raises this directly, by saying that present actions are in some way *constrained* by the past, whereas the second response relies on metaphor to make its point.[3]

So, Gellner and Mandelbaum are both extremely reticent to put forward an explicit social ontology. They both make reference to a social reality which is irreducible to purely individual factors, but neither is able to say exactly what this social reality actually is. The reason for this reticence – or 'sheepishness' – is that methodological collectivists are influenced by a moderate form of empiricism. To be sure, methodological collectivists do not want to say that what exists is definable in terms of what can be observed, and so they invoke a strata of reality which is 'more than' the actions of observable individuals. However, they are extremely concerned that putting forward an ontology of social structures will result in reified holism. To make a strong claim about structural factors which are unobservable in themselves would, for methodological collectivists, be to sail dangerously close towards the notion that structures controlled people, who were passive structural dopes. A residual empiricism pulls the methodological collectivists back towards the realm of observable facts, in the form of individuals' actions.

Methodological collectivism therefore cannot provide a clear ontology to guide methodology. Without any explicit formulation, there is no way that research could be criticised for misapplying a social ontology. Thus one could switch from: (1) an holist account of individuals being controlled by capitalist structures in an economic depression; to (2) give a description of individuals freely acting in a situational logic of economic growth, and refer to the latter position as methodological collectivism, because it makes reference to some undefined notion of social reality, and refuses to reduce S wholly into P (which methodological individualists would be happy with as they do not seek to reduce S into P, as that would be to endorse psychologistic reductionism).

In sum, a moderate empiricism cannot act as an underlabourer for sociology. An ontological underlabourer is required to link structure and agency, so that we may explain how individuals' agency is enabled and constrained by social factors; and to do so in a way that avoids the sociological logic of immediacy. Such an ontological underlabourer (as opposed to an ontological master-builder, as furnished by the sociological logic of immediacy) is required for sociological research because our access to the world is influenced by precepts, and these precepts include precepts about being. Our conceptual frameworks therefore need to make clear just how it is that structure and agency interact, otherwise we will fall into the problems noted above. More will be said about the efforts to link structure and agency, and the way an ontology may be used as an underlabourer, in Chapters 4, 5 and 6. Before this, though, we need to consider the views of Rorty, because if Rorty's views were accepted, there would be no need for social science as such, because there could be no truth about reality.

3 Post-Wittgensteinian pragmatism

Rorty, anti-representationalism and politics

Introduction

Rorty would not accept the view that philosophy can explain how knowledge is possible or how truth may be attained. Nor would Rorty accept the notion of using an ontology as a meta-theory that could guide empirical research and the formation of specific theories. The reason for this is that Rorty rejects the notion of positive underlabouring. Philosophy, and meta-theory too, would, for Rorty, be misguided attempts to step outside our socio-historically situated perspectives to try and gain some 'skyhook' or 'view from nowhere', in order to indulge in 'methodolatry', that could give a guaranteed access to The Truth.[1] Rorty does embrace a negative underlabourer function for philosophy, though, which means he wants to reject such 'realistic' attempts to 'represent' reality, in order to deflate the pretentions of philosophy, so that philosophers may stop seeing themselves as privileged guides to the truth (who can tell scientists what method to use), and start seeing themselves as people who may enrich us by developing new perspectives within the language game we are situated in.

For Rorty we can accept that natural science works without needing a philosophy to say why it works (let alone how it ought to work according to some methodological precepts), and we can accept that liberal democracy works (for 'us liberal democrats'), without turning to philosophical justifications concerning human being. We may add to this that social science would 'work' if it helped directly with policy formation to overcome practical problems. Social and political theory would not be science because it would concern grand speculation, which is not to say it is wrong, but it would be, for Rorty, to say that it ought to be viewed as something read in the private sphere outside work which may, like good literature, help educated and cultivated people by getting them to see things differently. We may read Marx at the weekend and ponder on how the poor may be helped and how silly the philosophy of history was, but we may not regard Marx (or any other text) as giving us *truth*, and we may not assume that the complexities of socio-historical reality can be 'boiled down' to a general formula. We may read Marx 'ironically' as a piece of 'poetry' for our 'edification' as people of letters, but reading Marx (or any theorist) literally would be a foolhardy realist misunderstanding which held that reality could be 'represented' (and changed via a theory's prescriptions). The other option would be to abandon the academy for a life of political involvement, if one did not want to be a 'literary figure' instead of a social scientist.

In this chapter I deal with Rorty's arguments in favour of anti-representationalism, and his arguments in favour of liberal democracy, together with his views on political activity. I argue that his post-Wittgensteinian position unfolds into the relativist and foundationalist philosophical logics of immediacy, and the structuralist and individualist sociological logics of immediacy. Rorty's post-Wittgensteinian pragmatism that would entail us accepting a view of social science as problem-solving policy work, or as literary work for private edification, need not therefore be accepted because his terms of reference end up replicating the problems he sought to avoid in his rejection of realism and representationalism. Rorty may maintain that realism and non-pragmatist philosophy are 'inflationary', in that they seek some God's-eye view, but, as was argued in Chapter 1, realist anti-foundationalism avoids such absolutist claims to knowledge (and relativism). We can therefore accept realism and reject the 'deflationary' approach to philosophy which puts the emphasis on practices within a language game and on seeing things differently, as the latter ends up predicated upon the logic of immediacy.

Realism and representation

Rorty regards (Western) philosophy (at least since the seventeenth century) as being realist, meaning that philosophy has sought to explain how human knowledge (in the form of ideas or propositions) may represent reality (that is external to beliefs or language). Philosophy sought to explain how knowledge was possible and therefore it would assume the mantle of a 'general theory of representation' (1994b: 3) which, *a fortiori*, meant that it could legislate upon different intellectual areas of enquiry, including scientific methodology. As Rorty puts it '[p]hilosophy as a discipline thus sees itself as the attempt to underwrite or debunk claims to knowledge made by science, morality, art or religion' (1994b: 3). To know the mind is to know that we can know, because to know the mind is to know how knowledge is constituted. From this it follows that the search for knowledge, in any area of study, must conform to the dictates of the philosophy of knowledge.

Rorty argues that

> The very idea of 'philosophy' as something distinct from 'science' would make very little sense without the Cartesian claim that by turning inward we could find ineluctable truth, and the Kantian claim that this truth imposes limits on the possible results of empirical inquiry.
>
> (1994b: 9)

To keep philosophy separate from science, and to secure a role for philosophy, given the *apparent* success of the nascent natural sciences, philosophy had to explain what it was that science was really doing, by saying how scientific knowledge could be *knowledge*. Without such an account of knowledge, the apparent success of science would be nothing but an illusion. Philosophy had therefore moved from being the handmaiden of theology to the master-builder of science, because given its unique understanding of how knowledge was possible, it could legislate upon empirical investigation of the world.

Once 'rational man' was the master of his mind he could then master the natural world. To *separate philosophy from science is thus to separate knowing from doing*, in order to explain why certain activities (such as science) were successful. The problem though is that in turning from the world to the mind, the result can only be a detached idealism, which is why the foundationalist search for certainty, in the form of a manifest truth, ended up with Kant's transcendental idealism. Hence Rorty argues that the defining feature of philosophy, after Descartes' turn to the mind, was 'methodological solipsism' (1994b: 191), because what could be known ended up being defined in terms of the individual's mind. Rorty notes that when Locke responded to Descartes' notion that knowledge was a priori, to argue that we had a posteriori knowledge via the senses, his distinction between primary and secondary qualities gave the game away. 'This distinction was so dubious as to lead us, via Berkeley and Hume, to Kant's rather desperate suggestion that the key only worked because we had, behind our own backs, constructed the lock it was to fit' (Rorty 1982: 192).

Thus the attempt to argue that we had an immediate access to a manifest truth via experience ran into problems, because the distinction between properties in the object itself and properties relative to the observer could not obtain. It could not obtain because all experienced properties were relative to the observer, in that we experienced ideas of sensation, and not the object 'speaking in its own language'. Kant's response to the problems of previous philosophy was to hold that we had a fixed set of categories, which decoded our disparate experiences. However, with Kant's transcendental idealism, the object of knowledge (the lock) was constituted partly by the categories in the mind (the key). This was not to argue for idealism, but given that we could never know the noumenal realm, and that the categories played quite a strong role in constituting the object of knowledge, the notion of a reality beyond our categories could easily become redundant.

Rorty does not restrict his critique of 'realism' to those philosophies which addressed how the mind may have knowledge. Rorty also criticises contemporary theories of truth which define truth in terms of correspondence. For Rorty the idea that truth is definable in terms of a linguistic proposition corresponding to a non-linguistic referent is absurd, because it would require one to 'step outside' language and all perspectives, to see reality-in-itself in order to compare the proposition with reality (1994a: 6). So, rather than hold that the correspondence theory of truth is at fault for making truth a property of a proposition (rather than its relationship to reality), Rorty is holding the view that the correspondence theory of truth requires the impossible task of seeing reality as it really is, before one can ascertain the veracity of any proposition. Indeed, as we will see, Rorty is not opposed to the idea that different language games 'carve out' different 'facts', even if he is opposed to the notions of knowledge, truth (as correspondence) and a reality-in-itself that we can 'represent' as it 'really is'.

At this point, one may be tempted to adopt an irrealism, such as: (1) the sceptical denial of knowledge (and science), (2) the truth-relativist view that all knowledge is wholly relative to contingent social norms (so science only exists for those who believe in the norms of science), or (3) the idealist view that there is nothing beyond our ideas (so science is just about ideas). Rorty would counsel against such a reaction, however, because such irrealism is still within the confines of what Rorty (1994a) refers to as the 'representationalist problematic'. The sceptical or relativist denial of knowledge, and the idealist argument that we know ideas, are operating within the frame of reference set by the realist conviction that beliefs can represent – or correspond to – non-beliefs. To argue for or against representation is to remain with the problematic that turns on the issue of beliefs being able, or unable, to represent something beyond them. What is needed, according to Rorty, is not an argument defending or rejecting the idea about beliefs corresponding to an external reality, but a break from this paradigm, to a pragmatic focus on ways for going on, within different forms of life.[2]

Anti-representationalism and the philosophical logic of immediacy

Instead of replacing realism with irrealism, we ought to swap the representationalist problematic for the anti-representationalist problematic. Whereas the representationalist problematic is concerned with the relationship – or not – between an individual's beliefs and reality, or propositions and reality, the anti-representationalist problematic is concerned with practices within different cultures. Whereas realism searches for 'skyhooks', to pull the mind beyond the corrupting influence of social and cultural beliefs *qua* prejudices which impede epistemic immediacy, Rorty's anti-representationalism has a pragmatic concern with improving our practices for going on. As Rorty puts it, '[b]y an anti-representational account I mean one which *does not view knowledge as a matter of getting reality right*, but rather as a matter of *acquiring habits of action for coping with reality*' (1994a: 1; emphasis added).

This does not mean that Rorty is arguing for a form of behaviourism whereby the body acts on practices which work (positive reinforcement stimuli) and avoids practices which do not work (negative reinforcement stimuli). Confusion may arise, though, when Rorty refers to his position as 'epistemological behaviourism' (1994b: 174). Rorty says this in the context of signalling his affiliation with the work of the later Wittgenstein. This may be doubly confusing as it may lead one to think that Rorty reads Wittgenstein as a behaviourist, and that he agrees with such behaviourism. Wittgenstein could be read as a behaviourist because he rejects any reference to an inner self, and argues that people's actions are based on following public rules within their language game. Thus social action is based on following public rules, concerning appropriate behaviour in particular circumstances. A behaviourist reading would hold that the social rules constituted the positive and negative reinforcement stimuli which determined the behaviour of the body, which did not possess an 'inner self'. Although there is not the space to go into a detailed interpretation of Wittgenstein, we can note the following. Unlike behaviourism, Wittgenstein would reject the denial of the self, and the view that the body was a determined mechanism (controlled by external stimuli). For Wittgenstein it makes no sense to deny the existence of a self because the notion of an inner self is itself empty. The denial of an empty proposition is itself empty.[3] Further, to say that the body was a determined mechanism would be to assume some form of meta-language game, via which one could explain all forms of individual behaviour, whatever the form of life, or community, involved. Against this, Wittgenstein would argue that one could not step outside a language game to assume such a master-view of reality-in-itself. One could not explain all forms of action via a master-ontology of the body.

This raises the spectre of relativism, and Wittgenstein's arguments are ambivalent on this topic. On the one hand, Wittgenstein argues that if a lion could talk we could not understand him (1995: 223), which means that language games are hermetic. Here normative relativism would lead onto truth-relativism, because one could not step beyond the community's norm to understand how others go on in a different language game, which implies that one could not recognise that one's views about an external reality were fallible. One would have no notion of truth that was external to the norms of the language game. On the other hand, though, Wittgenstein does make reference to human universals, when he talks of the common behaviour of mankind (1995: 82. ¶206). A similar divide occurs with Rorty's arguments, but before pursuing that issue, we need to connect Rorty's pragmatism to the above quick sketch of Wittgenstein's (later) philosophy.

Rorty's epistemological behaviourism is Wittgensteinian in the sense that for Rorty, actors' beliefs are connected to their social practices, which follow the rules of a language game; and beliefs do not picture or mirror non-beliefs *qua* discrete facts. Thus instead of having an 'atomistic' view whereby a proposition is justified if it 'corresponds' to a discrete fact, we have an 'holistic' view, whereby justification of beliefs is grounded in the community's norms and practices, i.e. its customary ways of going on. As Rorty puts it '[c]onversational justification, so to speak, is naturally holistic, whereas the notion of justification embedded in the epistemological tradition is reductive and atomistic' (1994b: 170). Such a position then is holistic in the sense that to understand a belief one must understand that it is a component of a broader language game. This is 'behaviourist' in the sense that we are dealing with beliefs as being connected with the practical activity – or behaviour – within a particular community, and that there is no transcendent essence for the self which can step beyond social perspectives to see that propositions do indeed correspond to atomistic facts. Instead of a transcendent self which has an immediate access to a manifest truth, there are people within different language games that go on in different ways.

Rorty argues that this anti-representationalism 'leaves one without a sky-hook with which to escape from the ethnocentrism produced by accultura-tion, [and] that the liberal culture of recent times has found a strategy for avoiding the disadvantages of ethnocentrism' (1994a: 2). So, what we believe reflects our spatial and temporal location within a particular community, and we cannot climb beyond this to see things as they 'really are', but liberalism rests on tolerance which helps foster new views and better practices for going on, by allowing for critique and the exchange of ideas. The argument here is close to Popper's (1962) notion that an 'open society' (i.e. liberal democratic society) allows science to flourish. Popper argues that as liberalism allows free speech, critique, and the open dissemination of ideas, science can freely develop without being retarded by having to conform to some politico-phi-losophical ideology, such as 'dialectical materialism'. Given free speech, science can freely develop.[4] Rorty is advocating a similar argument because he is saying that although we cannot escape our enculturation, liberalism fosters tolerance and indeed encourages dissent, so we can improve our prac-tices. We cannot find the finished Truth, and nor can we step outside the norms of our culture so our beliefs correspond to reality-in-itself, but we can have *progress*, in the sense that we can *improve our ways of going on*, and *liberalism allows the freedom to do this* (in science, and culture more generally).

This leads Rorty to argue that scientists should be regarded as moral exemplars, not because they have replaced religion to find The Truth in a secular way, but because science is based on 'unforced agreement' (1994a: 39). He says that

> On this view, to say that truth will win in [an open] encounter is not to make a metaphysical claim about the connection between human reason and the nature of things. It is merely to say that the best way to find out what to believe is to listen to as many suggestions and arguments as you can.
>
> (Rorty 1994a: 39)

We can go on in better ways, not by getting better representations, but by improving our practices in the light of open debate. Scientists are to be praised therefore as exemplary liberals rather than as Modern Schoolmen.

Before dealing with Rorty's views on liberalism, I will concentrate here upon the notion that we can improve our beliefs and practices. Such a notion requires some criteria by which to judge one way of going on more favourably than another. There are three forms of criteria by which one may make such a judgement. One may say that: (1) the standards for judgement are wholly internal to a conceptual framework/set of cultural norms, (2) the standards for judgement turn on beliefs corresponding to an external referent, with correspondence implying a relationship of epistemic immediacy, or (3) judgement turns upon correspondence between a theory and an object, with correspondence turning upon fallible conceptual schemes approximating to the truth (as argued for in Chapter 1).

Rorty's rejection of representationalism for pragmatism can be read as supporting position (1). He argues that

> All talk about *doing things to objects* must, in a pragmatic account of inquiry 'into' objects, be paraphraseable as talk about *reweaving beliefs*. [...] Once one drops the traditional opposition between context and thing contextualized, *there is no way to divide things up into those which are what they are independent of context and those which are context-dependent* [...]. For a belief is what it is only by virtue of its position in a web. Once we view the 'representation' and 'aboutness' relations (which some philosophers have supposed to 'fix the content' of belief) as fallout from a given contextualization of those beliefs, *a belief becomes simply a position in a web*.
>
> (1994a: 98; emphasis added)

Here then the object of knowledge is reducible into the conceptual scheme used to get knowledge. No reference can be made to anything other than the beliefs of the conceptual scheme. In which case, questions of reality would become questions of knowledge and questions of truth would be reduced into the origin of a belief within a conceptual scheme. What could be talked about would be what could be known, and what could be known were the beliefs that constituted a conceptual scheme. It follows from this that truth would also be reducible into a conceptual scheme, because to collapse the distinction between the object of knowledge and the beliefs about the object is to make beliefs self-referential. In which case, a belief would be true by virtue of its origin within a conceptual scheme. Thus we have: (a) the epistemic fallacy, as ontology is reduced into epistemology, by conflating the object to be known into the conceptual scheme with which we have 'knowledge'; and (b) the genetic fallacy, as truth turns on the origin of a concept in a self-referential conceptual scheme. In short, to collapse the distinction between the object of knowledge and conceptual schemes is to predicate explanation on the relativist philosophical logic of immediacy, the result being that any belief within a conceptual framework or language game would be justified because beliefs were self-referential.

Rorty would object by pointing out that truth-relativism was predicated upon the representationalist problematic and that as he was not concerned with issues of how beliefs did, or did not, mirror external non-beliefs, then he could not be a relativist. As he argues, '[n]ot having *any* epistemology, *a fortiori*, [the pragmatist] does not have a relativistic one' (1994a: 24; emphasis in original). The problem though is that relativism is an anti-epistemology rather than an epistemology. If epistemology concerns the relationship of beliefs with an external reality (whether the relationship is one of immediacy or not), and relativism holds that what is true is relative to a community's norms, then relativism is based on negating any reference to a reality beyond norms (or conceptual schemes). In other words, truth-relativism is opposed to any form of epistemology, whether foundational or anti-foundational, as it rejects the notion of truth claims being made about referents external to norms or concepts. Relativism reduces truth into norms, and thus renders the notion of truth redundant. Truth becomes a mere synonym for norms. Thus an enquiry into justification will turn on an enquiry into the origin of a belief within a particular set of norms. So, to reject epistemology *per se* is, in effect, the same as adopting a truth-relativist position, as both cut beliefs free from a relationship to an external reality. In which case 'progress' becomes a meaningless reference, as whatever beliefs obtain are true within one community, whilst other beliefs are necessarily false (except for those in different communities).

A better denial of relativism would be to say that as pragmatism is concerned with improving practices, or finding better ways of going on, then there must be some reference to an external reality. After all, Rorty is happy to admit that 'science works', as it helps us 'cope with reality', and he only takes issue with the attempt to explain why science works, using foundationalist epistemology. Without any reference to an external reality, with which our beliefs and practices connect, in some way, it would make little sense to argue that liberalism is good for promoting a culture of open discussion which will allow for the improvement of our ways of going on (including scientific practices).

Despite saying that there is no distinction between the context and thing contextualised, Rorty does actually make a distinction between the 'thing' itself and the context in which it is understood. Having put a lot of emphasis on denying that beliefs correspond to non-beliefs, Rorty argues that this should not be read as a form of idealism, whereby all we can refer to are self-referential beliefs. He argues that unlike idealism, pragmatism has

> a wholehearted acceptance of the brute, inhuman, causal stubbornness of the gold or the text. But they think this should not be confused with, so to speak, an *intentional* stubbornness, an insistence on being *described in a certain way*, its *own* way. The object can, given a prior agreement on a language game, cause us to hold beliefs, but it cannot suggest which beliefs to hold. It can only do things which our practices will react to with preprogrammed changes in beliefs.
>
> (1994a: 83–4; emphasis in original)

Similarly, Rorty argues that the pragmatist

> agrees that there is such a thing as brute physical resistance – the pressure of light waves on Galileo's eye, or of the stone on Dr. Johnson's boot. But

he sees no way of transferring this nonlinguistic brutality to *facts*, to the truth of sentences. The way in which a blank takes on the form of the die which stamps it has no analogy to the relation between the truth of a sentence and the event the sentence is about. When the die hits the blank something causal happens, but as many *facts* are brought into the world as there are languages for describing that causal transaction. [. . .] To say that we must have respect for the facts is just to say that we must, if we are to play a certain language game, play by the rules.

(1994a: 81; emphasis in original)

Now there is something beyond the context, or the web of beliefs, and it has some causal effect as regards those beliefs. The 'brute . . . causal stubbornness' of an object *exists prior to* any interpretative framework being brought to it.

It may seem that Rorty is now advocating position (3), which holds that we have a fallible and conceptually mediated access to reality. Rorty wants to say that although our beliefs do not mirror reality, there is still a reality beyond our beliefs, which means he is defending the metaphysical realist rejection of idealism.[5] So, whilst there can be no correspondence in the sense of having a direct access to an external reality, *our beliefs are about a reality that has a causal effect upon us*, even if it cannot cause us to have a belief which is an epistemic isomorph of a non-belief. The problem though is that beliefs become divorced from the external reality. Rorty may admit that there is a thing beyond the context, and that it has some causal influence over us, but this realm of reality becomes redundant. Rorty is so concerned with avoiding epistemic immediacy (i.e. position 2), whereby beliefs picture external essences, that he qualifies reality out of the picture, so to speak, by saying that *the object cannot suggest what beliefs to hold*. In other words, *all the work is done by the language game*. We thus have a form of post-Kantianism, with a divide between a knowable phenomenal realm, constituted by a language game, and an unknowable noumenal realm, which can 'cause' us to hold beliefs without suggesting what beliefs to hold. This is an odd use of the verb 'cause', given that not only does the holding of any belief require prior agreement on a language game, but having influenced us via a language game, reality still cannot tell – or even suggest – what beliefs to hold. Reality, in short, has no effective causal power at all, and instead all the explanatory work is done by a language game.

As Rorty puts it, when the die hits the blank there are *as many facts as there are languages* for describing this. All languages for describing this event are therefore of equal value. In other words, Rorty's argument entails the epistemic and genetic fallacies. What we can know is defined in terms of how we can know it (via language games), which is why there are as many facts as languages and, given the loss of any external referent, truth is reducible to a language game. There can be no better or worse languages for describing how the die hits the blank, because what we know is reducible to the language game we have to know it with. Therefore we cannot say that some practices are better than others, because there is no meaningful way to sustain any reference to an extra-discursive reality. We can go on as the language game dictates, but we cannot say that a language game is fallible, or that one language game is better than another because, given the loss of an extra-discursive reality, what we can know is wholly reducible to our language game. There may always be a perspective via which we interpret the world, but this does not mean that there can be no truth claims made about the world, as argued in Chapter 1.

In addition to this relativist form of the philosophical logic of immediacy, Rorty's work also adheres to the positivist/foundationalist version of the philosophical logic of immediacy. This much is suggested in the quoted passages above where Rorty implies that causal relations are to be defined in terms of observed regularities, such as the die hitting the blank and, presumably, leaving an imprint. Where the positivist definition of causal laws as observed constant conjunctions is clear in Rorty's work, is in his discussion of physicalism.[6] Rorty argues that '[p]hysicalism is probably right in saying that we shall someday be able, "in principle", to predict every movement of a person's body [. . .] by reference to microstructures within his body' (1994b: 354). Later on Rorty has less reservations, and the 'in principle' clause is dropped. He argues that

> Every speech, thought, theory, poem, composition, and philosophy *will* turn out to be *completely predictable* in purely naturalistic terms. Some atoms-and-the-void account of micro-processes within individual human beings *will permit the prediction of every sound or inscription which will ever be uttered*. There are no ghosts.
>
> (1994b: 387; emphasis added)

Rorty does not regard such a deterministic account of behaviour to be a threat to human freedom. This is because: (a) if we retain the 'in principle' version, then conditions will be too complex to carry out a real prediction, 'except as an occasional pedagogical exercise' (1994b: 354); and (b), if we drop this qualification, then there is still the fact that there will be many vocabularies to describe humans which are irreducible to atoms-and-the-void accounts (1994b: 388).

With the former account (account (a)), Rorty is arguing that causal laws can be observed in their effects, human behaviour is a result of causal laws, and the cause–effect relationship could be directly observed, *if it were not that there were many other factors at work*. Note though that the complexity clause is qualified itself, when Rorty argues that prediction could occur as an 'occasional pedagogical exercise'. In other words, if the number of causal factors influencing behaviour could be narrowed down, then we could directly observe a causal law by observing how a physical process produced certain types of behaviour. Thus if human behaviour were subject to experimental closure, we could observe causal laws at work. What this means is that Rorty does not just accept the obvious fact that science works, but tacitly proffers an explanation of *why* science works, using empiricism as an epistemological underlabourer. The message given out in the argument on empirical complexity is that causal laws are to be identified in their effects, as observed regularities, and that as observed events are complex, scientific method ought to be based on limiting the number of factors, so that we can just observe the relevant constant conjunction. *Scientific method is to be based upon experimental closure which limits the number of observable factors.*

As regards the latter account (account (b)) about irreducibility, Rorty argues that irreducibility does not entail incompatibility (1994b: 388). What this means is that vocabularies about aesthetic value, morals, political norms, etc., are irreducible to the physicalist vocabulary, but physicalism is still true. This argument though cannot prevent a determinist account of behaviour, because if behaviour *per se* is to be explained by physicalism, then it follows that different types of behaviour, such as formulating aesthetic, political, and moral arguments (etc.) will be subject to such a reductionist and determinist account too. Thus aesthetic, political, moral, religious, etc., languages will be epiphenomena that are explainable by a reduction down to observable physical causal laws. The languages are obviously incompatible in the sense that they have different frames of reference, yet they are reducible to physicalism, simply because if one accepts the physicalist view then it follows that other languages and ways of going on are to be explained by a reduction to the causal laws that control how individuals go on.

Rorty is, as Bhaskar (1991) notes, trying to have a Kantian conception of the self as both free and determined. As Kant held that the noumenal self was free, and the phenomenal/empirical self was determined, so Rorty holds that the social self that uses language games is free, whilst the physical self is determined (Bhaskar 1991: 47–69). In both cases the self that has free will is redundant, because there is no way to explain how it can influence the determined self.

So, Rorty rejects the representationalist problematic, defined in terms of realism and anti-realism, in favour of the anti-representationalist problematic. The former concerns the realist attempt to say how knowledge is possible, and the anti-realist (relativist or sceptical) denial of knowledge. The latter moves beyond defences and refutations of how beliefs represent reality, to shift the terms of reference to how we have different customary ways of going on. The problem though is that this pragmatic anti-representationalism collapses into truth-relativism, because beliefs become self-referential, as language games are prevented from being causally influenced by an external reality. Reality cannot 'suggest' what beliefs to hold, or which beliefs not to hold, and so language games become self-referential.

In addition to this, Rorty's account of physicalism indicates that he has a positivistic conception of scientific methodology. Rorty advocates such a physicalism in order to reject the notion that there is a transcendent self, or metaphysical mind, which stands above its location within a culture. Rorty wants to expunge the ghost in the machine (1994b: 387). More will be said about this rejection of the transcendent self below, and here we can say that the result was a determinism which would reduce all explanation of behaviour to brain states.[7]

Liberalism and ethnocentrism

In the rest of this chapter I will turn my attention from epistemological issues *per se* to discuss Rorty's arguments about politics and the ramifications of such arguments for social science. This discussion of politics will cover three topics: Rorty's 'ethnocentrism', Nietzschean liberalism and positivistic-conservatism. A discussion of politics may seem far removed from a discussion of epistemology, but for Rorty the anti-representationalist problematic has a political aspect, in that a concern with how we go on will necessarily concern how we go on in a social and political context. A concern with practices for coping with reality includes the social and political realm of dealing with others.

Rorty wants to defend liberal democracy, but given his anti-representationalism, he cannot argue for liberal democracy by making some truth claim about a universal, pre-social human essence. Thus Rorty cannot make a truth claim about human nature being materially acquisitive, in order to justify liberalism as a political system which allows people the freedom to engage in material competition, with the state regulating such competition to protect private property from being taken illegitimately by force or fraud. Nor can Rorty justify (representative) democracy in terms of individuals being rational, in the sense that they can apply some form of neutral method to select the best representative of their (perceived) interests. This is not to say that people can be characterised as irrational, but rather, it is to say that individuals have no defining essence, and that there is no way to step beyond one's enculturation, or ways of going on in an inherited language game, to base political decisions on the 'facts' about some pre-social human essence, or 'Reason'.

For Rorty the self is a decentred contingency. The self is decentred because there is no central defining essence which separates the self from its location within a particular language game, and so what the self *is* is contingent upon what the self *does* within a particular language game. Rorty argues that, as noted above, beliefs are 'habits of action' (1994a: 93), meaning that beliefs are connected to communal ways of going on in a language game. Thus to understand the self all one has to do is understand its socio-historical location within a particular language game. Against the metaphor of 'inner mental states' in the 'mind' Rorty argues that:

> For this traditional metaphor, a non-reductive physicalist model substitutes the picture of a network of beliefs and desires which is continually in process of being rewoven [...]. This network is not one which is rewoven by an agent distinct from the network – a master weaver so to speak. Rather, *it reweaves itself*, in response to stimuli such as new beliefs acquired when, e.g., doors are opened.
>
> (1994a: 123; emphasis added)

So, in contrast to the lone mind of foundationalism which transcends social norms to see the manifest truth, we have a self which is contingent upon its socio-historical location, and which reacts to its environment in ways deemed appropriate by the rules of the prevailing language game.

The position that Rorty is in then, is one whereby he wants to defend liberal democracy, whilst arguing that the self, together with, as we saw earlier, truth, is contingent upon the norms of a particular community. This means that the only defence of liberal democracy can be in terms of ethnocentrism. As there can be no reference to 'facts' independent of a given language game, especially facts about human being, there can only be reference to the rules of a language game, or the norms of a particular community. Political systems are therefore only assessable by reference to their own norms and customary ways of going on. In which case, the anti-representationalist concern for practices which work will, in the context of political practices, mean that *political systems can be defended if they work according to their own terms of reference*. So, providing that liberal democracy works according to its own terms of reference (i.e. providing that liberal democracy *is* actually liberal democracy), then it can be defended as good for liberal democrats. Or, to put it another way, liberal democracy is good for those who have been socialised into being liberal democrats, because liberal democratic practices are good for those who go on in liberal democrat ways. Such an argument is obviously circular, but for Rorty the circularity would be virtuous rather than vicious, because it merely acknowledges that we cannot step beyond our socially contingent perspectives, and that we must judge our political practices in terms of the perspective in which we are located. Just as there is no epistemic foundation for knowledge in the philosophy of mind, so there is no foundation for politics in an ontology of human being.

However, if there is no self which is an active spinner of a web of beliefs, i.e. a 'master weaver', then the decentred self, *qua* network, would be too passive. As Shusterman argues,

> this absence of a structuring centre prevents [the self] from being the sort of *Bildungsroman* it seems to want to be. [...] But without such a conception of the self that is capable of identity through change or changing description, there can be no self capable of self-enrichment or enlargement, and this would nullify the Rortian aesthetic life of self-enrichment, by rendering it meaningless.
>
> (1988: 346)[8]

If the self were a network devoid of a master weaver, then it would be a mere automaton. For to remove the master weaver from the web is to remove the creative force to change the web. Without such a self, the decentred self would be an epiphenomenon of the prevailing language game. The self *qua* decentred web would just be a reflection of the prevailing social norms.

Individuals would therefore have their behaviour determined by the rules of the language game. This is a problem not just as regards individual creativity, but as regards the defence of liberal democracy.

If we are in a position where not only is truth reduced into social norms as argued in the previous section, but the self is a passive epiphenomenon of the prevailing norms, then any political system would be 'justified', in the eyes of those who lived within that system. Liberalism would be justified along with state socialism and fascism. As regards this argument about truth-relativism, Geras argues that if we lose the notion of truth then we lose the notion of injustice. As Geras argues:

> if truth is wholly relativized or internalized to particular discourses or language games or social practices, there is no injustice. The victims and protesters of any *putative* injustice are deprived of their last weapon, that of telling what really happened. They can only tell their story which is something else. Morally and politically, therefore, anything goes.
>
> (1995a: 107; emphasis in original)[9]

Such a problem is compounded by the determinism which arises if one holds that the self is a mere decentred contingency. For in such a case there is no self which can be the possessor of universal human rights, and the self *qua* determined automaton will only regard its political system as correct. The result of this determinism would be tribalism, because at best there could be no communication between different groups and, at worst, there would be conflict between groups who would *necessarily* perceive other political systems as wrong. Difference would mean 'not us', and 'not us' would be wrong, because what it was to be right (epistemically and normatively) would be 'us – how we go on in our community'. Those in the wrong, by being different, may be tolerated, but then again, they may not.

Rorty would obviously not want to endorse ethnocentrism in the sense of blind nationalism, racism, etc.[10] Hence Rorty argues against Lyotard on the interpretation of Wittgenstein. He argues that '[w]hereas Lyotard takes Wittgenstein to be pointing to unbridgeable divisions between linguistic islets, I see him as recommending the construction of causeways which will, in time, make the archipelago in question continuous with the mainland' (1994a: 216). Rorty continues by arguing that

> On my reading, Wittgenstein was not warning us against attempts to translate the untranslatable but rather against the unfortunate philosophical habit of seeing different languages as embodying incompatible systems of rules. If one does see them in this way, then the lack of an overarching system of metarules for pairing off sentences – the sort of system which metanarratives were once supposed to help us get – will strike one as a disaster. But if one sees language learning as the acquisition of a skill, one will not be tempted to ask what metaskill permits such

acquisition. One will assume that curiosity, tolerance, patience, luck, and hard work are all that is needed.

(1994a: 216)

Thus on Rorty's pragmatic reading of Wittgenstein, we may not be able to have a meta-language game for translating different language games, but we can learn to *go on in different ways*.

Here Rorty would seem to be edging from his weak ethnocentrism, as opposed to strong tribalistic ethnocentrism (assuming that we can maintain such a difference), to a form of universalism. It would seem to be the case that Rorty is not just saying that different communities have different ways of going on. Rather, it would seem to be that he is adding another argument, which is that tribalism is bad, and that liberalism is good *for everyone*, because liberalism allows the requisite tolerance to help prevent conflict rooted in ethnic, national, religious, etc., difference. *The cornerstone of Rorty's argument with Lyotard over reading Wittgenstein is the belief that we (liberals) are tolerant of others, and that we want to, and ought to, understand others in their own terms.* We can therefore, according to Rorty, maintain a distinction between persuasion and force, when dealing with other cultures, because we can, to some extent, understand those cultures in their own terms. Whereas Lyotard 'would argue that the existence of incommensurable, untranslatable discourses throws doubt on this distinction between force and persuasion' (Rorty 1994a: 214), Rorty's liberalism allows such a distinction to obtain. What Rorty is doing, therefore, is presupposing liberal values, reading these into Wittgenstein, and using this as an argument about how different communities can avoid conflict, by not being locked into hermetic language games, where 'persuasion' entails imperialist violence. Without liberalism there would be 'unbridgeable linguistic islets', so liberal values underpin non-violent relations between *all* communities, with their different language games. Without a prior commitment to liberal values there is the very real danger that people may say that their spade has turned simply upon encountering difference. However, there is the danger that even liberals may not be able to understand how others go on, because they may not be able to get a reflexive distance from their own norms. Certainly Rorty seems to recognise this when he argues that those who question the Enlightenment liberal belief in a transcendent rational self are regarded as mad, because they are opposing the Enlightenment culture's norms. As he puts it, '[t]hey [e.g. Nietzsche] are crazy because the limits of sanity are set by what *we* can take seriously. This, in turn, is determined by our upbringing, our historical situation' (1994a: 188; emphasis in original). If people who question are 'crazy', in the sense that their arguments simply cannot be made sense of, because they are in contrast with the prevailing norms, then the same would apply to differences between cultures. Other cultures would appear crazy, even if one were a liberal, simply because one could not understand difference, and so one would not want to learn how to go on in a crazy way. However, if the limits of sanity are set by our culture or the rules of our language game, and if the self is decentred and therefore determined, then it is impossible for someone to acquire the requisite reflexive distance from their norms, in order to challenge those norms. It would not be individuals but only communities which were crazy. This means that there could be no understanding between linguistic islets, even if one were a liberal.

We can sum up this section as follows. Rorty's arguments about ethno-centrism are predicated upon the structuralist sociological logic of immedi-acy. This is because the argument places all the emphasis on the social object, in the form of an ontology of social norms, with the social subject being a passive and determined epiphenomenal puppet, or 'cultural dope'. To under-stand the behaviour of individuals it would be sufficient to simply refer to an ontology which described the prevailing norms. One would have a definitive master-ontology. This not only entails philosophical problems, because it turns on the notion that concepts have a relationship of epistemic immediacy to their referents (as argued in Chapter 2). It also results in a determinism that negates any justification for a particular political system, and this is compounded by the argument about truth which entails an anything-goes truth-relativism, thus rendering critique of injustice impossible.

Nietzschean liberalism

One way of summarising Rorty's position is to say that he wants to replace being (ontology) and knowing (epistemology) with becoming. In place of having truth claims which mirror discrete essences, such as a universal pre-social human essence, the emphasis is placed upon how people have differ-ent practices and how the self is different in different socio-historical con-texts. Instead of fixed 'realist' certainties, there is an emphasis on contingency.[11] Now as we have seen, contingency may imply relativism and determinism, producing results contrary to Rorty's intentions. To escape from this, the emphasis on contingency could be regarded as an emphasis on creativity. That is, instead of adhering to an *ontology of human being* which sought to define humanity in terms of a fixed essence, there is an emphasis upon individual self-creation, with the contingent character of the self allowing for a *continuous process of becoming*. Whereas certainties about the essence of the self impose constraint, recognising the contingency of selfhood allows for creativity.

However, to support the notion of the self changing its web of beliefs, and to avoid determinism, one must posit an essence for the self as a poetic master weaver. The creative self would not be a decentred contingency, but a poetic master weaver, acting upon its web of beliefs (which it was separate from), which means that whilst the web may be contingent, the self certainly is not. *For contingency to mean creativity and not determinism, there has to be a self separate from the web of beliefs.* Rorty seems to recognise this, and against his stated argument that there is no essence for the self, he tacitly imports an essence for the self, with which to justify liberalism, as an abstract political ideology. In place of an *ethnocentric defence of our liberal social practices* Rorty moves on to argue that liberalism, meaning the classical liberal abstract ideology which simply talks in terms of public and private spheres, is *justified because it is in accord with a universal human essence*.

We can see how Rorty ends up importing an essence for the self by turning to his discussion of Nietzsche's view on selfhood. Rorty approvingly cites Nietzsche's aphorism that truth is a 'mobile army of metaphors', in support of his claim that we cannot uncover the truth to arrive at a point of epistemic immediacy (1992: 27). This is extended to the issue of selfhood, with Rorty arguing that

> He [Nietzsche] did not give up the idea that an individual might track home the blind impress all his behavings bore. He only rejected the idea that this tracking was a process of discovery. In his view, in achieving this sort of self-knowledge we are not coming to know a truth which was out there (or in here) all the time. Rather he saw self-knowledge as self-creation. The process of coming to know oneself, confronting one's contingency, tracking one's causes home, is identical with the process of inventing a new language – that is, of thinking up new metaphors.
>
> (1992: 27)

Thus Rorty describes the identity of the self as its 'final vocabulary' (1992: 73), in order to illustrate his view that the self is a contingency: one *is* what one *describes* oneself as, using a particular set of words at a particular point in time, and there is no real essence behind this. The word 'self' is therefore a verb rather than a noun: there is no fixed essence which is named by the noun of 'self' (or 'I'), and instead selfhood is to be understood in terms of active on-going creation.

Of course, some individuals may mistakenly think that their contingent identity reflects some form of fixed truth. Those who can recognise the contingency of selfhood are referred to as 'ironists', because having recognised such contingency, they will not mistake their metaphors for literal descriptions, and so they will not regard identity issues as wholly serious (1992: 73). They will not be wholly serious about their identity because they recognise it is not a defining truth but a moveable feast, which they are free to recreate. Instead of being serious philosophers concerned with knowing about the nature of human being, ironists will be poets who will revel in the freedom to create and recreate what it is to be human. In place of taking identities seriously, poets will redescribe themselves, reworking the prevailing language game in novel ways, by taking an ironic approach to the language game.

Such poets will be engaged in a process of Nietzschean self-overcoming, meaning that they will overcome settled descriptions which others take unquestioningly as given: they will adopt an ironic attitude to the given, and recreate it in a novel, poetic way. To fail to do this is to fail to be human. As Rorty notes:

> To fail as a poet – and thus, for Nietzsche, to fail as a human being – is to accept someone else's description of oneself, to execute a previously pre-pared program, to write, at most, elegant variations on previously writ-ten programmes. So the only way to trace home the causes of one's being as one is would be to tell a story about one's causes in a *new language*.
>
> (1992: 28; emphasis added)

To be a poet, and thus to be truly human, one must invent a private language. Rorty's adherence to Nietzschean philosophy is thus at odds with his Wittgensteinianism, given Wittgenstein's argument that there can be no private languages, because meaning requires non-arbitrary verification, which relies on public rules.[12] Another way of putting this is to say that instead of the self being a contingent collection of beliefs, with no master weaver, the self has a defining essence as a master weaver. This enables the self to exercise a poetic ability to create private languages. Without a master weaver that was separate from the web of beliefs, the self would be a passive automaton. There would be no self which could stand back from the pre-vailing norms, take an ironic attitude to those norms, and then poetically create a private language.

As the self has a poetic essence it will benefit from being allowed the freedom to exercise its discursive agency, enriching itself by creating new private languages. Without the freedom for such discursive agency the poet could not practise poetry, and would therefore be impoverished. This means that the citizens of a liberal democracy benefit from the formal freedom allowed, and the informal culture of tolerance which is meant to accompany liberalism, whereas the subjects of an authoritarian state will be impover-ished. The subjects of an authoritarian state will not just lack the freedom to enrich themselves by poetically reworking their final vocabularies. They will also have their very humanity denied, because they will be subject to the worst form of pain, which is the pain of humiliation. In place of having the freedom to exercise their poetic ability and enrich themselves by creat-ing private languages, the subjects of an authoritarian state will have an identity imposed upon them, as members of the proletarian 'universal class', or 'master-race', etc.

On this issue of humiliation Rorty basically admits that he is dealing with a 'human universal', or essence, when talking about the self. He argues that

> She [the liberal ironist] thinks that what unites her with the rest of the species is not a common language but *just* susceptibility to pain and in particular to that special sort of pain which the brutes do not share with the humans – humiliation.
>
> (1992: 92; emphasis in original)

Whatever language game one is situated within, one is definable as a human by the susceptibility to redescription, i.e. humiliation. As various commentators note, this notion of harm appeals to a human universal, saying that such susceptibility applies to all people *qua* people.[13] However, this conception of harm trades upon another notion of human being. It is not simply that humanity can be defined as open to humiliation in terms of redescription. For that would beg the question as to why and how redescription functioned as a harming influence to humanity *per se*. To address this question, one must recognise that Rorty already has an essence for the self, in terms of poetic ability. Redescription is harmful because what it is to be human is to be a poet enriching oneself via the creation of private languages. If this expression of human nature is limited, individuals are impoverished as humans, and if poetry is denied, with individuals having an identity imposed upon them, then what it is to be human is violated. Rorty (1992: 91) may state that there is no universal human essence, and that people find solidarity through fear of humiliation, but unless there were a poetic self which would have its humanity abnegated by not being poetic, then there could be no such singular fear.[14]

One could say that if redescription is so harmful then liberalism ought to be harmful, because if individuals are free to create new languages, they could redescribe others, and thus harm them. However, Rorty defends liberalism by arguing that one may be a Nietzschean poet in the private sphere, and a liberal like J. S. Mill in the public sphere. Whereas Nietzsche was an anti-liberal elitist, Rorty gives us a Nietzschean liberalism, by demarcating self-overcoming away from the public realm, where one must not harm others. Enrichment need not be at the cost of humiliation. So, the argument then is a justification of *liberalism as an abstract political philosophy, using an ontology of human being as poetic, to support the liberal conception of politics as defending freedom, and preventing harm*. This justification of liberalism is very similar to the classical justification of liberalism put forward by the social contract theorists, holding as it does that individuals ought to accept the legitimacy of liberalism, because it is in accord with a pre-social human nature. Unlike the social contract theorists, though, Rorty's conception of enrichment and harm are discursive rather than materialist. Rorty talks in terms of individuals reworking their private identities rather than competing over material resources in the public sphere of the market. This Nietzschean argument about discursive enrichment though ends up in serious difficulty as we will soon see.

Poetry *contra* politics

Before developing my critique of Rorty's Nietzschean liberalism, I will note the two pertinent critical issues on this topic. The first issue is that Rorty is essentialising the public–private distinction.[15] That is, he is making a reference to the spheres of the state and the domestic sphere, without saying what these spheres are in substantive terms, or even recognising that the boundary between these spheres is permeable, and subject to change. Ironically, there is no recognition of the historical contingency of such a division. Instead, the implication is that the terms public and private pertain to fixed essences, in which case *a definition is being used to do the work of an intellectual defence.* Liberalism is *legitimised by fiat* if one holds that the justification for liberalism is in terms of a public–private divide which protects freedom and prevents harm, because one is simply accepting the claims of an abstract political ideology. One is not exploring concrete issues concerning power and social justice, but accepting a real system by accepting the terms of reference of an ideology.

The second issue is that there is a tension between Nietzschean poetry and liberalism. According to Fraser (1990), and Bhaskar (1991), who draws upon Fraser, there are three possible configurations, which I will quickly sketch out, using Bhaskar's rubrics. Firstly, there is the 'complementary position', whereby the poetic reworking of a language game results in a 'trickle-down' effect, to benefit all. Secondly, there is the 'opposition position', whereby poetry and liberalism are antithetical, with a marked tension existing between poets who want to expand poetic expression and liberals who want to prevent harm. Thirdly, there is the 'separatist position', whereby elitist poetry and liberalism are incompatible, but not in tension, as both can happily exist in their respective spheres. The third position is described as the 'Official Resolution of *Contingency, Irony And Solidarity*' (Bhaskar 1991: 89).[16] Against this, Bhaskar argues that

> it is not possible to distinguish redescriptions that affect actions with consequences for others and those that do not. Personal agency requires and uses social forms as its conditions, means and media and almost always has social consequences.
>
> (1991: 89)

In short, agency reworks a social context, and thus it cuts across the public–private boundary, which means that the tension between poetry and liberalism will be problematic, as poetic acts cannot be wholly confined to the private sphere.

My argument is that Rorty's Nietzschean liberalism is actually antithetical to liberal politics. With Rorty's Nietzschean liberalism the private sphere is where the poet creates private languages and the public sphere consists of the state and the public language game. The language game to which the self reacts ironically is a public resource open to all. The language game is public capital which may be utilised by any individual to enrich him/herself. This discursive capital cannot be appropriated by any individual, as no-one can appropriate a language, given the lack of its material character, and thus it remains a resource of *potentially* equal benefit to any individual. Thus to be enriched, an individual has to take a public resource and use it in a private way. In which case, politics would turn not on regulating social interaction, in the form of material competition in the market (i.e. on regulating material interaction in civil society), but on preventing one poet from humiliating another. It would prevent one poet invading the private sphere of another poet. Politics then would be based on *preventing inter-private sphere harm, rather than harm in the public sphere.* The liberal state would exist to prevent individuals invading another individual's private sphere and redescribing them, rather than to regulate public material relations in civil society.

This raises the question of why such inter-private sphere harm would occur. If every individual were a poet then every individual would be able to defend themselves from redescription. Some individuals may be less poetic than others, though, in which case the state may be required to protect the less able from the more able. Such a justification, however, would break down for two reasons. Firstly, it is hard to see why a poet would want to redescribe a non-poet, because s/he would literally gain nothing from it. If enrichment turns upon having a poetic language game then enrichment is based upon individuals improving themselves, using a public discursive resource that cannot be appropriated, and not on taking a material resource from another individual.

If a less poetic person were redescribed by a poet, then, and this brings us to the second point, the less poetic person would gain, not the poet. Such a position would be very odd, though. The poet would force an identity onto someone despite gaining nothing from it, and the individual would be harmed, despite being enriched, because they would not have created the identity themselves. Unless one works for one's enrichment, such enrichment will be a source of humiliation. The state may try to prevent such harm but there is the obvious difficulty of trying to separate an identity that is not entirely of one's making from that which is an utterly unique private language. For any poetic redescription will be a reworking of a public language game, rather than an entirely new invented language. When the less poetic draw upon the public language game they will, to some extent, be drawing upon a language game that has been modified by the more poetic. So, every identity will have some trace of another's influence in it and, further, if someone is able to complain about having an identity imposed upon them, then the imposition is far from total, in which case it would be difficult to ascertain how much harm, if any, had been done, without falling into sheer subjectivism.

There will be trickle-down because language crosses the public–private boundary. Language may be 'more than individuals', in which case it is 'public', but not only does the existence of language depend upon individuals using it in the private sphere, but the creation of private languages which ironically rework the prevailing language will feed back into the prevailing public language. Language is not static precisely because the ways that some people rework language in private end up becoming normal aspects of public language. Therefore, language depends upon the poetic for linguistic development. This means that in reworking the language game the poetic are not only enriching themselves, but are creating a richer resource for future use. Without such innovation, the public language game would cease to be a resource for enrichment, because it would eventually be exhausted. Without innovation, there are only a finite number of truly novel changes possible. Thus poets are needed to keep the possibility of enrichment open. This may result in harm for the less poetic, who depend on others to rework the public language game, but such harm would be a necessary evil, because without it, all of humanity would become impoverished.

Given this, complete protection from harm would require the less poetic to live in an impoverished separatist community. This however would make the liberal state similar to an authoritarian state, because although it would not force an identity onto individuals and abnegate their humanity, it would place them in a position of permanent severe impoverishment. This would harm such individuals because human nature is defined as essentially poetic, and some enrichment via trickle-down would be better than having nothing. Such separatism would also violate the liberal emphasis on equality of opportunity, as those in the separatist community would be, in effect, a lower caste, that were condemned as being unable to realise what it was to be truly human.

According to Ansell-Pearson, the upshot of Rorty's philosophy is a solipsistic retreat from the social world to a private sphere, where a pre-social, or pre-political, self indulges in private fantasy (1994: 170–1). This is too extreme, because we are dealing with language, which cuts across the public–private boundary. There is a poetic reworking of the public language game into a private language, not an *ex nihilo* creation of language, and this will affect others when they draw upon that language game. The public sphere will though be devoid of a civil society where individuals interact directly in person, and there can be no legitimate basis for the state to exist. Apart from the fact that individuals would have no motivation to harm others, the liberal state could not prevent such humiliation occurring to the less poetic anyway. A socialist state would fare no better either, as there could be no fairer redistribution of capital and resources, given individuals already had access to all the (discursive) resources they required, and enrichment turned upon innate ability. A state could separate the communities, but this is entering dangerous ground because it would amount to a form of proto-racism, whereby the less human (i.e. less poetic) were kept impoverished for their own security from the more human/poetic. The upshot of Rorty's Nietzschean liberalism therefore is a world with no substantive notion of a civil society, and a world divided into the more human and less human, with the less human being innately less human than those responsible for enriching humanity.

Pragmatism and female being

I now want to move the discussion from Rorty's justification of liberalism as an abstract political ideology to Rorty's treatment of substantive political issues, viz. ascribed status inequality limiting the life chances of women, and policy-formation by the state. In this section I will deal with the former issue, by discussing Rorty's arguments about feminism. In discussing Rorty's arguments about feminism we can see some of the practical difficulties that flow from the rather abstract discussion above about the self and enrichment. Specifically, we will see that inequality is privatised, meaning that inequality is taken to be a direct reflection of individuals' ability – or willingness – to enrich themselves by changing their identities, or final vocabularies, instead of a matter concerning objective social structures that impose, to some extent, gender identities upon people. There are not the conceptual resources to deal with social factors influencing individuals' life chances and attainment. Reference can only be made to the poetic essence of each individual. In which case any notion of unjust inequality would be inconceivable, because individuals are wholly responsible for their identities.

Rorty's (1998a: 202–27)[17] discussion of feminism is framed in terms of his anti-representationalist rejection of epistemology, and his rejection of the self having an essence. He argues that there can be no truth claims about the self, because the self is a contingency, and we cannot accept the idea of reality 'making beliefs true'. In which case, we cannot accept the view that feminism provides us with a truth claim about a really-existing injustice. We cannot say that there is a real injustice if some people are defined by another person as being subordinate. As long as that person is defined as subordinate they will be subordinate. One may not be able to say that this is 'objectively wrong', but one can recognise the potential for change. Although we cannot say that some practices are really wrong, because they damage human nature, or offend really-existing universal rights, we may say that people can escape from subordination by describing themselves differently. They can escape from subordination by being the author of their own final vocabulary: freedom stems from the authority of the author to create their own final vocabulary, or private language.

The first point to note about this is that, taken at face value, it ends up in the same position as the ethnocentric argument, whereby people were determined automata. Without a self that was separate from its web of beliefs the self would be a passive entity controlled and defined by the prevailing social norms. Or, specifically, women would be puppets controlled by a patriarchal language game. Thus there could be no harm in the form of humiliation, because there was no free and creative self which could be harmed by having an identity imposed upon it: the self would simply mirror the prevailing (patriarchal) norms. Patriarchy would be 'good' for those socialised into its gender roles (whether male or female), because patriarchy would work according to its own terms of reference, and individuals' behaviour would be determined by the prevailing norms. However, and this brings us to the second point, the ability to change oneself implies that there is a master weaver behind the contingent web of beliefs. What it is to be a woman (and a man) is a social construct, but such constructs can change (1998a:

210); which implies, as argued earlier, a constructor behind the veil of discourse, a self behind its web of beliefs.

Thus when discussing the poet Adrienne Rich, Rorty argues that the prevailing (patriarchal) language game makes women treat themselves like the dependent variable, and men as the independent variable, although Rich was 'split' between this public language game and her own private poetry (1998a: 221). She could not be a 'full-time poet' because she could not be a 'full-time female' (1998a: 221), meaning that she could not have a public voice as a poet. This gives the game away, so to speak, because instead of saying that women are wholly defined in terms of the patriarchal language game, Rorty is saying that (some) women have the ability to rework language. The *possibility* for change comes from the *potential* to poetically rework female identity, and this potential must be innate (in some women at least), otherwise women would passively remain defined in male patriarchal terms of reference, posited by the patriarchal language game.

To escape from inequality, then, women must redefine their final vocabularies. Women must become poets, to escape from inequality, and this means creating a new experience of what it means to be female, by creating a new language, tradition and identity (1998a: 212). By having a new voice women will have a new being (1998a: 226). To assist in this process Rorty acknowledges the need for separatism, as feminist practices would not 'work' in a patriarchal culture (i.e. they would be dysfunctional for the status quo). Rorty does not think, though, that such separation is permanent. It is just until the day when feminist practice seeps into the prevailing language game and becomes normal discourse. Although there is the risk of a permanent divide, Rorty says,

> it may also happen that, as the generations succeed one another, the masters, those in control, gradually find their conceptions of the possibilities open to human beings changing. [...] The new language spoken by the separatist group may gradually get woven into the language taught in schools.
>
> (1998a: 223)

Thus if men change then (feminist) women may be reintegrated into mainstream society, and the two forms of being could co-exist.

So, Rorty acknowledges that there is a problem regarding gender inequality. However, we are to explain this solely in terms of individuals' poetic ability. If women want change then it is up to them to change. If women do not exercise their poetic ability they will only have themselves to blame for the prevailing inequality, and from this we can infer that women are to blame for allowing themselves to be described as subordinates in the first place. Without a reference to how an ascribed status helps to create, sustain and legitimise unequal material/power relations, all we can say is that an ascribed status of inequality arises when one group allows an identity to be ascribed to it. Unless of course one group is intrinsically less poetic, in which case its inequality is, *ex hypothesi*, a direct expression of its less able state. In both cases, there is no unjust inequality, as women are to blame for not acting sooner, or women are innately less poetic than men. In short, all we can do is turn to a definitive ontology of human being, saying that humans are poetic, and that inequality is a direct reflection of innate ability, or the failure to realise that ability. One has the answer to questions concerning inequality by having access to a definitive ontology of human being which makes empirical investigation of the causes of inequality redundant.

As there could be no unjust inequality, liberalism would be legitimate because every individual would have equality of opportunity. All that individuals would have to do is rework the public language game to realise their innate ability and enrich themselves. The problem with women has been that they allowed the public patriarchal language game to define their identity, and that in private, or in a separatist community, they need to rework poetically their final vocabularies. Women cannot impose this change on men, because that would mean imposing a new final vocabulary upon men, and the liberal state would prevent men being humiliated in the public sphere. A change in male identity and practices could only legitimately occur if men allowed this to happen, and, after several generations, allowed the presentation of gender relations in schools to reflect this change. Even without such a change in the patriarchal language game, women would still benefit because in putting forward feminist critique they would be reworking the public language game into an edifying private language for self-enrichment. In which case, feminist *critique* would not exist *as critique*, because it would not be a public criticism of social relations but a private language for private enrichment. Thus, if our concepts to understand politics are just the self *qua* poet, and the public language game, we can reach the Panglossian conclusion that (in liberal states) all is for the best in the best of all possible worlds. This is because there is no unjust inequality, and women can enrich themselves without challenging the public language game of patriarchy. Thus political questions about the distribution of power and the legitimacy of power distribution, can be understood simply in terms of whether the self has exercised its ability, with liberalism allowing the necessary equality of opportunity.

In short, a discussion of a substantive political issue concerning equality of opportunity is addressed using a definitive ontology. Here the ontology deals with the subject rather than the object. Instead of an argument about the social object (i.e. social rules which determine behaviour), we have an argument about the subject, with a definitive ontology of human being. The ontology of human being holds that the self has a poetic essence, and that the self can enrich itself by poetically reworking the public language game into private languages. This functions as a definitive explanation of human behaviour because no other factors are adduced in the explanation of inequality. To understand different levels of attainment, we simply make reference to individuals' innate (poetic) ability *and nothing else*. Therefore there is no need to engage in empirical research to investigate if factors such as ascribed status inequality affect equality of opportunity, because one can simply say that attainment reflects ability. Thus a substantive political issue concerning social justice becomes an abstract issue, because the definitive ontology of the self is used to explain all forms of inequality in a wholly reductionist way, excluding any social factors to focus exclusively on individuals' innate ability. By holding to the individualist sociological logic of immediacy, no empirical investigation is required, because one can read-off, from the definitive ontology of human being, all forms of human behaviour, and 'know' that there are no non-individual (i.e. social) factors influencing individuals' agency.

From postmodernism to positivistic-conservatism

In this section I will turn my attention from the individualist sociological logic of immediacy to the foundationalist philosophical logic of immediacy. I will argue that although Rorty did align himself with postmodernism, his subsequent rejection of postmodernism ended up propelling his work on policy-formation into a positivism, which is also conservative because it deals with 'facts' that cannot be subject to legitimate normative critique or contestation. Rorty recoils from postmodernism, taking it to be trapped within the representationalist problematic, but the result is also squarely fixed within that problematic too.

Rorty defined himself as a postmodernist in his essay 'Postmodernist bourgeois liberalism'.[18] In this essay Rorty argues that his defence of liberal *institutions* can be separated from the Enlightenment *justification* of liberalism in terms of a universal human nature. Liberal practices are good for us liberals – because we are liberals – but we can dispense with what Lyotard referred to as 'metanarratives': there are no grand philosophical stories (about a Kantian transcendental self, or human nature) to justify any particular set of social practices. In this case, then, Rorty's postmodern rejection of metanarratives can simply serve as a synonym for anti-representationalism and ethnocentrism. Rorty also describes his position as 'bourgeois', because he accepts the Marxist view that liberal political institutions are historically contingent upon certain material conditions obtaining. Without any metanarrative to justify liberalism we can only justify it in its own terms, by saying that it works for us, in certain material circumstances.

Metanarratives represent an appeal to metaphysics, the purpose of which is to go beyond the social and historical contingency of lived practices, justifying (or rejecting) a political system by reference to something 'other'. To be a pragmatist is to give up the temptation of metaphysics and have courage to improve our practices for going on in the world. To overcome metaphysics is to overcome a self-imposed immaturity. Metaphysics is immature because it means that humanity tries to fetishise some non-existent non-human entity with human powers, in order to remove responsibility from itself to a superhuman 'moving force'. This metaphysical impulse to find meaning by turning away from the world characterised Christianity and political philosophies of history.[19] Rorty argues that

> By inventing 'History' as the name of an object that could be conceptually grasped, Hegel and Marx made it possible to keep both the romance of the Christian story about incarnate Logos, and the Christian sense of solidarity against injustice, even after we lost religious faith.
>
> (1998a: 235)

Against such fetishism we ought to focus on actual practices, but postmodernists took another route and replaced History, or the Universal Class, with Language and Discourse. If we accepted pragmatism though,

> We might then stop trying to find a successor to 'the working class' – for example, 'Difference' or 'Otherness' – as a name for the latest incarnation of the Logos. [... This] might help us avoid what Stanley Fish calls 'antifoundational theory hope' – the idea that a materialism and a sense of historicity more radical than even that of Marx's will somehow provide a brand-new, still bigger, albeit still blurrier, object   an object called, perhaps, 'Language' or 'Discourse' – around which to weave our fantasies.
>
> (1998a: 242)

So, although Rorty described himself as 'postmodern', he is not actually a postmodernist. If postmodernism is a synonym for anti-representationalism (and ethnocentrism) then Rorty obviously has no argument with it, but as we have just seen, Rorty is critical of the way that postmodernists have turned to metanarratives which reject actual practices to embrace metaphysics. This means that postmodernism is actually predicated upon the representationalist problematic, and is a form of realism (in Rorty's sense of the term), because instead of dealing with improving contingent practices, it seeks to move beyond practices, and base politics on epistemic certainty, by knowing some metaphysical moving force that is separate from actual empirical practices.

Postmodernists also adhere to the representationalist problematic when they use a methodology called 'deconstruction' to move from surface appearances to an underlying essence. At this point it is necessary to note Rorty's views on Derrida before discussing Rorty's critique of deconstruction. Rorty argues that Derrida is of use in the private sphere. It is useful to read Derrida's literary philosophy as a discourse of self-creation which we too may find edifying, but Derrida is not of use in the public sphere of politics (1996a: 15–17). Now although Derrida coined the term 'deconstruction', in putting forward a basically post-structuralist position, which held that as

meaning was endlessly deferred from signifier to signifier, the apparent stability of meaning in texts could be deconstructed, by pointing to its inherent
instability, this term has been used in a non-Derridean way, according to
Rorty.[20] Rorty notes that something called 'deconstruction' has been turned
into a (social/scientific) 'methodology', meaning that deconstruction has
become a way of unmasking an underlying essence (1996a: 15). Thus deconstruction is concerned with moving from illusory appearances to the underlying real essence, and so it is predicated upon the representationalist
problematic.

This means that such deconstructionists are adopting a position similar to
Marxist ideology-critique. Rorty argues that

> Many self-consciously 'postmodern' writers seem to be trying to have it
> both ways – to view things as masks going all the way down while still
> making invidious comparisons between other people's masks and the way
> things will look when all the masks have been stripped off. These post-
> modernists continue to indulge in the bad habits characteristic of those
> Marxists who insist that morality is a matter of class interest and then
> add that everybody has a moral obligation to identify with the interests of
> a particular class.
>
> (1998a: 209, footnote 17)

Indeed, Rorty notes that academic leftists, who were concerned with
unmasking 'bourgeois ideology', ended up drawing upon deconstruction to
take a more pluralistic approach which was still concerned with unmasking.
The result, Rorty argues, was an 'idiot jargon' of 'leftspeak', which is 'a
dreadful mishmash of Marx, Adorno, Foucault and Lacan [... that] resulted
in articles that offer unmaskings of the propositions of earlier unmaskings of
still earlier unmaskings' (1987: 570).

Rorty's reaction though is not to argue for the use of fallible theories to
interpret the social and political world, but to argue for a positivistic
approach to politics. Rorty's position is that theory ought to be confined to
the private sphere, with the public sphere of politics, and civil society, being
evacuated of theory for atheoretical factual problem-solving. Another way of
putting this is to say that in private we may read Derrida, or Marx for that
matter, but in public we will pursue what Popper (1989) called 'piecemeal
social engineering', meaning that politics is to be based on small-scale
improvements to a system which already functions well. Note that whereas
Popper would have allowed some room for theorisation (albeit in individualist terms, influenced by a moderate empiricism), Rorty's position is far more
empiricist, because it debars any notion of theory from the public sphere.[21]

Rorty argues that '[t]here is nothing sacred about the free market or about
central planning; the proper balance between the two is a matter of experimental tinkering' (1987: 564). Here then the public sphere has now been
broadened out from a rather disembodied and abstract language game

which people react to in private, to the material realm of civil society, in the form of economic markets. This argument about economic policy may seen unobjectionable – even truistic. However, it overlooks the problem that defining what is a successful economy is not simply a purely 'factual' matter. It is not just that monetarists and Keynesians etc., or pro- and anti-European single currency advocates, would disagree about the means to achieve sustained economic growth, but that people may disagree about going for maximum growth, given environmental concerns, or argue that more profits should be redistributed via progressive taxation, to help the less well-off and improve equality of opportunity. One cannot remove theoretical and normative issues as these inform our perspectives of the goals to aim for and the means to achieve those goals.

Rorty however would have none of this. For Rorty, politics is a matter of dealing with discrete atheoretical facts, and thus accepting the legitimacy of the given, with policies being generated *reactively* to overcome specific factual problems. Against Critchley (1996) who argues that Derrida ought not to be confined to the private sphere, Rorty argues that '[o]ur [pragmatic] attitude is: if it isn't broken, don't fix it. Keep on using it until you can find some other sort of tool which might do the job better' (1996b: 44). Hence we ought to 'save problematizing for the weekends' (1996b: 44); assuming that the weekends are when we are in the private sphere, and away from work. In the public sphere, then, the state would generate policies reactively, to overcome discrete factual problems in civil society as they emerged, in order to restore the status quo, and normative critique – or theorising more generally – would be confined to the private sphere, for personal use only (making it politically pointless). Thus Rorty wants to argue for a form of 'end-of-ideology' politics, whereby we can simply accept the fact that liberalism 'works', *contra* those committed to an ideological fantasy such as Marxism, who argue that there are unseen forces driving society, and distorting the truth.[22]

So, postmodernism and deconstruction are rejected for being based on the representationalist problematic and, against this, Rorty's anti-representationalist pragmatism holds that politics is a matter of factual problem-solving, to improve our practices. By removing theory *per se* from the public sphere, though, to focus on 'facts', the result is a positivism which is also based on the representationalist problematic. This is also conservative because it precludes any normative questioning of the given, maintaining that politics concerns the state reactively creating policies to improve an already good society. The result of this would be an elitist and technocratic conception of politics, with political action being instigated by the state, whereby 'experts' solved 'technical problems'. Against this, it could be argued that in his work on the 'American left' Rorty (1990b) does recognise the legitimacy of groups mobilising in civil society, to bring pressure upon the state, in order to achieve some specific policy objectives.

In this work, on the left in the USA, Rorty defines the left as seeking to improve social justice, whereas the right believes that the existing social and political relationships and institutions embody social justice. Rorty does not accept that the right is correct, but he does not think that the right is illegitimate. Rather, he believes that politics is – and *ought* to be – based on a constant argument between right and left. He argues that

> As long as our country has a politically active Right and a politically active Left, this argument will continue. It is at the heart of the nation's political life, but the Left is responsible for keeping it going. For the Right never thinks that anything much needs to be changed: it thinks the country is basically in good shape, and may well have been in better shape in the past. It sees the Left's struggle for social justice as mere trouble making, as utopian foolishness. The Left, by definition is the party of hope. It insists that our nation remains unachieved.
>
> (1998b: 14)

Rather than save problematizing for the weekends, confining it to the private sphere, it is now legitimate to question the given. Normative issues are allowed in the realm of public political discussion and, indeed, are perceived to drive politics. Without the left, politics would become rather static, and the importance of the left is that it provides the dynamism to seek out and resolve previously overlooked issues of social justice. The left is the force to improve society by pursuing reformist politics – but it needs to be 'held in check' by the right, otherwise the left would produce a monologue seeking change for the sake of change.

Rorty is quite critical of the left, though, because it has surrendered its public responsibility to improve society, and has become detached from the lived practices of real people. The left has become obsessed with theory for the sake of theory. The left is castigated for retreating from the public sphere of civil society, where its critical voice is needed. The problem (as regards the American left) is that the left moved from being a 'reformist left' to a 'cultural left'. Instead of being concerned with substantive issues concerning distributive justice, for instance, the left is only concerned with theorising cultural 'otherness'. The change in emphasis can be seen in 'cultural studies', which Rorty takes to mean 'victim studies'. The concern with 'otherness' has resulted in disciplines such as women's studies, black history, gay studies, Hispanic-American studies and migrant studies. There are no unemployment studies, homeless studies, or trailer-park studies, because these are not 'other' in the relevant sense (1998b: 79–80). Consequently the left has become 'spectatorial' because it only theorises culture, instead of getting involved with concrete policy issues, and so it has ceased to be a left (1998b: 14).

The left, to function as a left, needs to move from the private study and into (public) politics to try and influence the formation of policy. Rorty obviously recognises that the state will be influenced by monied interests, but he thinks that change in the interests of the less well-off is possible. That the state is not taken to be intrinsically – or necessarily – biased towards capital (or the rich 'overclass' as Rorty calls international capitalists), and with the help of the better-off middle class, the working class may mobilise successfully to effect improvements in pay and conditions (1998b: 54). This does not mean that the left ought to mount a general 'structural' – and theoretical – critique of society. There should be mobilisations over specific issues rather than general movements for radical change. As Rorty puts it, '[m]ovements are suited to onto-theological Platonists, campaigns to many-minded men of letters' (1998b: 118). The left can help Americans achieve their country by realising the potential within liberal capitalist America for people to 'get on', or at least have a decent standard of living, and it ought to pursue this rather than indulge in abstract theorisation of the 'other', or formulaic 'deconstructions'.

Now clearly Rorty does allow for 'bottom-up' (or bottom-with-the-help-of-the-middle-up) changes, which pulls sharply away from the technocratic elitism that only allowed for top-down reactive changes. Yet the change is not as radical as it may appear. This is because the approach is still positivist and conservative. It is positivist because it is still dealing with specific 'factual' issues. Campaigns form to seek a specific empirical change, and when this is achieved, the campaign concerned is redundant. To be sure, there may be some form of normative debate between right and left, but this would not amount to theoretical considerations about the structural features of liberal capitalism. Rather, it would be premised upon a shared acceptance of the defining features of liberal capitalism, and difference would arise from the left arguing that some specific empirical changes would be justified because they would improve equality of opportunity and the basic standard of living for the less well-off. In place of theory there would be facts, and norms would help select which set of facts one sought to obtain. Political discussion would not go beyond the observed realm of actual facts to question the context which structured the events which gave meaning to individuals' acts.

This implies that there is agreement over what the putative facts actually are, which brings us to the point that Rorty's argument is also conservative. The left is akin to a maintenance worker, making sure a machine works properly, by checking its oil levels and fitting new parts, rather than questioning the overall design of the machine. Whereas the right is complacent and reactionary, in that it dislikes change and has a tendency to romanticise the past, the left ought not to deal with *innovation* (i.e. change for the sake of change), but with *necessary* small-scale reforms/'repairs'. Instead of questioning the status quo, or pressing for structural change, localised and specific reforms are sought to maintain the socio-political equilibrium. Such reforms may come from groups mobilising in civil society, but this does not mean that they are challenging the legitimacy of the state. Rather, there is a classical pluralist view of the state in Rorty's work on the left in the USA, whereby the state is basically neutral, and creates policy outputs in response to rational well-argued inputs from pressure groups.[23] These groups are mature enough to focus on improving specific practices, rather than being immature, and turning to metaphysical metanarratives, to furnish some form of all-encompassing structural critique of liberal capitalist society. Thus instead of 'move-ments' joined by 'onto-theological Platonists' (who ought to keep their onto-theological Platonism in the private sphere), the responsible citizenry join pragmatic 'campaigns'.

So, in criticising postmodernism, the 'idiot jargon' of 'leftspeak', and a 'spectatorial left', Rorty argues for a pragmatism whereby the left seeks to enhance social justice by effecting policy-change, and the upshot is that Rorty's pragmatism becomes a form of positivistic-conservative social science, repeating the tenets of classical pluralism, as espoused in the 1960s (which, incidentally, is when Rorty charts the decline of a reformist left into a spec-tatorial left). In doing this, Rorty is basing methodology on a form of the positivist philosophical logic of immediacy, as explanations of the social world are reduced to observed events, carried out by individuals, with no reference to social structures, or a wider social context acting as an enablement and constraint upon individuals' agency.

An alternative to the above is to recognise that social science may use 'theory' without this being some attempt at 'onto-theological Platonism' which seeks to explain everything via some master-ontology of socio-politi-cal being. Indeed, given that what we perceive is influenced by presump-tions about being, it is necessary for us to develop an explicit theory of being to guide our research and critique of existing socio-political relations and structures. This would entail developing a general theory, or meta-theory, whose terms of reference could explain how individuals' agency was socially mediated, without holding that individuals had totally uncon-strained actions or totally determined behaviour. This social ontology, that resolved the structure-agency problem, could then be used to guide empiri-cal research and the formation of specific theories, in our research of all aspects of social, political and economic life. This is not to rule out the possibility that being well read helps us make decisions, but it is to say that theory is to be judged on its usefulness in helping us interpret the socio-political world, and not confined to the private sphere, where its rhetorical import may, or may not, enable an individual to 'see the world differently' when they are dealing with putative facts.

4 Post-Wittgensteinian sociology

Giddens' ontology of practices

Introduction

Although Wittgenstein would be opposed to the notion of a general ontology, as Wittgenstein believed that it would not be possible to develop a trans-cultural ontology which defined some 'general features' that somehow 'under-pinned' the specifics of every language game or form of life, Giddens draws upon the later Wittgenstein (amongst other thinkers) in developing his social ontology. Giddens seeks to resolve the structure-agency problematic using the notion of 'rule-following practices'. In seeking to define social reality in terms of rule-following practices, where agents have the practical knowledge to 'go on', Giddens seeks to avoid those social ontologies which adopt some master-ontology of structures, that makes agents 'structural dopes'. He also seeks to avoid methodological individualism for the reasons argued for in Chapter 2. Giddens therefore is keen to avoid the structuralist sociological logic of imme-diacy. (He is also opposed to psychologism and so he is opposed to the individualist sociological logic of immediacy as well.)

Giddens regards his approach to social ontology as (what we may call) more 'deflationary' than 'objectivist' accounts. What this means is that Giddens thinks his ontology of rule-following practices can link structure and agency without positing some definitive objectivist ontology of structures. He thinks the emphasis on knowledgeable social agents following practical rules about how to go on avoids the grand – and false – claims of other thinkers who over-emphasised structure. He also takes a deflationary approach to the application of the ontology, holding that his ontology may be applied in a piecemeal way. In making this claim about the application of his ontology, Giddens hopes to avoid the charge of essentialism: he thinks that a pragmatic piecemeal application will avoid the criticism that he is trying to build a definitive master-ontology. As will be argued, though, Giddens' post-Wittgensteinian ontology of rule following practices unfolds into both the individualist and structuralist versions of the sociological logic of immediacy. Further, the argument about the application of an ontology to empirical research and the formation of specific theories is untenable, because this results in an arbitrary application of the ontology.

The importance of ontology

We can begin to understand Giddens' ontological project by quickly noting his 'new rules of sociological method' (1976). These can be summarised as follows. Interpretative sociologies are correct insofar as they stress that the subject matter of sociology deals with a universe of actively created meanings (rule 1), and that the production and reproduction of society is carried out by knowledgeable social agents (rule 2). So we may say that social reality is 'socially constructed', in the sense that activities only have the meaning that agents ascribe to them. This does not imply that social reality can be understood simply in terms of the free development of meanings/norms. Instead, limits are set by the social context (rule 3). As Giddens puts it (making an allusion to Marx),[1] *'human agency is bounded. Men produce society, but they do so as historically located agents, and not under conditions of their own choosing'* (1976: 160; emphasis in original).

To understand agency we must therefore locate it within some structural context. This does not mean that structures will determine agency though, *as structures furnish the conditions which enable as well as constrain agency*. Agents may not choose their circumstances, but they can rework those circumstances. Thus for Giddens structures should be conceptualised as enabling as well as constraining, and this twin feature is referred to as the 'duality of structure' (rule 4). As structures enable as well as constrain for Giddens, it follows that *structures are the medium and outcome of agency*, because agency requires structures, and reworks structures (1995a: 374). That is, agency reworks the social context it is located within. This duality of structure means that

> Structures can always in principle be examined in terms of their *structura-tion* as a series of reproduced practices. To enquire into the structuration of social practices is to seek to explain how it comes about that structures are constituted through action, and reciprocally how action is constituted structurally.
>
> (1976: 161; emphasis in original)

What this means is that *structure and agency are mutually implicated*. Instead of agency meaning free will and structures being conceptualised as external determining forces upon the agent, structure and agency are definable only in relation to one another. Structures require agency not simply in the sense that without individuals there would be no social reality, but because structures are the medium through which agency is exercised: structures are the 'stuff' of agency. Agency does not exist in the form of discrete acts which occur in a social vacuum, devoid of social constraints or shared norms which give meaning to the acts. Rather, agency always exists in some social context, so to understand agency is to understand the structures which act as the medium for the practices of agents. Without regard for structures as the medium and outcome of agency, agency would be divorced from any social context, leaving us with an extreme atomistic individualism, that not even methodological individualists would endorse (given their reference to situations). The final rules (rules 6–8) amount to the view that social science has to entail 'immersion' in a form of life, and that social science concepts may react back upon lay knowledge: the so-called 'double hermeneutic' (1976: 161–2).[2]

Giddens' project therefore is concerned with placing ontology at the centre of social theory, to reconceptualise notions of, in his words, 'human being and doing, social reproduction and social transformation' (1995a: xx). To understand social change and continuity one must understand structure and agency, which means understanding agency in terms of situated practices, to see how agents may alter their customary ways of going on. In this case, 'human being' is defined in terms of 'human doing', i.e. situated practices, meaning that an agent is definable by their actions, and their ability to effect change. So, agents are not passive determined automata, because they have the capacity to act freely, but such actions are always mediated by social structures, which the agents' practices may reproduce or change.

Rule-following practices

Defining rules, resources and power

Having indicated that for Giddens structure and agency are mutually implicated, the next task is to define structure and agency. Giddens defines social structure in terms of rules and resources (1993a; 1995a). Rules can be subdivided into normative elements and codes of signification; and resources can be sub-divided into authoritative resources and allocative resources (1995a: xxxi). Giddens also describes the sub-division of rules as a division between the aspect of rules that relates to sanctions governing social conduct and the aspect of rules that constitutes meaning (1993a: 82; 1995a: 18). Or, to put it another way, all rules are both regulative and constitutive (1993a: 66). What this means is that rules both ascribe meaning to actions and delimit acceptable from unacceptable actions. This distinction though is an *abstract conceptual distinction, because in actuality, practices draw upon both aspects of rules* (1993a: 82). Turning to resources, a two-fold distinction between allocative resources and authoritative resources was noted. Allocative resources are defined as material resources which derive from the domination over nature (such as capital), whilst authoritative resources are defined as non-material resources (such as status), which result from the domination of some agents over others (1995a: 258, 373). It is important to note though that although *resources constitute structures of domination, because they entail the use of power, this is not to say that power is a resource.*

Instead of power being a resource, resources are used in the articulation of power, with power itself only belonging to agents. For Giddens, agents are definable as agents because they have power, meaning the ability to make a difference. *This means that everyone is an agent, because everyone can exercise some*

form of choice which will make a difference in some way or another. So, power char-
acterises all action, with resources being the media through which power is
exercised (1995a: 15–6). Therefore power is a capability and not a description
of affairs (1993a: 68). In other words, one cannot use the concept of power to
describe a set of resources, because power is the ability to be an agent, which
means that we can describe this capability, and its exercise via resources, but
we cannot define power by describing a fixed set of relations or resources.
Understanding power means understanding what agents do, rather than, for
example, saying that power stems from material resources, such as capital.[3]
As Giddens puts it, '[p]ower is generated by definite forms of domination in a
parallel way to the involvement of rules with social practices and, indeed, as
an integral element or aspect of those practices' (1993a: 69). We can describe
the use of resources, such as capital, in terms of how agents use these resources
in relations of power, but we cannot conflate power into resources, and say
that capital is itself a *source* of power, as capital is a *medium* for the exercise of
power.

Giddens rejects the Nietzschean reduction of truth to power (1995a: 257;
1995c: 259–68), which influenced Weber with his belief that there was no
rational way to adjudicate ultimate values (and giving us, according to
Giddens, 'normative irrationalism' (1993a: 68)), and more recent (post-structuralist) thinkers like Foucault, for whom truth is the will-to-power.
However, Giddens does argue that 'power is logically prior to subjectivity,
to the constitution of the reflexive monitoring of conduct' (1995a: 15). What
this means is that the agent must possess the ability to make a difference, i.e.
the ability to make decisions and act upon them, before that agent can engage
in practices and monitor those practices. Putting power before subjectivity is
not a recipe for irrationalism if one holds that agreement can be reached,
rather than imposed via force, on the basis of agreements made in particular
contexts, according to Giddens. Instead of power being a force to impose on
people, power allows decisions to be made, so power in this sense allows
agreement to be reached.

So, to be an agent is to have power. Power is the power to act in the world,
and this power enables agents to use rules and resources. Moreover, power
qua agency requires rules and resources because rules and resources (structures) are the medium and outcome of agency, which means that for power to
be exercised (i.e. for agents to act as agents), they must act using some rules
and resources. This is not to say that agency will necessarily result in social
change, but it is to say that social continuity is not a result of structures (rules
and resources) determining behaviour, but, rather, of at least some agents
actively reproducing the existing rules and resources. People make history,
but not in circumstances of their own choosing, and these circumstances
(understood in terms of structures *qua* rules and resources) are the medium
and outcome of agency (meaning the realised ability of agents to act), which
may or may not change the circumstances, even though history is 'made' by
practices (agency), not circumstances (structures).

Rules: formal and practical

Having defined structures and rules and resources, noting that power is irreducible to resources because it is a capacity of agents to use resources, I will now say more about the definition of rules. Giddens argues that most social rules cannot best be understood as analogous to formal rules, such as rules in games like chess. This is not just because the legitimacy of such rules is not (usually) subject to chronic contestation, as social rules often are (1993a: 67). It is also because rules cannot be regarded as 'isolated formulae', which pertain to discrete 'moves' (1993a: 65). There are two reasons why rules cannot be regarded as isolated formulae. Firstly, instead of a 'singular relation' between an activity and a rule, practices are subject to numerous rules. The way that people go on in a specific circumstance requires them to draw upon a plurality of practical rules concerning appropriate conduct. Secondly,

> Rules cannot be exhaustively described or analysed in terms of their own content, as prescriptions, prohibitions, etc., precisely because, apart from those circumstances where a relevant lexicon exists, *rules and practices only exist in conjunction with one another*.
>
> > (1993a: 65; emphasis in original)

Giddens argues we should regard rules

> as techniques or generalizible procedures applied in the enactment/ reproduction of social practices. Formulated rules – those that are given verbal expression as canons of law, bureaucratic rules, rules of the game and so on – are thus codified interpretations of rules rather than rules as such. They should be taken not as exemplifying rules in general but as specific types of formulated rule, which, by virtue of their overt formulation, take on various specific qualities.
>
> > (1995a: 21)

These specific qualities are the determination of practices according to formal criteria, rather than the mutual implication of rules in practices. Or to put it another way, instead of rules being the medium and outcome of practices, as the duality of structures suggests, there is a clear *dualism between object (formulated rules) and subject (agents and their practices)*, with rules *qua* structure being external and constraining, rather than enabling and constraining. The reason for this is that all the examples given by Giddens of formalised rules (bureaucracy, games and law) are prescriptive rules which define what is appropriate in terms of agents following those rules *to the letter*. When confronted by formal rules the agent simply has to conform, if s/he is to follow the rule, which means that in such cases practices mirror the rules, leaving little or no room for deviation.

Wittgenstein and sociology

The issue of a subject–object dualism replacing the duality of structure advocated by Giddens will be explored later on. Here I wish to continue the exegesis of Giddens' ontology, by noting that the conception of agency as rule-following practices, with rules being regarded as the practical ability to go on, derives from the philosophy of the later Wittgenstein. Such a conception of rules as the practical ability to go on overcomes, Wittgenstein argues, the paradox of rule-following. The paradox would be that if one based action on rule-following, then any observed act could be taken as an illustration of both rule-following and rule-breaking. Wittgenstein's resolution of this paradox is, Giddens notes, to argue that it is based on a misunderstanding, 'a confusing of the interpretation or verbal expression of a rule with following the rule' (1995a: 21). The point behind this resolution of the paradox is that rule-following turns on the use of practical knowledge about how to 'go on' within a form of life, whereas discussion about how practice P is an example of rule R turns on using discursive knowledge to interpret and codify a rule, which results in the paradox. The paradox only arises if one tries to approach rule-following in terms of discursive rather than practical knowledge, because trying discursively to codify on-going practices will result in different rules being read-into observed practices by different observers. Consequently one type of action may be held to follow one observer's rules whilst breaking the rules of another observer. The on-going flow of practices would be broken up to fit a set of categories that were then defined tautologically to fit the practices that were supposed to be examples of the rule.

Underlying this of course is the argument that meaning is linked to use.[4] Or, as Giddens puts it,

> 'Don't look for the meaning, look for the use' does not imply that meaning and use are synonymous, but that the sense of linguistic items can only be sought in the practices which they express and in which they are expressed.
>
> (1993a: 38)[5]

To parody Cartesian terminology, we may say simply that 'I go on, therefore I am'; as one's being and knowledge arise from, and are defined in terms of, the practical ability to go on within a form of life. Agents have the power to act in the world and exercising the power in on-going practices defines what the agent is: human being is definable in terms of human doing, which is understandable in terms of rule-following practices.

This is not to say that Giddens is in agreement with much post-Wittgensteinian discussions of social reality. Such post-Wittgensteinian positions would hold that there could be no general ontology (such as Giddens' 'structuration theory'), because that would mean reifying the concept of 'form of life', or 'language game', by moving from some specific ways of going on, to a meta-theory, which tried to find some underlying universal essence. So instead of trying to explain structure and agency in general terms, the emphasis would be on *understanding the meanings of individuals*. The approach would turn on *understanding*, and this would be juxtaposed to *explanations* which discussed individuals' behaviour in causal terms, by reference to deterministic structures.

The result of such an approach is to produce a sociology which presumes consensus and which, in effect, conceptualises agents as cultural dopes, because it lacks any understanding of how agents may change the prevailing rules. The emphasis is on how agents conform to an unexplained background of social norms and conventions. On such Wittgensteinian theories, Giddens argues that

> Established rules set the boundary of investigation, and while the conduct of agents is portrayed as purposeful and cogent, the origins of 'conventions' are shrouded in mystery, and perhaps even as *necessarily inexplicable; they do not appear as 'negotiated', as themselves the product of human action*, but rather as the backdrop against which such action becomes intelligible.
>
> (1976: 51; emphasis added)

Similarly, Giddens says that

> as expressed in forms of life, institutions are analysed only in so far as they form a consensual backdrop against which action is negotiated and its meanings formed. Wittgensteinian philosophy has not led towards any sort of concern with social change, with power relations, or with conflict in society.
>
> (1993a: 50)

One of the thinkers Giddens has in mind here is Winch who, according to Giddens, simply takes rules as given, without dealing with conflictual responses to rules. For Giddens, rules may be contested, which has the consequence that following a rule could have very different meanings for different agents, so Winch is wrong to conflate meaning into occurrence (1976: 48). If we are to understand social reality then we must switch from a perspective which takes institutions and norms as simply given, in order to analyse and explain social institutions and the contested nature of institutions and norms.

Giddens' sociology is therefore post-Wittgensteinian because whilst it conceptualises agency in terms of rule-following, and rules in terms of practices (not formal discursive rules), it goes against Wittgenstein's philosophy by trying to give a general ontology. *Instead of making reference to different ways of going on, Giddens introduces meta-concepts such as structure and agency, which are abstracted from any specific practices.*[6] This is meant to enable Giddens to break from the interpretative approach of Wittgensteinian philosophers such as

Winch, because such a general ontology, or meta-theory, seeks to connect agents' actions within a broader context. Rather than seek to understand why a specific act is meaningful, for the individuals concerned, Giddens' ontology would link a practice to a prevailing structure, which means linking the meaningful acts of an individual to a broader social context, defined in terms of rules and resources. It also means that social conflict may enter into the explanation, because instead of seeking the meaning of individual acts against an unexamined backdrop of norms, the norms themselves would be explained, and it would be recognised that different groups may respond to rules in different ways.

The ontological status of structures

Giddens argues that structures only have a 'virtual existence'. What this means is that structures have a virtual existence outside time and space, becoming real as memory traces, or when 'instantiated' in practices situated within time-space (1993a: 63–4). Structures only 'really' exist in the form of 'structural properties'. Structures (rules and resources) are virtual, and exist outside time-space, until they are put into practice, whereupon they become structural properties, and structural properties are simply the instantiated structures which are repeated in social practices. The structural properties most deeply embedded in time-space are called structural principles. The instantiated structures constitute social systems, which are defined as recursive social practices (1993a: 65–6; 1995a: 23–5). So, rules and resources are virtual until instantiated in praxis, where upon they become 'real', and form structural properties, of social systems (which are repeated practices). As Giddens puts it:

> To say that structure is a 'virtual order' of transformative relations means that social systems, as reproduced social practices, do not have 'structures' but rather exhibit 'structural properties' and that structure exists only in its instantiations in such practices and as memory traces orienting the conduct of knowledgeable human agents.
>
> (1995a: 17)

In more simple language, we may say that society is based on repeated practices, and these practices are based on rules and resources which only have an existence as such, when used in interaction. For example, the institution of the family is deeply embedded in time-space, with individuals repeatedly engaging in the practices that constitute family relations. The rules which constitute meaning for and which sanction such practices are virtual until drawn upon by individuals in the appropriate context, whereupon they serve to continue a way of going on which is ubiquitous (i.e. which is deeply embedded in time-space). So, this way of going on is a structural property (it exists), and the continuous practices that sustain it draw upon rules (structures) which are virtual (they exist 'in suspension' when not acted upon). As regards structural principles, these concern the interconnection of different institutions or structural properties, such as the modern nuclear family and industrial capitalism.

This conception of social structure is rather different from the established usage. Often, the term structure is used to mean an objective entity which is external to, and constrains, subjectivity and agency. This usage began with Durkheim's (1993a) definition of social rules as objective, external and constraining, which was coupled to the methodological injunction to study one social fact by another, because the social facts were *sui generis*. Hence the study of suicide (1993b), which was in terms of explaining the national suicide rate (one social fact) by reference to 'suicidogenic currents' (another social fact), without any reference to individuals.[7] Durkheim's later work (1995), though, stressed the importance of internalised norms, which eroded to some extent the subject–object divide. The problem here was that the notion of collective values, and the later development of this idea in Parsons' 'normative functionalism', placed the emphasis on how behaviour conformed to internalised social norms, which compromised the notion of agency (Giddens 1993a: 51). In other words, the subject was held to be a 'cultural dope', who *reacts to the constraining pressure of internalised norms, rather than acting upon rules which allow change* (Giddens 1993a: 53). Giddens relates this to contemporary sociology, referring to the structuralist work of Blau, and Althusser's structuralist Marxism. On Blau, Giddens makes the same point he made against Durkheim, which is that in defining structures as external and constraining (1995a: 210), agents become passive dopes. Against Althusser, Giddens argues agents are 'structural dopes' of even more stunning mediocrity than Parsons' cultural dopes, because agents are just bearers of structures; or subjects are just vehicles for the object (1993a: 52). In other words, whereas cultural dopes have some agency, even though it is to conform, structural dopes are just decentred reflections of structures.

This rejection of structures as being only external and constraining leads Giddens to reject the notion of emergent properties, which Durkheim used to define social facts. For Giddens, as we have seen, social structures are not ontologically distinct from individuals' practices. He argues that

> Social systems do have structural properties that cannot be described in terms of concepts referring to the consciousness of agents. But human actors, as recognizable 'competent agents', do not exist in separation from one another as copper, tin and lead do. They do not come together *ex nihilo* to form a new entity by their fusion or association.
>
> (1995a: 171)

Thus Cohen argues that it would be entirely inconsistent for structuration theory to talk of emergent properties, because the emphasis is on interrelated practices, not individuals confronting some mysterious – and undefined –

stratum which 'emerges' from the interaction of individuals to then exert an 'objective' constraint upon them (1990: 42).

For Giddens, one may say that structures are real, which is why he notes, in passing, that his concepts concerning structures are compatible with a 'realist epistemology' (1993a: 63), but one should not juxtapose objectivity to subjectivity, nor externality to internality. The point that Giddens wants to make is that structures are the medium and outcome of interaction: this is the duality of structure (1995a: 25). Virtual structures become real once instantiated, but this is not to say that structures, or rather, structural properties, are emergent properties as emergent properties would be, for Giddens, reified 'things' that existed outside people and which deterministically 'shoved' people about.

Giddens has little sympathy with the methodological individualist counter to structuralism (or holism). Such individualism is criticised for making reference to social factors without being able to define them or even accept them (1993a: 95; 1995a: 213–21).[8] Giddens may argue that '[s]tructure has no existence independent of the knowledge that agents have about what they do in their day-to-day activity' (1995a: 26), but this is not meant to commit him to methodological individualism. His point is that *instead of being cultural or structural dopes, social agents are knowledgeable, in the sense that they have the practical knowledge, i.e. the practical ability to 'go on', by knowing what practices are appropriate.*

Problems with rules

An individualist ontology: conflating structure into agency

Switching from exegesis to critique, we can say that Giddens' general ontology unfolds into individualism on the one hand, and a subject–object dualism on the other hand. In this section I will explore the former issue and, as a way into describing Giddens as an individualist, I will begin by discussing Archer's (1995) view that Giddens elides structure and agency together, with structuration theory being guilty of 'central conflationism'.[9] Archer, who will be discussed in more detail in the next chapter, begins by criticising methodological individualism for upwards conflationism, which denies the existence of a non-individualist social reality, and Durkheimian collectivism (as opposed to Gellner's and Mandelbaum's methodological collectivism) for downwards conflationism, which makes agency epiphenomenal. Following this, Archer then notes that Giddens' attempt to resolve the structure-agency problem, by moving from a subject–object dualism to a duality, results in structure and agency being elided, or run together. Rather than prioritise structures or agency, '[c]entral conflationism instead deprives *both* elements of their relative autonomy, not through *reducing* one to the other, but by *compacting* the two together inseparably' (Archer 1995: 101; emphasis in original). This is regarded as a strength by 'elisionists', because it is thought to resolve the structure-agency dilemma without reducing structures to individuals or reifying structures.

Such central conflationism is erroneous for Archer though, because it fails to conceptualise structures as emergent properties. Without such a notion of emergent properties, structures are activity-dependent in the *present tense*. As Archer puts it, '[a] leap is made from the truistic statement, "no people: no society", to the fallacy, "[t]his society because of these people here present" and its necessary by-product, a sociology of the present tense' (1990b: 86). So although Giddens is correct to stress the activity-dependence of structures in order to avoid reification, we should recognise that *structures are activity-dependent in the past tense*. What this means is that instead of conflating structure and agency together, as practices in the present, we should recognise that structures are emergent properties that were created by past acts, and are now ontologically distinct from agency.

For Archer, social structures may enable and constrain agency as Giddens argues, but we can only study this by conceptualising structures as being ontologically separate from agency. By eliding structure and agency together, one prevents the possibility of studying how structures furnish a social context which will provide objective constraints upon individuals' practices (and which may nonetheless be eventually modified by agents). Or, to put it another way, with this sociology of the present tense, there is no way to analyse how people make history in circumstances not of their own choosing, as the said circumstances become conflated into agents' practices in the here and now: circumstances are identical with individuals' choices in the present tense. So when Craib (1992b: 3–4) notes that for Giddens structure and agency are two sides of the same coin, with observed practices being conceptualisable as either structure or agency, we may paraphrase this as 'individuals make history, and they do so in circumstances of their own making and choosing, in this instant'. To disavow the notion of emergent properties is to endorse a sociology of the present tense, which will evacuate any notion of an historically derived social context, leaving us with just individuals' practices in the here and now.

Moving from the issue of structure and agency in general, to the specific issue of defining structures in terms of rules, Archer argues that rules ought to be considered as emergent properties. There are three reasons for this (1995: 108). The first is that many rules, such as laws, contracts, constitutions, etc., have *autonomy* from their instantiation, because they have an independent existence in time and space. The second is that rules are *anterior* to practices, because rules pre-exist practices. The third reason is that rules have an independent *causal influence*, so that the law will be applied to a miscreant even if the miscreant is ignorant of the law. This does not reify rules, according to Archer, as rules are activity-dependent in the *past tense*, as emergent properties. What this means is that emergent properties may be created by people in the past, but they then have an independent existence. Rules therefore have a real existence outside present practices, because individuals made the rules in the past, and those rules now exert an independent influence over individuals.

Now it may have been noticed that the examples of rules given by Archer are the sort of rules that Giddens refers to as formulated rules, or discursively codified rules, which are not the normal type of rule. Rules concerning the law, bureaucracy, contracts, games, etc., are not typical of social rules according to Giddens. This is because such rules rest on a subject–object dualism, given the formalism of the rules concerned. When confronting the rules of law, or the rules of a game, for instance, one is confronting formulated rules, prescribing what one ought to do, and what one ought not to do. The rules are external and constraining. In this case, such rules may be characterised as emergent properties, as Archer argues, because such rules are not reducible to individuals instantiating them in practices. This is not to imply that conceptualising structures as emergent properties necessarily results in a subject–object dualism, for as we will see in the next chapter, social realism links structure and agency without making structures just external determining constraints upon agency, by using the notion of emergent properties. Rather, the point here is just that formal rules, as Giddens notes, have a prescriptive function and, as Giddens fails to note, this means that such rules are ontologically distinct from agency in the present tense. Such rules would be the object, which was separate from the subject, and which functioned as an external constraint upon the subject.

My concern in this section though is not with the issue of a subject–object dualism arising from behaviour corresponding to formal rules, but with the way in which Giddens' argument about non-formal rules ends up as a form of individualism. If we consider what Giddens takes to be archetypal social rules, then we are dealing with informal rules. These informal rules are only understandable in terms of practices. That is, such rules are to be understood in terms of agents' practical knowledge about how to go on in different situations, rather than discursive codifications of rules. This could imply a concern with an interpretative sociology that dealt just with agents' meanings and understanding of the world. As we have seen though, Giddens wants to move beyond interpretative sociology, in order to link agency to structure, so as to emphasise the importance of the prevailing social context (as an enablement and constraint) upon agency. In which case, it is incumbent upon Giddens to operationalise the concept of structure in a way that will enable us to analyse how rules influence practices. We need to understand how the historical circumstances influence the individuals who make history, whilst not being able to choose their circumstances.

However, this is precisely what Giddens cannot do. If we try and analyse rules then we meet the problem that rules are definable in terms of practices and practices are definable in terms of rules. Rules are not something separate from agents' practices, but are intrinsic to agents going on. That is, rules are to be understood not as enablements, but as enabled action: rules are not to be understood as entities with the potential to enable action, but as the action itself. Rules are practices-in-action. This could seem like a 'chicken-and-egg' situation, with rules being defined as practices and practices being defined in terms of rules. The chicken and the egg though are ontologically distinct, and the point behind the paradox concerns the temporal sequence of events. In which case such an analogy will not work, for we cannot begin to ask how rules *qua* pre-existing structure influence the course of agency over time (by providing a context which is eventually reworked by agents), because rules are reduced into agency.

This means that we have a sociology of the present tense as Archer argues, but it does not mean that Giddens' ontology may be described as elisionism, or central conflationism. Non-formal rules cannot be regarded as being ontologically distinct from agents' practices. The result of this is that rules become conflated into practices: structure is conflated into agency. There is no way to operationalise the concept of rules, except to use it as a synonym for individuals' practices, in which case 'structure' would be a synonym for agency, meaning that structure would be redundant as a concept in its own right (and misleading as a noun). Structure and agency are *not elided* simply *because structure is reduced into agency*: rules are nothing more than individuals' practices. *This produces a sociology of the present tense because we could not understand how individuals made history in circumstances not of their choosing.* We could not explain how structures furnished a social context which enabled and constrained individuals' practices. Instead, all we could refer to would be individuals' practices. Such a position would clearly be individualist, because there could be no reference to anything other than individuals and their acts. Hence it would appear that Giddens' social ontology would put us in the same position as those theories he criticised for focusing on agents' meanings without linking this to a broader social context. We may analyse agents' practices, and their meanings, but we cannot move beyond this to examine how a social reality, which is irreducible to individuals, constrains as well as enables agency. *In short, we have upwards conflationism (rather than central conflationism), which can only explore individuals' acts and meanings in the here and now, because it cannot conceptualise the existence of a broader social context influencing individuals (and changing only slowly).*[10]

Rules and the subject–object dualism

In this section I will shift the concern, to argue that a subject–object dualism can emerge in Giddens' ontology. To see how this arises we can begin by noting that for Giddens, we may conceptualise practices as having either a pluralist or a singular relationship to rules. With the pluralist conception of rules *vis-à-vis* practices, one would argue that in the *flow* of on-going *practices*, agents draw upon *multiple rules*, as each context requires different practical *skills*, in which case, we cannot hope to identify rules by deriving *a rule* from *a practice*. For example, a male factory worker may have to be able to conform to the employer's orders (formal rules), but he would also have to go on within a male workers' subculture, which links into social life, with gender norms about appropriate 'masculine conduct' pertaining to both work and social spheres. In acting as a masculine worker, the male factory worker would be using different practices to continue reproducing his gender iden- tity. These practices may be regarded as embodying multiple rules, because the agent concerned would draw upon sets of practical skills in each specific circumstance: it would not be the case that the worker mechanically followed a rule, to which his behaviour conformed. Instead, he would draw upon sets of practical skills about how to go on. As argued above, though, unless we can distinguish rules from practices, by saying that structures are ontologically distinct, the result is an individualism which reduces structure into agency.

Alternatively, one could argue that a singular relationship obtains between *a rule* and *a practice, with a practice necessarily conforming to the rule* qua *causal factor*. In this case one could turn to the structuralist sociological logic of immediacy, in order to procure a definitive social ontology. With such an ontology one could have a 'filing cabinet' of discrete essences, or rules, and one would then either read-off behaviour from the ontology, or read the ontology into observed events. The paradox of rule-following would not arise, because one would be using an essentialist conception of rules, which maintained that *a discrete act* corresponded directly to *a rule*. One could not hold up an act as an illustration of breaking and following a rule, because to know a rule would be to know the discrete act which would necessarily correspond to it.

Of course Giddens would not endorse such a view. However, such an issue arises when we consider how Giddens' account of rules can imply a subject– object dualism. To recap, Giddens holds that social rules are not to be thought of as analogous to rules in a game, because social rules only exist in conjunction with practices: rules are ways of going on (1993a: 65). Subsequently Giddens qualifies this, saying that there are formal rules, such as laws, bureaucratic rules and the rules of games, etc; although he equivocates, saying in the same paragraph that such rules are (a) 'codified interpretations of rules rather than rules as such', and (b), that they are 'specific types of formulated rule', which do not 'exemplify rules in general' (1995a: 21). An example of formal rules being 'codified interpretations' would be laws, using juridic discourse to codify different forms of practices according to prevailing norms. What this means, then, is that laws *qua* dis- cursive codifications of rules *qua* practices are just restatements of accepted norms: they are discursive knowledge which repeats practical knowledge.

Another way of putting this is to say that laws follow practices, and that laws are not ontologically distinct from practices (which follow norms), because laws are just reinterpretations of really-existing ways of going on. *Against this, we can say that even if laws are initially developed to codify accepted ways of going on (by, for instance, upholding contractual obligations), laws do become ontologi- cally distinct, because they exert an objective influence over practices.* So if some people decided not to uphold contractual obligations, they would be not just violat- ing a set of cultural norms, but in violation of a rule, which would have very real consequences, in the form of legal penalties. The law would pre-exist their action and act as an objective effect upon it. We may also note that laws may be used in changing norms rather than tracking the prevailing consensus. Thus laws could be put in place to help counter widespread discrimination based on racism and sexism for instance. Here the ontological separation of laws *qua* rules from practices would be clearly illustrated with laws being objective constraints upon previously accepted ways of going on.

So, laws *qua* formal rules have to be regarded *as rules in their own right*, rather than as discursive codifications – or interpretations – of rules, and these 'specific types of formulated rule' may be regarded as emergent properties. They have an ontological status which is not dependent in the present tense upon instantiation: formal rules exist before the acts they may constrain. Of course past actions will have created formal rules, but now they are not reducible to individuals' practices. Whether we are discussing laws (as above) or other types of formal rules, such as bureaucratic rules, these rules really exist outside instantiation, as Archer argued. Whereas Archer defends the conception of structures as emergent properties, in her realist attempt to link structure and agency (as described in Chapter 5), Giddens would regard the conception of structures as emergent properties as an illustration of the subject–object dualism. Giddens has an ontological dichotomy between: (a) the duality of structure, whereby structures exist in their instantiation within practices, and enable as well as constrain agency; and (b), the subject–object dualism, whereby structures are Durkheimian emergent properties which are external constraints upon agency. The recognition that formal rules were emergent properties would, given this dichotomy, mean that structure and agency became separated, resulting in structures being constraints upon agency, with agents' practices simply conforming to the external and determining influence of structures. The notion of purposeful social agents would be lost as the emphasis shifted onto the way that behaviour conformed to structural determinants.

Note that when Giddens says that rules are not like formal rules in games such as chess, because social rules are contested, he is implicitly saying that rules can be objective constraints upon practices, and that these rules may be resented, because they are perceived as unjust *impositions*, i.e. unjust restrictions upon freedom. This could, as has been suggested, apply to legal rules, as laws are often the site for conflict over values precisely because laws exist as ontologically distinct entities from practices, which can restrict agents' practices.

Moreover, it can also apply to informal rules, or practices. If we reject the emphasis upon consensus, as Giddens does, in order to recognise that the social world is made up of a plurality of groups, some of whom will actively question prevailing norms and practices, then we will recognise the ubiquity of conflict (in the broadest sense of the term). The corollary of this is that whilst some agents will see the accepted ways of going on (i.e. informal rules) as normal, and will probably take them for granted, others may see the existing practices as an unjust constraint. Mouzelis (1989) argues that a subject–object dualism will emerge as soon as some agents 'step back' from prevailing norms, in order to question and criticise (or even analyse) such norms. As he puts it, '[w]hen specialists or lay-persons use metalanguages, their orientations to rules and resources [i.e. structures] can be understood better in terms of a subject/object dualism than in terms of duality' (1989: 617). In other words, when social scientists, or agents, produce a questioning or critical language, they are stepping back from a structure which then becomes external to them.

We can develop this point by saying that *rules are an external object, whether perceived as such or not. Structures can be external constraints (as well as enablements) before they are recognised or perceived as such.* So, if some regard the prevailing gender norms as normal and 'natural', and take them for granted, whilst others analyse, question and/or criticise such norms, then it is not simply the case that such norms only have an objective existence for the latter group, *especially given that the said norms would have a stronger causal impact upon the identity and agency of uncritical agents.* Rather, such norms or rules about how men and women ought to go on would exist as (to use Archer's 1995 terms) an objectively real *cultural emergent property.*[11] Whatever one thought about gender, one would be born into a pre-existing system of rules concerning appearance, sexuality, rights to employment, rights to birth control, the acceptance of homosexuality, etc., which would be irreducible to the practices of particular individuals, and which would constrain one's actions. Therefore in order to understand the ubiquity of conflict, meaning the pressure for change (or the ability of agents to be agents, using Giddens' notions of power and agency), we need to talk of emergent properties, which for Giddens means talking of a subject–object dualism.[12]

So, on the one hand, structure is reduced into agency, with structures being rules which exist as the actions of individual agents. In this case, we would have an individualist sociology which would mean putting the emphasis on individuals' meanings; which is what Giddens tries to move beyond. On the other hand, when Giddens accepts that formal rules exist, their existence would be as entities that are external constraints upon agents' practices. Such entities would be emergent properties, which, according to Giddens, results in a subject–object dualism, whereby the individual subject has their behaviour determined by the social object. Further, we may extend this point to informal rules, or customary ways of going on, using the example of gender norms as *cultural emergent properties.* As emergent properties entails a subject–object dualism for Giddens, this means that he escapes from interpretativist sociology by imposing a subject–object dualism. This dualism would entail the structuralist sociological logic of immediacy because it would be a definitive list of the social essences. One could simply read-off different forms of behaviour from the ontology of emergent properties which determined individuals' behaviour. In place of a flow of practices using a plurality of rules/social skills, there would be a singular causal relationship between a rule and a discrete form of behaviour which was determined by that rule/essence.

Problems with linking the micro and the macro levels

Voluntarism

In this section I will deal with Giddens' arguments concerning social systems and methodological *epoché*. As with the argument about rules, my case against Giddens will be that his work unfolds into an individualism and a subject–object dualism. Giddens argues that social systems are to be understood as '[r]eproduced relations between actors or collectivities, organised as regular social practices' (1993a: 66; Fig. 2.2). Such reproduced relations can, in turn, be broken down into 'social integration', concerning relations of reciprocity between actors, and 'system integration', concerning relations of reciprocity between groups or collectivities (1993a: 76–7). Further, he talks of 'institutional analysis' and the analysis of 'strategic conduct', referring to the study of 'system properties', and individuals, respectively; whilst stressing that this division is just a 'methodological *epoché*' that does not correspond to system and social integration, respectively (1993a: 80).

Another way of putting this is to say that Giddens wants to connect individuals into a wider social context, not just by talking of individual acts as following social rules, but also by linking individual practices to broader social continuities, or 'social systems'. He seeks to do this, obviously, in terms of a duality, rather than a subject–object, or structure-agency, dualism. Therefore when Giddens talks of social systems he is not referring to systems in the sense used by structuralists and functionalists, whereby social systems are emergent properties that are constraints upon agents (1993a: 50). External and constraining emergent properties are not to be set up in a dualism with individuals. Instead, '[s]ocial systems involve regularised relations of interdependence between individuals or groups, that typically can best be analysed as *recurrent social practices*' (1993a: 65–6; emphasis in original). Structures are virtual, and are therefore characterised by 'an absence of the subject' (1993a: 66), but when individuals instantiate structures in particular practices, they contribute to the continuance of social systems, which are 'more than' particular individuals and their acts. So systems are not objectively real structures that are external to agents' practices.

The problem though is that if emergent properties are denied, on the grounds that they necessarily result in a subject–object dualism, then it is hard to see what prevents the concept of 'social system' becoming redundant. For if social systems are not emergent properties then, *a fortiori*, they are not ontologically distinct from agents' practices, which would mean that social systems were simply synonyms for agents' practices. Or, to be more accurate, they would be synonyms for the practices which agents *chose* to repeat. This position would not just be individualist, focusing upon individuals, but also voluntarist, because there would be very little (if any) constraint upon individual acts.

If we accepted such an individualist and voluntarist sociology, it would be difficult to explain how there was any form of social continuity, or 'recurrent social practices', i.e. social systems. As Craib argues, one could not explain continuity or regularity in terms of 'unintended consequences', because chaos is just as likely (if not more so) than order (1992a: 116). To put it another way, if ten individuals were told to speak a word in private it is unlikely that their words would collectively come close to forming a coherent sentence. If those individuals were removed from their isolation though, then they would be able to produce sentences which were appropriate to an on-going dialogue. That is, individuals would be able to 'mesh' their practices in with others, resulting in continuity. In this case, social systems may be understandable via a linguistic analogy, with the reproduction of society being akin to the reproduction of language.

Although Giddens denies that he thinks of society as akin to a language, because he wants to distance himself from structuralism and interpretative sociologies (1993a: 4), he does draw upon the linguistic analogy, when describing how the utterance of a grammatical English sentence contributes to the reproduction of the English language as a whole, and how the same may apply to social reality (1993a: 77). Giddens draws upon this analogy when discussing the relationship between social and system integration. He argues that

> the systemness of social integration *is fundamental to the systemness of society as a whole*. System integration cannot be adequately conceptualised via the modalities of social integration; none the less the latter is always the chief prop of the former, *via the reproduction of institutions in the duality of structure*. [...] The duality of structure relates the smallest item of day-to-day behaviour to attributes of far more inclusive social systems: when I utter a grammatical English sentence in a casual conversation, I contribute to the reproduction of the English language as a whole.
>
> (1993a: 77; emphasis in original)

This turn to the linguistic analogy does not resolve the matter though. We are still left with a very individualist and voluntarist account which cannot really explain how the social context may be ontologically distinct from individuals, and how this context may constrain agency. Just as agents may choose to speak French rather than English tomorrow, so it follows that agents may just change their social practices and thus transform society, simply by an exercise of unconstrained free will; assuming that they agree on the outcome, so as to avoid chaos, given that social order cannot be a fortuitous 'unintended consequence'. Individuals may choose to mesh their sentences into an on-going dialogue, but the dialogue, or even the language itself, can be changed simply by exercising free will. In which case, the social system, or continuity, is to be understood in terms of an *intended consequence*: continuity obtains because different individuals choose it. *The existence of social systems therefore seems to be entirely dependent upon individuals consciously deciding to reproduce certain ways of going on.* Thus social systems depend upon actions in the *present tense*, as there is no way to conceptualise social reality as a pre-existing emergent property, that acts as a mediating constraint upon agency, and can only be changed slowly, given that it is ontologically distinct from agency. In short, social systems depend upon agents' dispositions in the present here and now.

What this means is that to understand social relations a reduction is necessary, whereby social reality is explained by reference to psychological dispositions. As social systems are not to be understood in terms of emergent properties which are separate from individuals' practices in the present tense, and as systems cannot be understood in terms of accidental unintended consequences, it follows that systems are an intended consequence, produced by agents choosing to act in a particular way *en masse*. Social systems, i.e. continuing practices, obtain because individuals desire this to be the case. If individuals 'changed their minds', the practices would change, and the existing social system would simply cease to be. Layder picks up on this point about the dependency of social systems with the practices of knowledgeable agents. He argues that

> This seems to imply that reproduced practices are virtually the same thing as people's reasons and motivations. If this is so, it strongly suggests that social reality is dependent upon psychological phenomena – something which Giddens is otherwise strongly against.
>
> (1994: 141)

This implies not only that the discussion of social systems in a way that is antithetical to the notion of emergent properties implies an individualist conception of social reality. It means that the argument turns on the individualist sociological logic of immediacy. This is because one would be turning to a psychologism, whereby an ontology of human being would be a definitive master-ontology, whereby all social phenomena could be explained by an explanation which reduced social relations down to expressions of psychological states. Thus to know the ontology of psychological states is to know all the causes of human behaviour.

Parallel universes

Having noted this, we can say that a subject–object dualism also appears in Giddens' discussion of systems. Giddens contrasts social integration, defined in terms of reciprocity between individual agents, and system integration, defined in terms of reciprocity between groups or collectivities. This means, as Mouzelis argues, that co-presence becomes the defining feature, with individual co-presence defining social integration (1995: 124), and lack of co-presence defining system integration. Therefore social and system integration are the same, in effect, as the micro- and the macro-level units of analysis, where the micro is defined in terms of face-to-face interaction, whilst the macro level is 'above' this (Mouzelis 1995: 124). Now some defend such a micro–macro divide, such as Wagner (1964), who argues that sociology can be divided up according to small-scale studies of individuals, and large-scale macro quantitative studies, with the units of analysis pertaining to 'size', i.e. individuals, or social processes (measured in a quantitative way). Against this, as Alexander (1987) argues, it is misleading to formulate the issue as one of size. Alexander argues that '[t]here can be no empirical referents for micro and macro as such. They are analytical contrasts, suggesting emergent levels within empirical units, not antagonistic empirical units themselves' (1987: 290). So we should try and link macro or systemic factors to the micro level of individual agency, as the two are intertwined, and separating them would result in a marked subject–object dualism. To use a micro–macro divide would necessarily result in a subject–object dualism, because one would be trying artificially to contrast the realm of actual individuals with the realm of social processes cut off from, and 'above the heads of', individuals.[13]

With such a subject–object dualism there would be parallel universes, whereby agents scurried around in an unconstrained way at the micro level, whilst social reproduction, in the form of macro-level processes or statistical regularities, simply 'occurred', presumably as some form of unintended consequence. *This is important to note, because it means that instead of the social subject being determined by the social object, the two realms would be cut off from each other.* Such a view is reinforced by Giddens' argument about the analysis of strategic conduct and institutional analysis. The study of strategic conduct is the study of agents' discursive and practical consciousness, whilst institutional analysis brackets agents' practices, to focus on the 'chronically reproduced features of social systems' (1993a: 80; 1995a: 288). As Archer argues, '[t]his methodological bracketing has produced a pendular swing between contradictory images – of chronic recursiveness and total transformation' (1995: 88). On the one hand we have agents and their ways of going on, or their discursive and practical consciousness, meaning agents acting on the basis of their knowledge, or dispositions and changing practices; and on the other hand, we have systems which are, by definition here, characterised in terms of continuity. With institutional analysis we are dealing with social systems that are unchanging, and with strategic conduct, we are dealing with unconstrained free will and change. Strategic conduct turns on such a voluntarist notion of agency because the emphasis is just on the individual's consciousness and practices, meaning that actions could be derived from dispositions. There could be no reference to a social context influencing the individual, because given the methodological dualism, reference to non-individual factors commits one to the study of regularities which are unchanging and separate from individuals. Agency therefore is unconstrained by a wider

social context, and this unconstrained agency, whereby acts mirror dispositions, would result in an emphasis on change. We would be dealing with how
individuals *chose* to act in different ways. There could be no 'middle way' as
there is no way, given this methodological dualism, predicated upon macro
continuity and micro change, to say how a social context influenced and
constrained agency, and was, in turn, eventually altered by agency. We
just have a dualism between unchanging systems and individuals' practices,
meaning a dualism between structural continuity and individuals effecting
change.

So, whilst the definition of social systems resulted in individualism and
psychologism, the discussion of social and system integration, together with
the arguments for methodological bracketing, resulted in a subject–object
dualism. This dualism did not mean, as it usually does, that the object dom-
inates the subject, but that there were parallel universes. This divide between
the micro and macro levels is overcome though, when Giddens considers how
social systems may influence individuals' practices. *Giddens may define social
systems in terms of recurrent social practices, rather than emergent properties, but he
does go on to say that social systems may act as external constraints upon individuals.*
He argues that 'the greater the time-space distanciation of social systems – the
more their institutions bite into time and space – the more resistant they are
to manipulation or change by any individual agent' (1995a: 171). Admittedly
Giddens does move straight on to talk of enablement, saying that although
time-space distanciation may close some possibilities off, it will nonetheless
open up others. This may well be true, as individuals could, for instance,
accept legislation on some issue or mobilise to change it.

Nevertheless, the point has been conceded that there are strata of social
reality which are ontologically distinct from individuals, and which can act as
external constraints upon individuals. In which case, it must be an emergent
property of some sort, which is not necessarily a problem, unless one holds, as
Giddens does, that emergence implies a subject–object dualism whereby
emergent properties are only external constraints and not enablements,
with the object determining the subject. As Layder comments, Giddens'
account of institutional durability (in terms of routinisation) is not convincing
(or internally coherent), because Giddens lacks the conceptual resources to
explain how there can be 'objective structures' which pre-exist and post-date
the life of particular individuals (1994: 141–2). So Giddens' concepts are
premised upon a sociology of the present tense, meaning that the focus is
on the practices of individual agents in the here-and-now. His attempt to
overcome the voluntaristic implications of this led him to talk of contextual
constraints, which are irreducible to present acts, and we can only escape
from the present tense by invoking an ontology of emergent properties, which
for Giddens would mean a subject–object dualism.

With such a subject–object dualism, the agency of the individual subject
would be an epiphenomenon of the object, and Giddens comes to admit as
much. When discussing the issue of structural constraint, Giddens argues that

'it is best described as *placing limits upon the range of options open to an actor, or plurality of actors, in a given circumstance*' (1995a: 176–7; emphasis in original). Giddens goes on to talk of the capitalist labour market, where the propertyless worker has to sell his/her labour power. This is described as the agent's 'only one feasible option' (1995a: 177). Giddens then notes that '[a]ll structural properties of social systems have a similar "objectivity" *vis-à-vis* the individual agent [... although] the feasible options open to agents may be greater than in the labour contract example' (1995a: 177). Concern that all the emphasis is upon constraint leads Giddens to state that there are enablements as well.

However, his example is of workers being enabled to get a living from having to enter the labour contract on the terms of the capitalist. What this means, as Thompson argues, is that there has been a move from defining agency in terms of the power to make a change, to defining agency in terms of 'feasible options', meaning recognition of lack of choice (1991: 73–4). Instead of being able to 'make a difference' the agent has only one option – or one *feasible* option – which is, in effect, the same as having no options (Thompson 1991: 73). One has to accept that one has no real choice. Consequently the concept of agency is, for 'practical purposes', irrelevant (Thompson 1991: 74). Thus Thompson argues that 'Giddens manages to preserve the complementary between structure and agency only by *defining* agency in such a way that any individual in any situation could *not* be an agent' (1991: 74; emphasis in original).

In a reply to this, Giddens argues that what constitutes a feasible option will change if agents' 'wants' and 'motivations' change, and that potential new courses of action may emerge as a result (1991b: 259). This is not a satisfactory rejoinder, though, because in addition to the psychologistic reductionism it entails, conflating the outcome of agency with dispositions, it redefines 'feasible options' as any option, by failing to admit that the objective constraints of a situation will limit the realistic courses of action. One may avoid the constraints of the labour market and the 'rat race' by becoming a New Age traveller, which is an option if one's wants and motivations adapt to this, but it is not a feasible option for most people. To maintain the meaning of feasible options, we have to realise that realistic options are embedded into contexts which may severely limit the freedom of an individual. Recognition of such objective constraints would mean a subject–object dualism for Giddens, though, because social reality would be an external constraint upon freedom of choice and action. The discussion of structural constraint therefore entails the structuralist sociological logic of immediacy, because one would be dealing with an objective structure that was conceptualised as a determining factor upon agency.

What is the purpose of structuration theory? Or, what is the link between ontology and methodology?

For Giddens a social ontology is required to inform a critical attitude towards previous research, and to guide on-going research. On the point about reading previous research, Giddens reads selected parts of his ontology into several pieces of completed research. One of the pieces of research chosen is Willis's study of working-class school boys, whilst another discussion is about a study of how the City of London came to economic prominence (1995a: 281–354). In Willis's (1977) study, the working-class boys are not simply deviant, but are knowledgeable social agents. These agents realise that formal schooling will make little difference to their life chances, and they draw upon the macho culture inherited from their fathers to distance themselves from the school culture, and to adopt a 'tough' attitude, appropriate to their future working environments. The unwitting outcome of this is that their rebellious attitude ends up making them accept dead-end jobs with no chance of career progression. Giddens uses this study as an example of the analysis of strategic conduct, with 'institutional' concerns being bracketed off. He agrees with Willis's study, dismissing a functionalist interpretation of the boys' conduct in terms of 'imperfect socialisation', to say that the boys – or the 'lads' – are knowledgeable social agents who are engaged in rule-following practices. The unintended consequence of the lads following a rebellious macho way of going on, though, is to reproduce the institutional relations of the capitalist labour market.

The problem here is not that Giddens distorts Willis's work, but that he does not add anything to it. All Giddens has done, basically, is to redescribe certain aspects of Willis's study in new language. For Willis's 'counterculture' we now have Giddens' 'knowledgeable agents' engaged in 'rule-following practices', and whereas Willis talks of the oppositional culture reproducing capitalism, Giddens talks of unintended consequences, and the activities of knowledgeable social agents reproducing the 'structural properties' of 'social systems', which are 'embedded in spans of time-space'. This may redescribe Willis's study, but it does not challenge or reinterpret Willis. Indeed, we may apply Ockham's razor and remove the supplementary layer of (structuration theory) concepts, as they add nothing to the understanding of the original work. As Giddens' concepts are just supplementary rather than complementary, they may be removed because the supplement merely replicates the main body of research.

Against the charge of redundancy we can note that Giddens states that reading (some of) his ontology into completed research will allow for 'various quite basic criticisms and emendations to be made to the research work analysed' (1995a: 326). However, apart from the fact that Giddens does not criticise or emend Willis's work, we can note that Giddens' ontology is not specific enough to be used in such a way. Taken at 'face value' we get the problem that the concepts are truistic, unfalsifiable and circular. Or, as Baert puts it, 'Giddens on the whole abstains from providing bold conjectures – quite a few of the basic statements actually verge on the tautological. [...] Many aspects of Giddens's carefully worked-out theory are simply immune to refutation, being as self-evident as logical formulae' (1998: 108–9). These points apply to the notion that for agents to act, agents must be knowledge-

able (they know how to go on – i.e. they must have social skills), and that
agents deal with limits and (potential) opportunities in a particular social
context. Arguing against this would commit one to either a determinism or an
unconstrained voluntarism, so we have to accept these points, but they do not
tell us much. Therefore rather than have a specific detailed ontology, we have
a set of rather truistic and elastic concepts, which are general enough to be
operationalised in numerous ways, which means that the ontology will just
create synonyms for already established research findings. If the ontology
were to allow for 'basic criticisms' and 'emendations' it would need to have
a specific set of concepts which could be contrasted against those used in the
research; unless, that is, the general concepts of structuration theory were
given meaning in an arbitrary way, with the concepts simply being defined
in ways antithetical to the research being studied.

I say if we take Giddens' ontology 'at face value' then the above problems
emerge. If, though, we analyse the ontology, as I sought to do in the previous
sections of this chapter, then it is the case that Giddens' work unfolds into
individualism and a subject–object dualism. In the former case, we have the
individualistic sociological logic of immediacy, because the individualism
results in a psychologistic reductionism. In the latter case, we have the structuralist sociological logic of immediacy, with the object determining the subject, as social structures become emergent properties which, given Giddens'
ontological dichotomy between practices and determining structures, means
that structures are external constraints upon agent. What this means, apropos
finished pieces of research, is that the ontology would be specific enough to
criticise and emend the research in question. The problem, though, is that if
ontology were predicated upon the sociological logic of immediacy, then it
would be definitive: there would be a relationship of epistemic immediacy
between a concept and a really-existing essence in reality which determined
behaviour. The ontology would be a filing cabinet of essences from which all
forms of social behaviour could be explained. Therefore, if one did adopt such
an ontology, the implications as regards finished pieces of research would be
two-fold. On the one hand, one could dismiss the work as redundant, because
behaviour could be read-off from the definitive ontology. On the other hand,
one could read-into the research one's concepts to verify the ontology, for if
one took the ontology to be definitive, then research would either be utterly
erroneous or read as a verification of the ontology.

Giddens is certainly concerned about his ontology being essentialist, i.e. a
definitive master-ontology. He is concerned that in developing a general
definition, or meta-theory of social reality, it may be thought that his ontology is definitive, meaning that it is predicated upon the structuralist sociological logic of immediacy, with each concept pertaining to a discrete
empirical essence. To avoid this, Giddens stresses that his ontology is not
meant to furnish a new research programme in its own right (1991b: 213;
1995a: 326–7). So instead of trying to get methodology to mirror the ontology, with research setting out simply to verify the filing cabinet list of con-

cepts, Giddens is keen to stress that empirical investigation would not be a verification of a definitive ontology. In fact, the link between the ontology and actual methodology (i.e. to the development of specific theories and empirical investigation) is so loose that Giddens holds that his concepts are to be used as 'sensitizing devices, nothing more' (1995a: 326).

Outhwaite (1990) and Bryant and Jary (1991b) support this stance. They argue that a social ontology may be complex, but one must not mistake the complexity of concepts for an attempt to mirror reality. Thus Outhwaite argues that Giddens has a 'cautiously realist approach' whereby a plethora of concepts are developed, and designed to be used in a selective/flexible way (1990: 71). This prevents the 'reification of hypothetical structures', which occurs when a less cautiously realist approach presumes that there is a relationship of identity, or immediacy, between a concept of a structure and a really-existing essence. Similarly, Bryant and Jary note that '[u]nlike Parsons, Giddens has never wanted empirical researchers to incorporate his whole conceptual vocabulary in their work' (1991b: 27). So, Giddens' ontology may be complex but only certain aspects will be drawn upon, because to draw upon the entire ontology would be to assume that social reality mirrored the concepts. Further, in drawing upon selected concepts, it would not be the case that these concepts mirrored discrete referents, but that the concepts were heuristic, or sensitising devices, which could be interpreted in different ways, allowing the researcher to be sensitive to the context, rather than dogmatically applying a previously worked-out definition of a structure, etc.

Bhaskar, and Archer, who will be discussed in the following chapter, also develop an elaborate social ontology, and some see Bhaskar and Giddens as having very similar positions. Outhwaite takes such a view, holding not only that Bhaskar has a similar ontology to Giddens, but that Bhaskar's realist ontology (of emergent properties) is also meant to function, in effect, as a sensitising device (1990: 69–71).[14] Bhaskar is held to be 'ontologically bold and epistemologically cautious' (Outhwaite 1987: 34), meaning that his ontological concepts, like those of Giddens, do not mirror reality. Conversely, Bryant and Jary say that Giddens is a 'naive realist', in the sense that he accepts that there is a reality beyond ideas, discourse, etc., but that he does not want his ontology to be used like Bhaskar's 'scientific realist' ontology (1991b: 26–7). They contrast Bhaskar's scientific realism with Giddens' naive realism, to say that Bhaskar's ontology is not a sensitising device, but more of a claim to epistemic certainty. Bhaskar's ontology, unlike Giddens' ontology, is held to seek a definitive explanation of social reality, with concepts mirroring discrete essences.

The issue here is not the correct interpretation of Bhaskar; although it must be noted that Giddens' explicit rejection of emergent properties does not sit well with Bhaskar's realist defence of emergent properties.[15] Rather, the key point to note here is that Giddens, Outhwaite, and Bryant and Jary are confusing the issue of *how much ontology to apply* with the issue of *how to apply an ontology*. It is not the case that if one seeks to apply an entire ontology then one is drawing upon a form of essentialism in the form of the sociological logic of immediacy, whereby a definitive ontology of structures (or human being for that matter) is held to mirror reality *qua* discrete essences. Of course functionalists like Parsons may argue for a filing cabinet approach, with a complex set of concepts being used to map social reality, but the use of a whole ontology need not be based on the assumption that the ontology is definitive. *One may apply a whole ontology of emergent properties (as will be discussed in the next chapter) without saying that this ontology mirrors social reality: a theory of being does not imply a being–knowing identity, or immediacy.* As soon as one says that an ontology need not be definitive, with the concepts mirroring social reality, then one is able to apply the ontology to guide methodology. The issue about applying selected components of an ontology to avoid essentialism and reification is wholly specious, because if the ontology does not presume to mirror reality it may be applied *in toto*, and if its concepts are thought to mirror discrete referents/essences, then applying only selected concepts will not circumvent this problem.

There is also the problem that if one applies an ontology in a piecemeal way the application will be arbitrary because one is admitting that research does not need an ontological underlabourer, and so there can be no justification for applying any ontological meta-theory. One would be in the position of holding that presumptions about being do not influence research. In which case there could be no reason to draw upon a meta-theory that supplied some precepts about being; especially if those precepts were elastic enough to 'fit' anything one wanted to say. All one would be doing is introducing a supplementary layer of words that Ockham's razor could shave off.

A supporter of Giddens may say that we could 'pragmatically' apply the ontology when it was 'useful', and that we ought to avoid the urge to develop grand ontologies that explained everything. Yet this raises the question of what the adjective 'useful' could mean, and the problem that the justification for the ontology could move from epistemic to rhetorical grounds, with it being maintained (in effect) that the concepts were useful additions to parts of an argument, because they 'sounded right'. Yet the point of sociological research, which is to create some knowledge about how individuals' agency is influenced by the social context, compels us to resolve the structure-agency problem, and to use the ontology that resolves this problem to inform all social research, as all research is influenced by our presumptions about being. This does not necessarily result in the sociological logic of immediacy as we will see in the next chapter on social realism, and using the terms of reference that say how agency is socially mediated will be more useful in our search for new knowledge of social reality, than a set of concepts that, at first glance, can be used in any way one wishes, and which, upon closer inspection, turn out to entail the sociological logic of immediacy.

5 Social realism

Overcoming the sociological logic of immediacy

Introduction

In this chapter I argue that realist anti-foundationalism may be complemented by a social realist meta-theory, that resolves the structure-agency problem. This will entail arguing for the ontological positions developed by Bhaskar and Archer.[1] Social realism, it will be argued, is developed via an immanent critique of alternative accounts of being. This immanent critique started with Bhaskar's critique of 'empirical realism' in the philosophy of natural science, and the critique of individualism, collectivism and what Bhaskar calls the 'dialectical position' (of Berger and Luckmann), with regard to social ontology. Bhaskar's ontology was fairly schematic though (which is why some mistakenly assumed Bhaskar and Giddens to have similar social ontologies), and Archer elaborated this into a more nuanced ontology, emphasising the role of emergent properties, and the activity-dependence of structures in the *past tense*. Rather than discuss how this social realist meta-theoretical ontology may inform methodology (i.e. empirical research and the formation of specific theories) and thus act as a positive underlabourer (which is the task of the next chapter), I will move from exegesis to consider some Wittgensteinian and Marxist criticisms of social realism. Such critiques of social realism hold that it is, basically, a form of essentialism, positing the idea that some universal essences can explain all human behaviour. Such a view, which would make social realism turn on the sociological logic of immediacy, is rejected by showing that a social realist ontological underlabourer is different from an ontological master-builder, because it supplies fallible precepts to guide research, and not a list of 'facts' or essences.

Bhaskar on the philosophy of science: from empirical realism to transcendental realism[2]

Empirical realism

With regard to the philosophy of natural science, Bhaskar argues for a 'transcendental realism'. Such a transcendental realist concern is with the condition of possibility for science, and the ontological precepts used to explain the condition of possibility for scientific knowledge formation are derived from an immanent critique of an alternative position, viz. 'empirical realism'. Empirical realism pertains to both positivism and post-Kantian philosophies of natural science, and the discussion will start with Bhaskar's critique of the former.

Bhaskar's project in the philosophy of science is to avoid the reduction of ontological questions into epistemological questions. Bhaskar wants to avoid what he terms the 'epistemic fallacy' (which was defined and discussed in Chapter 1). This leads Bhaskar to reject positivism, on the grounds that it commits the epistemic fallacy of reducing being into knowing, i.e. for reducing, or transposing, ontological questions into epistemological questions (1986: 6, 1993: 13, 17–18, 1997: 36). Ontological questions are transposed into epistemological questions with positivism, because the object of science, viz. causal mechanisms, is defined in Humean terms, as observed constant conjunctions. Thus *what* exists, and *what* is knowable, is defined wholly in terms of *how* we may have knowledge: an account of knowledge formation based on experience is used to define the objects of knowledge for natural science.

This results in what Bhaskar (1997: 64) refers to as an 'actualist' ontology. What this means is that any account of (natural) being must confine itself to propositions concerning actual observed, or observable, states of affairs, rather than causal mechanisms which are unobservable in their effects. A description of observed discrete 'facts' would be taken as an accurate account of being, with laws being manifest in their effects *qua* observed constant conjunctions. Thus the actual is constituted by the realm of empirical events (i.e. the contingent effects of causal laws) and the experience of this; but with no account of underlying causal mechanisms producing the observable events.

An actualist ontology is also an ontology of 'closed systems'. Laws and their effects would be thought to correspond exactly, with laws being observed constant conjunctions, and so it would follow that natural reality was a closed system, because it would be made up of a fixed set of unchanging observable regularities. There would be no 'openness' in the sense that there would be no difference between laws and their observable effects, with observed effects being the result of different (unobserved) laws interacting. In place of unobserved causal laws having observed effects which were *contingent* upon a particular set of changing interactions between causal laws, an actualist closed systems ontology would hold that observed regularities were manifestations of *universal* causal laws. To observe a regularity would be to observe a relationship of natural *necessity*.

The problem with this is that closed systems do not (for the most part) obtain, unless one is creating artificial closure in an experimental situation (and even then unknown factors may intervene). Therefore the positivist could not explain how an identified putative law could be held to exist outside the experiment, or the use of closed system identification of putative laws, if open systems exist. As Bhaskar argues:

> The empiricist is now caught in a terrible dilemma: for the extent that the antecedents of law-like statements are instantiated in open systems, he must sacrifice either the universal character or the empirical status of laws. If, on the other hand, he attempts to avoid this dilemma by restructuring the application of laws to closed systems (e.g. by making the satisfaction of a *ceteris paribus* clause a condition of their applicability), he is faced with the embarrassing question of what governs phenomena in open systems.
>
> (1997: 65)[3]

So, if one used an empiricist epistemology to inform positivist scientific methodology, empiricism would act as a master-builder. By committing the epistemic fallacy, empiricism defines ontology in terms of an epistemology which is premised upon the notion that we have a direct access via experience to the manifest truth. Thus the ontology of natural reality produced by this is one which holds that causal laws are identical with their effects, with causal laws being defined via observed regularities: given an empiricist epistemology the ontology produced is an actualist closed systems model of being.

The empiricist-positivist philosophy of science described above is one version of what Bhaskar refers to as empirical realism. The other version of empirical realism is post-Kantian (1997: 26).[4] Bhaskar argues that post-Kantian philosophies of science 'reject the empiricist account of science, according to which its valid content is exhausted by atomistic facts and their constant conjunctions' (1997: 27). However there is an ontological similarity between the two, which is that neither can sustain the notion of causal structures being definable in terms other than that of how the knowing subject may have knowledge (1997: 25–6). Both are predicated upon the epistemic fallacy, with both empiricist and post-Kantian accounts of natural science turning upon an actualist closed systems ontology. As Bhaskar argues,

> It is in their shared ontology that the source of this common incapacity [i.e. the epistemic fallacy] lies. For although transcendental idealism rejects the empiricist account of science, it tacitly takes over the empiricist account of being. This ontological legacy is expressed most succinctly in its commitment to empirical realism, and thus to the concept of the *'empirical world'*.
>
> (1997: 28; emphasis in original)

With post-Kantianism the emphasis changes from a manifest truth, which is directly experienced, to our concepts, with experience being mediated via categories/conceptual structures. Nevertheless the view remains that causal laws are definable in terms of empirical regularities, even though these are constructed via our categories. So, instead of defining causal laws as observed constant conjunctions which are taken to be the manifest truth, causal laws are definable as perceived constant conjunctions, which are the products of our categories. Consequently post-Kantianism is, like empiricism, predicated upon the epistemic fallacy, because questions of being are reduced into questions of knowing: causal laws are defined in terms of the regularities perceived by the knowing subject. Further, post-Kantianism also adheres to an actualist closed systems ontology because causal laws would be defined as fixed regularities with no conception of causal laws being separate from their perceived effects.

The root of the problem with empirical realism is that it is predicated upon a relationship of epistemic immediacy, or being–knowing identity, because with both empiricist and post-Kantian philosophies of natural science, there is no way to avoid defining causal laws as anything other than the regularities which are observed or perceived via categories. Which leads us straight into the difficulty of explaining how causal laws can exist when regularities fail to obtain. Or to put it another way, the object of natural science (causal laws) is dependent for its existence upon the subject perceiving universal regularities in a closed system, and as the natural world is not a closed system, *the object of science disappears with the subject's failure continuously to perceive universal regularities.*

The non-identity of being and knowing

Against empirical realism, Bhaskar argues for the anti-foundational non-identity of being and knowing. As Bhaskar puts it, his realism 'explicitly asserts the non-identity of the objects of the transitive and intransitive dimensions, of thought and being' (1993: 23). In other words, Bhaskar is complementing an argument for anti-foundationalism with an argument for a metaphysical realist ontology, by maintaining that our knowledge is conceptually mediated, and that this knowledge is of an external reality which cannot be known with epistemic immediacy.

As knowledge claims do not directly mirror a manifest truth there is no relationship of identity between the realms of being and knowing. Thus knowledge claims constitute a *transitive* realm because given the lack of a direct epistemic access to an external reality – the intransitive realm – our knowledge claims will be *fallible*. Therefore what constitutes scientific knowledge will necessarily change over time, as theories with better approximations to the truth are developed. This leads Bhaskar (1997) to describe his position in terms of 'epistemic relativity', and to argue against the correspondence theory of truth. Bhaskar advocates epistemic relativity, simply because given the lack of a direct access to a manifest truth, our knowledge claims are relative to some fallible theory or perspective. This is different from truth-relativism because the anti-foundational emphasis on the conceptual mediation – or relativity – of truth claims is complemented by a metaphysical realist ontology. That is, the truth content of a concept is not reducible to its origin within a conceptual scheme because if it has any truth content, this will arise from its relationship to an external reality. As Collier puts it, we are trapped inside the transitive realm, but

> This is no real trap, since we can always *change* the transitive dimension, and that we do so in the ways that we do is (in the best case) explained by the fact that the transitive dimension is not an end in itself, but produced entirely in order to explain what occurs in the intransitive dimension.
>
> (1994: 82)

We may not be able to break outside our perspectives, but this does not mean that all perspectives are equal in usefulness or truth, because if they *correspond* to an external reality, then they will do so in different ways, with differing degrees of verisimilitude.

Bhaskar would, as noted above, object to the correspondence theory of truth, but I have just described the relationship between the transitive realm and the intransitive realm in terms of correspondence, because Bhaskar's rejection of the correspondence theory of truth is erroneous. It is possible, *pace* Bhaskar, to adhere to both the thesis of epistemic relativity and the correspondence theory of truth. Before saying why this is so we can survey Bhaskar's view to the contrary. Bhaskar notes that for the correspondence theory of truth, a proposition is truth iff (if and only if) it corresponds with a state of affairs. He continues,

> But propositions cannot be compared with states of affairs; their relationship cannot be described as one of correspondence. Philosophers have wanted a theory of truth to provide a *criterion* or stamp of knowledge. But no such stamp is possible. For the judgement of the truth of a proposition is always intrinsic to the science concerned. *There is no way in which we can look at the world and then at a sentence and ask whether they fit.* There is just the expression (of the world) in speech (or thought).
>
> (1997: 249; emphasis added)

This argument against the correspondence theory of truth is erroneous. For as was argued in Chapter 1, the correspondence theory of truth need not entail the relationship of epistemic immediacy that Bhaskar maintains it does. Hence Popper adhered to the correspondence theory of truth, whilst advocating the notion that truth claims had varying degrees of verisimilitude: truth claims could approximate to the truth, and this would occur if they corresponded to the truth, in some fashion, but there was definitely no notion of a direct access to a manifest truth. The source of Bhaskar's error lies in his view that the correspondence theory of truth furnishes a *criterion* of truth when, as Collier argues, it may furnish a *definition* of truth (1994: 239). Truth may be described as occurring when a proposition corresponds to reality, but there is no abstract philosophical a priori algorithm to define how beliefs may correspond to an external reality, and given the lack of such an algorithm, correspondence does not necessarily imply that propositions directly mirror external reality. Propositions about gravity will be true if (or 'iff') they correspond to the physical processes involved with gravity, but this does not necessarily imply a special philosophical 'method' to explain how sentences can directly express the world in its own (pre-linguistic) terms.

A stratified ontology of emergent properties in open systems

Turning from Bhaskar's critique of empirical realism and his anti-foundational conception of epistemology, to his ontology, we can note that Bhaskar (1997) argues for a stratified ontology of emergent properties existing in open systems. The ontology is 'stratified' because it maintains that there are different strata of being, with the higher strata being dependent upon other strata for their existence whilst being causally independent of the lower strata. To give what may well be the 'classic example', water is an emergent property of hydrogen and oxygen: water depends for its existence on the existence and admixture of hydrogen and oxygen, but it is causally independent of both properties. The properties of water cannot be understood in terms of the properties of hydrogen and oxygen alone. Thus natural reality is stratified because higher strata properties *emerge* from lower strata properties.

Causal laws *qua* emergent properties exist in open systems because causal laws can interact in a number of ways, with the result that the observed effects of causal laws are always contingent upon a particular configuration of causal laws having effects which, at one particular point in time, happen to interconnect with the effects of other causal laws. So instead of perceiving a causal law in an observed regularity, an observed event will be contingent upon the effects of several causal laws interacting.

Given this ontology of natural being it follows that one could not adopt a methodology derived from empirical realism. One could not maintain that scientific methodology ought to seek knowledge of causal laws via an inductivist methodology or a deductivist methodology. Inductivism would mean defining a relationship of natural necessity in terms of a finite number of observed regularities. This is not only logically fallacious because it bases a proposition about a event recurring into infinity upon a finite number of observations; it is also erroneous because it confuses the observed contingent effects of causal laws with the laws themselves. Similarly, deductivism is predicated upon an actualist closed systems ontology.[5] A deductive approach to methodology would mean making a distinction between the *explanans* and the *explanandum*. The *explanans* pertains to the law (for example, all metals conduct electricity), and the 'initial conditions' (for example, that there is no insulation or other form of circuit-break). That is, the *explanans* pertains to the premises.[6] The *explanandum* pertains to the conclusion which, in this case could be that copper, as a metal, conducts electricity. This deductive methodology is based upon an actualist closed systems ontology because causal laws are defined in terms of empirical regularities. It is assumed that if an observed event conforms to the premise (*explanans*) then a causal law has been observed. As the realm of natural being is an open system, though, one cannot draw a conclusion about a causal law existing, from such observed events. In sum, methodologies based upon the empirical realist actualist ontology of closed systems cannot explain causal laws, because causal laws do not exist as empirical regularities in closed systems; contrary to the ontological presumptions of empirical realism, and the epistemic presumptions concerning the philosophies of mind (empiricism and post-Kantianism) which underpin this.

Instead of inductivism and deductivism, scientific methodology has to be based on the notion of seeking out knowledge of causal structures, or 'generative mechanisms', which 'underlie' their observed and contingent effects. This means that science ought to be based upon what Bhaskar calls the RRRE methodology; and this methodology has four stages. The first stage is the *resolution* of a complex event into its causal components. The second stage is the *redescription* of component causes into the perspective deployed. The third stage is to *retrodict* the possible antecedent causes. The final stage is the *elimination* of alternative possible causes of components, which will remove alternative explanations, by appealing to independent evidence about antecedent causes (Bhaskar 1997: 125; 1998: 129; Collier 1994: 122–3). Rather than seek a manifest truth, methodology has to be based upon constructing theoretical interpretations of complex empirical events, to define the underlying non-observable causal mechanisms at work, and to criticise alternative accounts of natural laws, which place too much emphasis on the realm of the actual.

So, whereas empiricist epistemology functioned as a master-builder, with the possible objects of scientific enquiry being delimited by a philosophy of mind, the transcendental realist ontology of emergent properties existing in open systems functions as a meta-theory, or underlabourer. This meta-theoretical ontology of emergent properties existing in open systems can be used to guide scientific methodology, meaning that it may guide the formation of specific theories and empirical research. Scientific investigation is to be premised upon the notion of searching out underlying causal structures which are ontologically separate from their contingent effects, hence the RRRE methodology in place of inductivism and deductivism. Further, knowledge of such causal structures will be conceptually mediated and fallible because there is no epistemic immediacy, or relationship of being–knowing identity.

Now it may be objected, especially by those of a more (post-Wittgensteinian) 'pragmatic' position, that this ontology is, like empiricist epistemology, very dogmatic. Whereas empiricist epistemology – and empirical realism generally – had an actualist closed systems model of being, to which science methodology had to adhere, by seeking out constant conjunctions, Bhaskar's realism, it may be argued, presumes to mirror natural being. In the former case a philosophy of mind provides a master-builder for science and in the latter case an essentialism is used, whereby a definitive master-ontology is a master-builder because it lists all the discrete essences which constitute natural being. With such a charge of 'essentialism' it would be presumed that *any* form of ontology *necessarily presumed* some form of epistemic absolutism, by seeking what Putnam called a 'God's-eye view', and what Rorty called a 'skyhook', as any definition of reality would be presumed to be a detailed 'map' of reality which was total. The general point to make here is to repeat the argument made by Searle in Chapter 1, which is that ontology, or at least realist ontology in the form of metaphysical realism, is not an epistemological position, concerning how we may know reality. Of course our specific concern here is with an ontology which does seek to say something about reality, other than the metaphysical claim that reality exists beyond our representations of it. However, the realist meta-theoretical ontology (of emergent properties in open systems) does not presume to be an essentialist master-ontology, which mirrors (all the) discrete essences in the realm of natural being. For realism is part of the transitive realm, meaning that it is a fallible theory itself, and its ontological precepts are general precepts and not descriptions of discrete essences. It may seek to guide the formation of specific theories and empirical research, but this does not presume immediate access to (all the) 'facts'.

The transcendental argument and the method of immanent critique

Bhaskar is aware that the charge of circularity may be made with regard to his 'transcendental realism'. This is because often transcendental arguments about X being the condition of possibility of Y are tautological, with X being the condition of possibility of Y because Y is defined in such a way that it must conform to X. Against this Bhaskar argues that

> this snare [i.e. circularity] can be avoided only if philosophical enquiry assumes the form of immanent critique, so that transcendental arguments paradigmatically become, or at least are always supplemented by, transcendental refutations of pre-existing, and more generally alternative accounts.
>
> (1986: 14)[7]

This immanent critique takes as its starting point the assumption that 'science works', and then moves on to develop an alternative account of natural being (in terms of emergent properties existing in open systems), from the immanent critique of the empirical realist actualist ontology of closed systems. As Bhaskar puts it,

> one assumes at the outset the intelligibility of science (or rather of a few generally recognized scientific activities) and asks explicitly what the world must be like for those activities to be possible. This programme

not only yields new insight into the structure of scientific knowledge (the form that it must take if it is to be knowledge of a world investigated by such activities), but enables us to see the tacit presupposition (of a closed world, completely described) on which the traditional problem of its rationality was hung is *inconsistent with its very possibility*.

(1998: 8; emphasis added)

So, transcendental realism asks what the condition of possibility for natural science is. A circular answer is avoided because the answer is developed via an immanent critique of an alternative paradigm, viz. empirical realism. The precepts developed from this immanent critique are ontological precepts about the natural world being a stratified open system. Given this ontology, the inductive and deductive methods have to be replaced with the RRRE method. The precepts from this ontology constitute a meta-theory, that can be used as a positive underlabourer to inform empirical research and the construction of specific theories. In short, the condition of possibility of science is that it seeks fallible knowledge of emergent properties in open systems that are known via theoretical interpretation.

Transcendental realist naturalism: Bhaskar's social ontology[8]

Turning to the issue of social ontology, Bhaskar sets out three approaches to the structure-agency problem, and provides an immanent critique of each approach (1998: 25–34), which is similar to the critical points raised in Chapter 2. The first approach he discusses is 'voluntarism' (meaning methodological individualism), which is rejected because it fails to account for social reality, for reasons which were discussed in Chapter 2. In short, the social context is reduced into individuals, and so we cannot say how individuals are influenced by their socio-historical location, which means we can say nothing, as individuals are not acontextual atoms. The second approach is 'collectivism' (which it may be more helpful to call 'holism', as it is different from the methodological collectivism discussed in Chapter 2) that is illustrated by Durkheim's ontology of social facts, and this is criticised for being deterministic. This cannot account for the condition of possibility of social science, because agents are conceptualised as passive structural dopes, and social facts are reified as entities beyond human control. For Bhaskar collectivism – or rather holism – is to be rejected for putting all the emphasis on factors beyond individuals when individuals do have some form of free will.

The third position criticised is the 'dialectical' position of Berger and Luckmann (1991). This view is rejected because it begins with free agents creating, *ex nihilo*, social structures, and then presents social structures as external and constraining. In other words, it replicates the problems of both voluntarism/individualism and collectivism/holism.[9] As Bhaskar puts it, such a model 'encourages, on the one hand, a voluntaristic idealism with respect to our understanding of social structure and, on the other, a mechanistic determination with respect to our understanding of people' (1998: 33).[10]

Bhaskar seeks to overcome these problems, which we can refer to as the 'traditional critiques' given their ubiquitous existence within the literature on the structure-agency issue, with his 'Transformational Model of Social Action' (henceforth TMSA). He argues that unlike the model of social reality argued for by Berger and Luckmann, with the TMSA model it is not the case that individuals *create* (*ex nihilo*) social structures (which then act upon them), but that individuals *recreate* social structures, which provide the social context for action. Here social structure, like the natural environment, is *always already made* (1998: 33). According to Bhaskar,

> It is true to say that society would not exist without human activity, so that reification remains an error. And it is still true to say that such activity would not occur unless the agents engaging in it had a conception of what they were doing [...]. But it is no longer true to say that agents *create* it. Rather one must say: they *reproduce* or *transform* it. That is, if society is always already made, then any concrete human praxis, or, if you like, act of objectivation can only modify it; and the totality of such acts sustain or change it.
>
> (1998: 33–4; emphasis in original)

Hence the task of sociology is to understand how agency refashions the social context in which it is situated, in a way analogous to a sculptor fashioning a piece from the material available (1998: 34). This conception of social reality leads Bhaskar to make a distinction between the *duality of structure* and the *duality of praxis*. The duality of structure refers to the dual character of society as the ever-present condition (material cause) and continually reproduced outcome of agency. The duality of praxis refers to the dual character of agency, as both conscious production and often unconscious reproduction of society (1998: 34–5).

So, unlike the voluntarist position which fails to deal adequately with constraint upon the individual, and the Durkheimian-collectivist position which under-emphasises agency, by reifying structures as external constraints, Bhaskar is arguing that *individuals' actions always recreate a pre-existing social context, whether such reproduction is intended or not.* He gives the examples of marriage reproducing the institution of the nuclear family, and work reproducing capitalism, noting that people getting married or going to work do not (usually) consciously intend to reproduce those institutions (1998: 35). This is not to focus exclusively on reproduction/continuity, though. For Bhaskar also wants to explain change as well, although he states that change is not a direct consequence of a consciously intended plan. That is, one may act to change society in some way, but the changes created (if any) will create unintended consequences, and may only be partially realised. For example, if divorce were made more difficult to obtain in order to protect the institution of the family, then fewer people might get married and more people might live in unhappy marriages, or live apart, all of which might possibly create emotional turbulence for their children. So an attempt to strengthen the family would weaken it, by leading to fewer families forming and by creating dysfunctional family units. Thus '[s]ociety does not exist independently of human activity (the error of reification). But it is not the product of it (the error of voluntarism)' (1998: 36). That is to say, society is reproduced by agents working within a pre-existing context, rather than produced *ex nihilo* by unconstrained practices.

This TMSA model of social ontology turns on an ontology of emergent properties existing in open systems. Social structures are objectively real and irreducible down to the level of individuals because structures are emergent properties: social structures exist as an objectively real context which agents reproduce, or change, via their agency. These emergent properties exist in an open system because as individuals have free will, and as actions have unintended consequences, structures do not produce fixed regularities whereby agents' behaviour continuously conforms to a structural determinant.[11] So, from an immanent critique of alternative accounts of social being, Bhaskar is able to advocate the use of a meta-theoretical ontology of emergent properties in open systems, which means that Bhaskar is able to advocate the doctrine of naturalism. *The natural and the social sciences ought to share a unity of method, because they have a similar form of object and, as Bhaskar argues (1998: 25), it is the nature of the object that defines its cognitive possibilities for us. Thus transcendental realism can explain the condition of possibility of the natural and social sciences in terms of science gaining (conceptually mediated and fallible) knowledge of objects of study which are emergent properties in open systems.* Note that this may be called a 'contingent naturalism' because the argument for naturalism was contingent upon the immanent critique of alternative social ontologies, rather than being an argument to the effect that the social sciences ought to copy the methods of the natural sciences if they are to be 'scientific'.

Obviously there are differences between laws of nature, or relations of natural necessity, and social factors; and Bhaskar responds to this issue by qualifying his naturalism, noting some ontological, epistemological, and relational limits to the possibility of naturalism. The ontological limits on the possibility of naturalism are as follows. (a) Social structures, unlike natural structures, do not exist independently of the activities they govern. (b) Social structures, unlike natural structures, do not exist independently of the agents' conceptions of what they are doing in their activity. (c) Social structures, unlike natural structures, may be only relatively enduring (so that the tendencies they ground may not be universal in the sense of time-space invariant) (Bhaskar 1986: 130–1; 1993: 79; 1998: 38).

The epistemological limit on the possibility of naturalism, it is argued, is that there can never be any equivalent to experimental closure in the natural sciences (1986: 133–4; 1993: 82–4; 1998: 45–6). Lacking any decisive test-situations for theories, the criteria for rational replacement and development of theories 'must be *explanatory and non-predictive*' (1998: 45–6; emphasis in original). This is held to be of no ontological import, though, as 'social laws', like natural laws, are not to be confused with their empirical effects. In other words, only someone who adhered to an actualist closed systems ontology would deny the existence of social laws or social structures on the epistemological ground that we cannot observe the social structure either in itself, or via Durkheimian 'objective indicators' (such as the legal system being an indicator of the type of social solidarity in a society).[12]

The relational limit on the possibility of naturalism is that the social sciences are part of their own field of inquiry, so 'they are *internal* with respect to their subject-matter in a way in which the natural sciences are not' (1998: 47; emphasis in original). What this means is that (a), social objects of study may be affected by social science and conversely (b), social reality will affect the formation of sociological knowledge (1986: 134; 1993: 84; 1998: 47). This could mean that the very distinction between the intransitive and transitive realms broke down, in which case social reality would cease to consist of emergent properties and it would be dependent for its existence on agents' perspectives, or meanings. Bhaskar argues, though, that this does not happen, and he does this by making a distinction between causal interdependency and existential intransitivity. His argument is that social structures may be affected by social science knowledge, and actors' conceptions, but that social reality remains an emergent property. Thus 'the concept of existence is univocal: "being" means the same in the human as in the natural world, even though the modes of being may radically differ. The human sciences, then, take intransitive objects like any other' (Bhaskar 1998: 47). As social structures are not conceptualised as reified determining forces upon agency, it is possible for agents to alter structures, by acting upon certain forms of knowledge: change would occur as a result of conscious agency (which is not to deny the possibility of unintended consequences too). Yet even though such agency may potentially change structures, it would be a logical error to infer from this that structures are reducible to agents' acts, meanings or instantiation. Agents may mobilise for a minimum wage, accepting arguments about social justice over supply-side arguments about economic decline resulting from the supply cost of labour increasing, and realise their objectives; but capitalist structures would continue to exist as objectively real factors.

Developing the ontology

Problems with the limits to naturalism

In this section I will discuss the sympathetic critiques concerning Bhaskar's 'ontological' qualifications to his naturalism, made by Benton (1981), and Archer (1995), before moving on to discuss the subsequent emendations made to social realist ontology. Turning to the first ontological limit to naturalism, Benton argues this notion is rather vague, and if we focus on the verb 'govern', then the argument does not work, because in the natural world there are powers which are real and yet may remained unexercised. An example, given by Benton, is the power of an organism to reproduce, which may remain unexercised although it still exists (1981: 17). The analogy in the social world that Benton gives is that of the state having extensive military power which still exists when unexercised. Having indicated that this first ontological disanalogy between social and natural reality is not necessarily a disanalogy after all, Benton presses on to argue that for social structures to be a stratum of reality that is not reducible to individuals, social structures must, to some extent, be independent of individuals' activities. Yet given the argument that structures are not independent of individuals' activity, the notion of structures as emergent properties is lost. Thus Benton states that 'Roy Bhaskar is, it seems, committed to a variant form of individualism in social science' (1981: 17).

Archer (1995) reads this qualification in a slightly different way, following up the point about the natural–social disanalogy *vis-à-vis* structuration theory. Her point is that we can retain the notion of activity-dependence, provided that we say that social structures are activity-dependent in the *past tense* because to make structures activity-dependent in the *present tense* is to reduce structures down to individuals' practices (i.e. the instantiation of rules). In developing her point, Archer begins by noting that Benton

> left a loophole for activity-dependence, through allowing for those activities necessary to sustain the *potential* for governance. Thus in the case of a State, its full coercive power may remain unexercised but actions such as the (current) raising of taxes and armies may well be necessary for it to retain its potential power of coercion.
>
> (1995: 143; emphasis in original)

The state then may have powers which remain unexercised (military power) but which are still activity-dependent (upon the raising of taxes for instance).

Archer goes on to show how, in his reply to Benton, Bhaskar uses the loophole to retain his argument about activity-dependence, although he still fails to avoid an individualistic position. Bhaskar's reply is that

> a structure of power may be reproduced without being exercised and exercised in the absence of any observable conflict [...] so long as it is sustained by human practices – the practices which reproduce or potentially transform it. In this sense the thesis of the activity-dependence of social structures must be affirmed. *Social structures exist materially and are carried or transported from one time-space location to another only in virtue of human praxis*. This does not, *contra* Benton, entail commitment to methodological individualism: it is merely a condition for avoiding reification.
>
> (1998: 174; emphasis added)

For Archer this rejoinder is reminiscent of Giddens' argument about instantiation, where structures have a 'virtual' existence until instantiated. In which case, structures cannot be emergent properties, because they would exist outside time-space until instantiated in individuals' practices. Conversely, for Archer, social structures are activity-dependent, but the activities are the *activities of the long dead*. What this means is that social structures exist as emergent properties, created by past agency, which condition present agency, and which cannot be significantly transformed, except over time. This is why for Archer social structures are activity-dependent *in the past tense*. More will be said about Archer's ontology presently, and for now we need to move on to the next problem, as regards the ontological limits to naturalism.

The second ontological limit to naturalism was the argument that social structures, unlike natural structures, do not exist independently of agents' conceptions of what they are doing in their activity. As Benton and Archer argue, this can be read in three different ways. The first reading is that structures depend upon agents having some conception of what they are doing, which is nothing more than a truism (Benton 1981: 17; Archer 1995: 145). If structures require agents, and agency requires a notion of agents being conscious beings, then the point is sustained, but simply noting this is not epistemically important (Benton 1981: 17). It is simply acknowledging that agents are not cultural or structural dopes. The second reading is that *some* social relationships, such as friendship, require the agents involved having *particular* conceptions of what they are doing (Benton 1981: 17; Archer 1995: 145–6). In this case, if the parties involved change their conceptions, then the relationship is finished. However, most social relationships are not like this. 'Where society surrounds and sustains a relationship with sanctions, including coercive powers, social relationships can be, and are, sustained through immense changes in participating actors' conceptions of what they are doing' (Benton 1981: 17). Benton gives the examples of employer–employee relationships, imperial domination and marriage, whereby social sanctions sustain a relationship or institution, despite conflicting values, or changed beliefs. Thus unlike friendship or commitment, which require a consensus of conceptions, many social relations and institutions can – and do – survive, and function, with a conflict, change or divergence as regards beliefs/conceptions. Archer extends this point, noting that unless we sustain the notion of social reality as an emergent property, which constrains (as well as enables) agency, then Bhaskar's position is the same as Giddens' and thus, for her, results in central conflationism (1995: 145–6). This is because the notion of social structures as emergent properties would be lost, giving us just individuals, their beliefs, and their practices; which brings us to the third reading.

The third reading concerns the relationship of agents' beliefs to social change. According to Benton, we may read the second ontological limitation as telling us that if agents change their minds, then this would be a cause for structural change, although the consequences may be unintended. As Benton argues, though, whilst this is not obviously wrong 'it hardly counts as an a priori demonstrable truth about society as such' (1981: 17). Rather, such questions, about the relationship between changed conceptions and changed structures, is an open question, which requires empirical research for each specific issue, as there are always unintended consequences (1981: 17–18). Archer argues that the notion of concept-dependency may mean that certain structures have to be misconceived in order to continue (1995: 146). Her conclusion is the same as Benton's, though, viz. that if such a claim is a universal a priori claim, then it cannot be sustained. Thus, 'there are no grounds for demonstrating this as an a priori truth; the matter seems to be one for empirical investigation, particularly since we can find evidence of large conceptual shifts (feminism) which existing structures have withstood largely unchanged' (1995: 146).[13]

Bhaskar's elaborated social ontology

To avoid the charge of reification Bhaskar was over-cautious, which meant he over-qualified his realist ontology, compromising the principle of structures being emergent properties, by putting an erroneous emphasis on the activity-dependency and concept-dependency of social structures. Another problem with Bhaskar's initial social ontology was that it was too schematic. In this section I will discuss how, in relation to these two problems, Bhaskar's social ontology was developed to link structure and agency in a more adequate way.

Bhaskar's original TMSA model (see Figure 5.1), as set out in *The possibility of naturalism* (1998)[14] was, as Archer notes, 'too fundamentalist' (1995: 155). It is too fundamentalist because as it is a rather schematic model it fails to explain the actual link between structure and agency. Archer gives three reasons for such a failure (1995: 155). The first is that it lacks any sense of historicity, despite containing a 'before' and 'after' moment, because it could be used as an heuristic device, to represent any moment, rather than a phase in an on-going historical process, where structure and agency are intertwined. The second reason is that it seems 'overpersonalized', as 'structural influences appear to work *exclusively via socialization* and seem to exert their influence directly upon (all) individuals' (1995: 155; emphasis in original). The third reason is that the before and after are unconnected by interaction. Thus, the notions of emergence, history and the social mediation of agency are downplayed (1995: 155). What

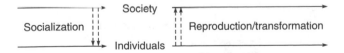

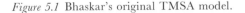

Figure 5.1 Bhaskar's original TMSA model.

we have then is a rather abstract model, which lacks a sense of how individuals are embedded into social contexts which condition individuals' agency, with structures preceding all present actions.

Bhaskar moves on though, in *Reclaiming reality* (1993),[15] to give us a more nuanced model, as set in Figure 5.2. This model overcomes the three problems noted with the original. Firstly, it introduces prior emergence and the current influence of structural properties at points 1 and 2, as the unintended consequences of past actions, and as the unacknowledged conditions of present actions (Archer 1995: 155). Secondly, the influence of social structures limits agents' understanding, and this is compounded at points 3 and 4, by limitations on self-understanding, which means that the 'production process' (of agency) is a mediated product of agents (Archer 1995: 155–6). In other words, agency is mediated by structures, and the outcome is not a direct expression of an original conscious intention. Thirdly, the model now includes temporal phasing, with time point 1 being the outcome of an antecedent cycle, point 1' (Archer 1995: 156); meaning that agents reproduce a context that always already pre-dates their actions, with the reproduced (or changed) context being the new *milieu* for the next stage of action.

Thus Bhaskar improves his original ontology by replacing a model of structure and agency as rather separate entities, with a model which emphasises how agency is always already embedded within a context furnished by pre-existing structures (created by past actions), which are modified by agents, and which furnish the new material for later agency. Hence emergence is important, because it allows us to sustain the notion of past activity creating the context for, and limitations upon, present activity. Without such an emphasis upon emergence (meaning the activity-dependency of structures in the past tense), we would be left in the position of saying that putative structures are activity-dependent in the present tense only, which would reduce structure into individuals' actions or instantiations. Hence, by putting a stronger emphasis upon structures as emergent properties, Bhaskar can distance himself from Giddens (and individualism), by saying that 'I am inclined to give structures (conceived as transfactually efficacious) a stronger ontological grounding [than Giddens] and to place more emphasis on the *pre*-existence of social forms' (1983: 85). So, by emphasising emergence we emphasise how social structures are formed *prior to present interaction*, and how present interaction may change those structures, which then become

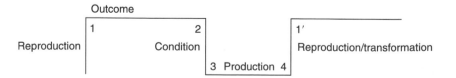

Figure 5.2 The improved model.

the starting point for the next cycle of structure-agency interaction. Emergence, that is to say, has to be grasped via 'analytic histories of emergence'; which is to move onto the realist position developed by Archer.

Archer's social ontology

Archer (1995) argues that the refined TMSA model set out in Figure 5.2 maps onto her model of morphogenesis and morphostasis (or the MM model), and that the MM model is more elaborate. Archer's MM model is set out in Figure 5.3.[16]

Archer notes that she prefers her model to the refined TMSA model,

> for the simple but important reason that my T2 and T3 period (where prior structures are gradually transformed and new ones slowly elaborated) shows diagrammatically that there is no period when society is *un-structured*. In a purely visual sense, Bhaskar's T2–T1' (contrary to his intention) *could* convey that structural properties are suspended for this interval, whilst they undergo 'production'.
>
> (1995: 157–8; emphasis in original)

Archer's MM therefore allows the *dramatis personae* to retain the stage setting which contextualises and gives sense to their actions. Bhaskar's refined TMSA model may allow this too, but Archer's model has removed the potential figurative ambiguity concerning the location of structures.

Archer's ontology is also more elaborate than Bhaskar's, because it has a more complex conception of social reality. For Archer, there are three types of emergent properties: Structural Emergent Properties (SEPs), Cultural Emergent Properties (CEPs), and People's Emergent Properties (PEPs). SEPs are material-structures, and CEPS are belief-systems which are not reducible to individuals' beliefs. CEPs as emergent properties constitute a Cultural-System (or CS), and the use of beliefs within a CS is referred to as Socio-Cultural Interaction (or S-C) (Archer 1995: 172–94). Finally, as

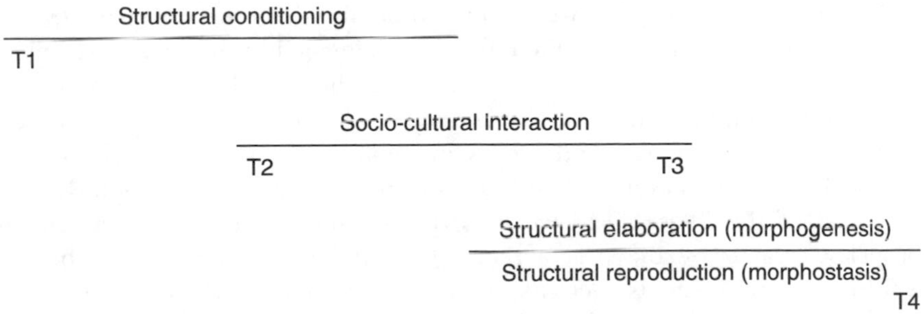

Structural conditioning
_____

T1

Socio-cultural interaction
_____

T2   T3

Structural elaboration (morphogenesis)
_____
Structural reproduction (morphostasis)

T4

Figure 5.3 Archer's morphogenetic/static cycle and its three phases.

regards PEPs, Archer makes a distinction between the Person (as biological and psychological entity), the Agent (a plural concept referring to a group), and the Actor (meaning a role-incumbent within a group) (Archer 1995: 247–57). Agents are sub-divided into corporate agents and primary agents, with the former pertaining to organised groups pursuing a goal, and the latter pertaining to groups which do not express interests or organise to pursue a goal; and an individual may well be a member of both (1995: 258–9).

There are two key points to note with regard to Archer's social realism. The first is that, to recap, in order to retain the notion of social structures being irreducible to individuals' activities in the present tense, we need to argue that social structures are emergent properties, which means they are activity-dependent in the past tense. Structures were the product of past interactions, and serve as the context for present interaction, providing both enablements and constraints for individuals' interactions; with such interactions resulting in either change or continuity.

In order to understand how individuals' activity results in either change or continuity, we need to begin by noting the construction of an analytic dualism between structure and agency, which brings us to the second point. The dualism here is *analytic* rather than *philosophical*, because the distinction between structure and agency is one of theoretical artifice. Thus the above diagram is not meant to imply that at T1 there are just structures, whilst at T2–T3 there are just agents (i.e. groups), with T4 ushering out agents. So whilst in reality structure and agency are always already embedded, with agents always acting in some form of social context, we have to separate – or abstract – the structural factors from a preceding series of events, in order to explain how agency was enabled and constrained by those structures, and how such agency led to either change or continuity. Thus we have a 'dualism' rather than a 'duality', because instead of conflating structures into practices (as with Giddens' duality), structures are separate from practices (as different forms of emergent property). This does not result in a 'philosophical dualism', or a subject–object dualism, whereby structure is an external and determining constraint upon agency, because structure and agency are interconnected in reality, and their separation is in the form of a theoretical/artificial dualism.

By using analytic dualism we can operationalise the 'morphogenetic cycle' methodology, to explain how the outcome of agency is either morphogenesis (change) or morphostasis (continuity). Using the morphogenetic cycle, an artificial distinction is made between structures (the context) and (corporate) agents, with the cycle having the following moments: structural conditioning, socio-cultural interaction, and structural elaboration or reproduction. In the first part of the phase (T1) we have the context, which is an emergent property created by the past actions of agents, and which will enable as well as constrain agents' activity in the present tense, which occurs with socio-cultural interaction (T2–3). This activity either reworks the pre-existing context producing change, or it results in continuity (T4).

Time is used to make the analytic dualism between structure and agency, and *time is used to link structure and agency*. The interplay of structure and agency is analysed by separating structure and agency into discrete analytic units, pertaining to different time phases within a cycle, and then contrasting the initial phase (the original social context) with the last phase (the social context which is either the same or changed, following agents' activity). This does not of course imply that the time phases are discrete entities, any more than it implies that structure and agency are discrete essences which are in reality separated from each other. Rather, the time phases in the morphogenetic cycle are premised upon analytic dualism, meaning that they are used as analytic abstractions, from an on-going flow of continuous structure-agency interaction.

The picture can be made more complex by introducing CEPs, and discussing how S-C agency may draw upon, contest and change a CS. That is, in addition to discussion of how agency responds to the structure context within which it is located, we may also talk of belief systems as emergent properties, with different agents interpreting one CS in different ways, or different agents mobilising different CS in support of their claims. In pursuing such an analysis one would still be using the morphogenetic cycle, because one would explain that belief systems (CS) were irreducible to activities in the present tense, and explain how belief systems may change, or may not change, over time, depending upon how agents were able to mobilise. This is not to imply that CEPs are epiphenomena of SEPs, as a crude materialism would maintain, but it is to say that there can be an 'elective affinity' between ideas and (material) vested interests; although Archer notes that individuals may go against their vested interests, because of a prior ideational/normative (CS) commitment and, in so doing, such individuals incur 'opportunity costs' (Archer 1995: 195–246).

Using this ontology of emergent properties, social scientific methodology will be based upon developing 'analytic histories of emergence'. What this means is that: (a) the formation of specific theories and empirical research ought to be based upon the *precepts* (SEPs, CEPs, and PEPs) supplied by Archer's ontological meta-theory; and (b) the way in which social research will *use these precepts* to explain social phenomena will be *historical*. In order to understand social phenomena, social scientists will have to reconstruct the interplay of three ontologically independent factors (SEPs, CEPs and PEPs) which, despite the fact that each factor exists in its own right (i.e. it is not epiphenomenal upon another emergent property), are always already interconnected. This means that social scientists will have to base social scientific explanation upon a conceptually mediated and fallible reconstruction of how, over time, the social context and individuals (acting as actors within agents) interacted, with agency resulting in change or continuity. Such a reconstruction will use analytic dualism to operationalise the morphogenetic cycle, and, having explained the interplay of structure and agency over time, using this cycle, one will produce an analytic history of emergence, i.e. a history of the interaction between different emergent properties.

Challenges to social realism

Realism and epistemic immediacy

Bhaskar approves of Outhwaite's description of his work as 'ontologically bold and epistemologically cautious' (Outhwaite 1987: 34; mentioned by Bhaskar 1998: 176). What this means is that in order to avoid the epistemic fallacy of transposing ontological questions into epistemological questions we have to recognise that it is the nature of the object that influences our knowledge of it (rather than defining what is known in terms of how we have knowledge), although such knowledge will always be mediated by some fallible theory – there is no epistemic immediacy. However, for some, the very notion of developing an ontology implies a commitment to epistemic immediacy. Thus Fay argues that realism is a form of essentialism, and Layder argues that realism is a form of empiricism.

Fay (1990) argues that realism should be linked to a correspondence theory of truth, rather than the notion of epistemic relativity, and that such a correspondence theory would seek a God's-eye view.[17] As Fay puts it

> Realism asserts that Ultimate Reality is structured and formed 'in itself', in much the same way the coloured pegs in Mastermind are. In doing so, it encourages the belief that there is only One True Picture which corresponds with this pre-existing, pre-formed reality. (This in turn encourages the notion that there is an Ultimate Codebreaker who has created this already-ordered Reality – realism is, I think, a continuation of the Christian view of the world.)
>
> (1990: 38)

So, the 'bold' claims about social ontology must, *ex hypothesi*, entail essentialism, which contradicts the thesis of epistemic relativity, because the ontology would purport to mirror all the fixed discrete essences. Realism is based upon locating a finite number of fixed essences: a bold ontology leads to a bold epistemology. 'For realism asserts that there is an underlying causal structure at work behind surface phenomena, and such an assertion certainly suggests an essentialism to the effect that this underlying causal structure is unitary and invariant' (Fay 1990: 39). This essentialism would mean that, as regards the use of social ontology, realism was predicated upon the structuralist sociological logic of immediacy; the reason for this being that the social ontology would have to list all the causal mechanisms *qua* fixed discrete essences. In short, ontology seeks to be a master-science of being, which implies epistemic immediacy and absolutism.

Similarly, Layder (1985) argues that realism results in empiricism. Layder's point is that realism places such a strong emphasis on ontology (in the form of generative mechanisms) that knowledge has to be construed as mirroring reality. Layder affirms that he is a (metaphysical) realist, because he denies 'radical idealism', and affirms that there is a real world. He goes on to insist that 'knowledge of this world is impossible without conceptual instruments, which, more often than not, derive from, or are connected with, wider theoretical parameters of discourses' (1985: 255). Thus Layder makes a distinction between dogmatic claims about 'ontology' (read: reality itself), and 'ontological schemes' (read: theories about reality) which are constructed within a particular discourse; whilst stressing that discourses are about the world, *contra* 'radical idealism'. Social realism is held to be a dogmatic realism, which results in a 'sophisticated empiricism', because by privileging ontology (in the sense of reality-in-itself), 'Bhaskar is implicitly claiming there is an extra-theoretical givenness to the structures of reality which, as a result, determines our knowledge of them' (Layder 1985: 268). Knowledge is 'determined' because knowledge has to mirror these fixed atheoretical features. For realism, we must remove the veil of theory/perspectives to see atheoretical/aperspectival reality as-it-really-is. Against this, Layder argues that we cannot seek direct knowledge of reality, or ontological features, without realising that ontologies are always constructed within a particular discourse. In short, we should recognise the discursive relativity of ontology (as ontological schemes), in order to avoid the empiricism that stems from the belief that beliefs ought to mirror reality directly (1985: 273).

Realism as an empty abstraction

An alternative line of criticism holds that realism offers empty abstractions that are divorced from substantive engagement and study of the social world. This brings us to the arguments of Shotter (1992) and Magil (1994). Shotter (1992) criticises Bhaskar from a Wittgensteinian perspective, arguing that we can understand practices within forms of life, but we cannot explain such practices by abstract ontologies. Thus Bhaskar's realism is only a 'theoretical realism' which is 'monologically articulated' (Shotter 1992: 171), because it is an abstract fiat about reality. Shotter argues that

> In the 'bustle' of everyday life, there is no order, no one single, complete order. Hence the meanings of events in the living of our lives cannot be properly understood within the confines of an order; they are only to be found in the not wholly orderly, practical living of our lives.
>
> (1992: 167–8)

Shotter goes on to agree with the view (as put forward by Fay, for instance) that realism seeks a God's-eye view, because to define a general ontology, which is abstracted from practices, is to seek a view from everywhere and nowhere, which no-one could actually have (1992: 168). As no-one can attain this view, then realist ontology remains an empty abstraction.[18]

A similar point is made from a Marxist perspective by Magil (1994). For Magil '[n]o universal ontology can resolve specific ontological problems within particular sciences or social sciences' (1994: 121). He makes this point by drawing an analogy between social realism and dialectical materialism. Dialectical materialism served well as the orthodox philosophy of Stalinism, because it was general enough to be interpreted in virtually any way one chose: it was elastic and general enough for Stalin to interpret it in any way which suited him. One could make the realist philosophy more specific, but then it could not function as a general guide, so its purpose would be undermined (1994: 124). Instead we should accept that '[t]here are no universal ontological truths or principles that can supplant, alleviate or guide the work of concrete investigation' (1994: 125). We can have detailed and specific knowledge from detailed and specific empirical studies, and ontology is of no use for this, because it achieves generality by being abstract and vague.

Realism and circularity

The problem, according to Gunn (1988), is that if first-order categories were taken to explain themselves, then circularity would result, whereas if we pursue second-order justifications, then we invite an infinite regression, by asking for the justification of the justification *ad infinitum* (1988: 89). Gunn argues that Marx escapes this problem by fusing meta-theory and theory. Marx achieves this because his work was based on immanent critique. So, rather than turn to a philosophy/meta-theory to provide the guiding principles for social investigation, Marx set out to examine capitalism in its own terms, and to see what problems emerged. Gunn argues that such immanent critique is 'dialogical' in form. What this means is that '[i]mmanent critique converses with its critical targets, in contrast to external critique which holds no brief for answerability in any conversational (or "dialogical") sense' (1988: 98). External critique would require one to talk *at* one's opponent using prior meta-theoretical convictions, whereas immanent critique would require one to talk *with* one's opponent, to unravel their position from within. Thus, for immanent critique, '[t]he categories which meta-theoretically "control" discourse are also the categories which at a first-order level discourse "finds"' (1988: 107).

Gunn takes Bhaskar to task, arguing that his ontological underlabourer gives us a model of external relations, which results in tautology (rather than infinite regression). Tautology occurs because to identify a generative mechanism one must say that it explains observed phenomena, but these phenomena can only be explained by appealing to a generative mechanism (1988: 109). Gunn argues that

> Tautology arose because two allegedly separate things were supposed to make sense of one another within a causal-explanatory frame. [...]

Nothing is explained by anything else or, put differently, there are no 'generative mechanisms'. Instead there is a determinate abstraction: the existence of unity in difference and of the abstract in the concrete.

(1988: 112–13)

So, for realism we identify a generative mechanism by turning to empirical data, but the criterion for saying what data identify a generative mechanism can only be made by reference to a generative mechanism. As Gunn puts it, 'appearances become the criterion of generative mechanisms (of reality) while generative mechanisms (reality again) become the criterion of phenomena or appearances' (1988: 110). Against this meta-theoretical ontology of 'external relations', Gunn argues for an ontology of 'internal relations'. Instead of looking for a causal relation between A and B, the notion of internal relations holds that A and B (and C, etc.) are part of an interlinked totality, and concepts refer to real features, but not by locating causal relations between objects that are external to one another. Concepts locate different aspects of the same interconnected phenomena, and they do so by locating the practical presuppositions of existing practices.

Rejoinder to the challenges

The critiques levelled at realism by Fay and Layder are reminiscent of the critique of realism made by post-Wittgensteinian pragmatists such as Putman and Rorty, who argue that ontology (and metaphysics) *necessarily* presumes to be a master-science of being, and that a correspondence theory of truth implies a relationship of epistemic immediacy. My response to the critiques of Fay and Layder is similar to my response to Putnam's 'internal realism', and Rorty's argument about knowledge claims, viz. that such positions entail the relativist philosophical logic of immediacy.

Such a conclusion may seem extreme. Indeed, Layder does say: 'I share with realism a commitment to the idea of an independent and objective material world' (1985: 255). In other words, Layder supports the metaphysical realist denial of metaphysical idealism. In which case, it should follow that Layder holds that perspectives give us a mediated and fallible access to an external reality. Instead of self-referential discourses, discourses would provide some form of access to an external non-discursive reality. Layder cannot sustain such an argument, though. The reason for this is that Layder draws a dichotomy between 'ontology' meaning reality-in-itself, and 'ontological schemes' meaning theories of reality which are internal to a discourse. The corollary of this is that either we have direct access to reality-in-itself, or our beliefs about reality are self-referential components within a discourse: we have either empiricism or truth-relativism. We cannot say that ontological schemes provide a conceptually mediated and fallible access to an external reality, because any reference to a reality other than that construed by a discourse, as an 'ontological scheme', is a reference to reality-in-itself (or 'ontology'). Given this, all we have left are self-referential ontological schemes, which means that a concept becomes true simply by virtue of its origin within a discourse. There is no way to sustain the notion of fallibilism, and thus avoid truth-relativism, because there can be no reference to reality other than that construed by the discourse.

Layder argues that

> the ontological features and structures that are the objects of (realist) knowledge, do not exist entirely independently of [theoretical-perspectival] knowledge [...]. I want to show that such objects are always embedded in, and in a significant sense *constructed* by, discursive parameters, i.e., that knowledge of these objects largely depends upon *prior* theoretical commitments.
>
> (1985: 260; emphasis in original)

The problem of course is that the objects of knowledge, and therefore truth claims about such objects, are *wholly* constructed by discourse with Layder's argument. The objects of knowledge, and truth claims about such objects, are self-referential aspects within a discourse, because to hold otherwise (i.e. to invoke notions of an extra-discursive referent) would, for Layder, be to try and step outside discourse to see reality-in-itself.

The same sort of dichotomy underpins Fay's argument that the rubric 'critical realism' is oxymoronic. Fay notes that the epistemically *critical* aspect of realism pertains to epistemic relativity and fallibilism, with beliefs being always open to critical review (given the lack of foundationalist certainty), and this, he argues, is in stark contrast with the *realist* emphasis on ontology, which presumes an uncritical epistemic certainty. As Fay puts it,

> The difficulty with critical realism, then, is that its critical aspects (by calling into question the notion of a preordered world) is at odds with its realist aspect (which asserts the existence of such a pre-ordered world). Because of this difficulty it is not at all clear that critical realism is a coherent philosophical position.
>
> (1990: 38)

So, the 'critical' aspect of 'critical realism' pertains to knowledge being anti-foundational, whereas the 'realist'/ontological aspect of 'critical realism' pertains to an essentialist doctrine, whereby concepts directly mirror fixed discrete essences. On the one hand we have perspectives, or discourses, and on the other hand, we have reality-in-itself. The upshot of Fay's position is truth-relativism too, because Fay draws a mutually exclusive distinction between anti-foundationalism and essentialism, meaning that there are either different discourses, or theories which purport to mirror being-in-itself. As with Layder there is no way to sustain the notion of a reality beyond discourses, which means that discourses become self-referential, resulting in truth-relativism and the genetic fallacy.

Against the arguments of Fay and Layder we may note that one may complement anti-foundationalism, or the thesis for conceptual relativity, with the argument for external or metaphysical realism, without the latter implying direct or absolute knowledge. As Searle argued, realism is an onto-logical thesis and not an epistemic thesis (1995: 154–5). In other words, ontology, as used in the arguments for metaphysical realism, simply pertains to a metaphysical conjecture about reality existing outside our representa-tions of it. It does not say anything specific about the world, let alone presume to be a master-science of being. Fay and Layder may not be idealists, but they fail to argue for metaphysical realism, because they presume that 'realism' and 'ontology' are essentialist doctrines predicated upon epistemic immedi-acy. Consequently they argue for the thesis of conceptual relativity without complementing this with the thesis of external/metaphysical realism; and the result is truth-relativism, because the object of knowledge and truth claims about it are wholly reducible to a discourse, perspective, language game, etc. Furthermore, it is erroneous to assume as Fay (and Bhaskar) do that a correspondence theory of truth implies a relationship of epistemic immediacy. So we may agree that realism does have a correspondence theory of truth, without this supporting Fay's conclusions about realism.

Hence, given this generic suspicion of ontology, Fay and Layder are even less disposed to accept ontology in the form of the social realist meta-theore-tical ontology of emergent properties, which is *presumed to mirror specific aspects of reality-in-itself*. This, obviously, misunderstands realism. The ontology of emergent properties is a *theory* of reality, and so it is a fallible conjecture, which is in the transitive realm. Ontology does not, *contra* Layder, mean 'reality-in-itself', and theories are not taken to mirror the intransitive realm. This realist ontology is developed via an immanent critique of alter-native positions, rather than via an argument about it having some form of privileged epistemic access; so it is not construed as some form of algorithm for epistemic immediacy. From the process of immanent critique the concepts developed are taken to be *general precepts* and cannot be taken to refer to specific empirical features of reality: the theory is of emergent properties and not specific emergent properties. In which case, one may use realism as a guide for empirical research without realism negating such research by acting as a master-science of being or presuming a direct access to reality-in-itself.

Of course for Shotter and Magil the very notion of a meta-theory is untenable because it is too general to be used in interpreting specific aspects of research. This is not the case though because all research has presump-tions about being, and therefore it is better to develop some explicit pre-cepts about being in a non-dogmatic way via an immanent critique of other paradigms. The alternative is to presume we have a direct access to reality-in-itself, or an arbitrary approach to ontology. As we have seen, positions influenced by some form of post-Wittgensteinianism make reference to 'practices', but this unfolds into the individualist and structuralist sociological logics of immediacy, because the ontological precepts are not fully worked out and explicitly stated. Similarly, Marx developed no clear ontology, which has led to numerous materialist accounts of being, ranging from crude economic reductionism, to 'organic' theories that see all aspects of social reality as parts of an interconnected whole, where there is no clear identifiable causal force.

Turning from the issue of ontology to the method of immanent critique in developing precepts, we can note that with Gunn, immanent critique is levelled not at *theoretical consideration of the object of study* (meaning issues concerning the structure-agency debate, and how social science knowledge represents the object), *but at the object of study itself*. For Gunn, one begins with an immanent critique of capitalism (the object of study), rather than, say, methodological individualist or positivist conceptions of social reality. So, to understand capitalism we do not need to explain putatively discrete relationships in terms of generative mechanisms, with the meta-theory of generative mechanisms being needed to explain specific relationships in its own meta terms of reference. Instead we need to begin with an immanent critique of capitalism (the object of study) as a totality. From this, a meta-theory and specific theories will be developed in tandem. The concepts developed in such a fashion are developed as 'determinate abstractions'. What this means is that concepts are abstractions, or theoretically artificial ways of dividing up an interconnected totality; although such abstractions are determinate, in that they reflect substantive aspects of the whole. Whereas realism would allegedly use a meta-theory of specific general essences to explain (tautologically) discrete causal mechanisms, Gunn's method would allow theory to capture the complexity and interconnectedness of the object of study, in its own right.

It is disingenuous of Gunn to argue that he approaches the object of study with no prior theoretical convictions, in order to develop his concepts via an immanent critique – or 'dialogue' – with the object of study. Gunn approaches the object of study from a position influenced by a form of Marxism known as 'Open Marxism'. The principles of Open Marxism are set out in Bonefeld *et al.* (1992). Here a distinction is made between different conceptions of form. One definition of form is that whereby form is a specific manifestation of a broader generic entity, so a fascist state is a specific *form* of the modern nation-state (Bonefeld, *et al.* 1992: xv). An alternative, Hegelian-dialectical definition of form takes form to be a 'mode of existence', and commodities which exist through the money and credit form are given as an example (ibid.). The difference in the two meanings of form, then, is that in the former case we are dealing with general laws being applied to specific situations, whilst in the latter case, the generic is inherent in the specific, and the abstract is inherent in the specific (Bonefeld *et al.* 1992: xvi). What this difference means is explicated thus:

Putting the matter in the bluntest possible fashion, those who see form in terms of species have to try to discover something behind, and underlying, the variant social forms. Those who see form as a mode of existence have to try to decode the forms in and of themselves. The first group of theorists have, always, to be more or less economic-reductionist. The second group of theorists have to dwell upon critique and the movement of contradiction as making clear, for its own part, the 'forms' that class struggle may take.

(1992: xvi)

Any position which is not open is closed and therefore to be rejected for crudely defining the world of social relations and processes as being epiphenomena of some ultimate 'thing', or 'first cause'.

Gunn takes his position to turn on immanent critique, rather than 'external critique' where a meta-theory is justified by reading the empirical data to fit the theory, which is then held to explain the data. However, Gunn is giving us a dogmatic meta-theory, because he is assuming the truth of his Marxist pantheism which regards everything as a moving force, and then his putative immanent critique of capitalism amounts to nothing more than a description of capitalism according to the terms of reference he already took to be true. In short, he verifies an ontology of everything (in the form of the structuralist sociological logic of immediacy) by defining capitalism according to the ontology. This conflates specific theory/empirical research into the meta-theory because knowledge about the socio-political world is simply read-off from the latter, so any research will simply repeat the pantheistic ontology.

So, a 'fusing' of meta-theory and theory resulted, as it must, in the latter being conflated into the former, given that there are always some precepts which influence the construction of specific theories, and so one cannot develop a theory 'from nowhere' (unless one held that a theory could directly mirror facts). Therefore one needs to maintain a clear distinction between meta-theory and theory This does not mean that meta-theory will 'by-pass' specific theories, to be justified tautologically by being read-into any empirical findings, which are then taken as verifications of the meta-theory. To be sure, this may happen with the use of general precepts but, as I argue in the next chapter, this can be avoided by developing 'domain-specific meta-theories', based on an immanent critique of some theories that deal with a substantive topic, and the development of an alternative that draws upon the general ontological meta-theory (of SEPs, CEPs and PEPs).

6   Social realism and the study of chronic unemployment

Introduction

In this chapter my concern is with the issue of how a social realist meta-theory may be applied. My argument is that to apply a social realist meta-theory (i.e. the ontology of SEPs, CEPs and PEPs in open systems) one needs to develop a 'domain-specific meta-theory'. A domain-specific meta-theory is constructed by developing an immanent critique of existing paradigms that deal with a particular research area. In this case the research area is that of chronic unemployment. So, I will describe various socio-logical approaches to the issue of chronic unemployment; together with politically driven ideological arguments about a deviant 'underclass', which sociological research into chronic unemployment ought to dispel. The sociological approaches will be subject to an immanent critique to see to what extent the terms of reference used can help us understand the issue of chronic unemployment, and from this immanent critique a general theory will be constructed to overcome the conceptual problems, by draw-ing upon the general social realist meta-theory. There could be no direct application of the general meta-theory, it will be argued, because this would result in circularity.

Defining the underclass

Origins of the term 'underclass' and the politicised concept of an underclass

Gans writes that

> When in 1962 Gunnar Myrdal took an old-fashioned Swedish word for 'lower class' to describe a new [US-] American 'underclass', little did he know what immense effects his brief, seemingly offhand, new conceptua-lization would have on America's view and treatment of the poor. Indeed, had he known, I am sure he would have chosen another term, if only because some subsequent distortions of his idea ignored his crucial

insight into the future of the US economy and those whom he saw as its latest victims.

(1993: 327)

Gans (1993) argues that Myrdal was prescient in arguing, in effect, that the USA economy was going to enter a 'post-industrial' age, whereby the decline of manufacturing would create structural unemployment. In this prognosis there was no Panglossian service-sector panacea whereby people would move from 'old-fashioned' manufacturing jobs to 'modern' service-sector jobs. Rather there would be an increasingly large number of people who were excluded from the labour market, because the old industrial labour market would contract severely. Without wishing to enter the debates over the definition and veracity of the notion of a post-industrial economy, we can note the important point that here the concept of an underclass was a structural concept. The problem, as Gans argues, is that the word 'underclass' was then taken up by those on the political right. The word was retained but the meaning altered, as right-wing commentators started talking of a 'dangerous black underclass', thus changing a structural concept about chronic unemployment being caused by the decline of manufacturing into a behavioural (or normative) concept about criminal and deviant behaviour by black people (Gans 1993: 327–8).

The use of the word 'underclass' to refer to a group that are held to be deviant in some way is not surprising, given the number of commentators, not all of whom are necessarily right wing, who have held that there is a sub-normal deviant group 'beneath' – or 'under' – normal society. Thus Marx talks of

> The 'dangerous class', the social scum, that passively rotting mass thrown off by the lowest layers of old society, may, here and there, be swept into the movement by a proletarian revolution; its conditions of life, however, prepare it far more for the part of a bribed tool of reactionary intrigue.
> (McLellan 1990: 229)

Whilst the proletariat are the 'universal class' who will free all of humanity by replacing capitalism with communism, thus ending the existence of class-divided society, the lumpenproletariat (or ragged proletariat) are, for Marx, the remnants of the previous lower class and, as such, they have no necessary compunction to fight against the exploitation of capitalism, as experienced by the proletariat. Rather, they will fight for whoever pays them, which is why they are the 'dangerous' class.

What it is important to note for our purposes are the metaphors used: the lumpenproletariat are *thrown off* from the lowest layers of (the old) society, and they are *passively rotting*, because they are the *déclassé* remnants of a previous social formation, and are thus outside the active class dynamics of nineteenth-century industrial capitalism. This notion of there being a *déclassé* group rotting under normal society has been the defining feature of all the arguments that hold that an *under*class (or whatever term is used for this concept) is somehow deviant from normal society and a threat to normal society. The difference though between Marx's views on the underclass and those of other nineteenth-century commentators is that whereas Marx posits an economic-structural cause for the creation of a *déclassé* group (i.e. the change to an industrial capitalist social formation) that is dangerous because it is mercenary, the latter people posit a biological cause for the creation of a *déclassé* group that was perceived as a threat (in Britain) to Victorian society, because it threatened to 'contaminate' the working class with deviant (anti-work) ideas.

The underclass as a deviant sub-'race'

In the mid-nineteenth century, debate turned on the issue of a 'substratum', and how this was different from the working class. As Morris states, one mid-nineteenth-century commentator, Mayhew, noted how casual and sweated work in London created conditions of economic distress, whereby work was insecure and gruelling (Morris 1994: 16). However, Morris notes, Mayhew went on to draw a distinction between casual labourers and vagrants, which was difficult to sustain given the nature of casual labour, and which Mayhew tried to support by turning to biology. Mayhew divided 'humanity broadly into two races: the wanderers and the settlers; the vagabond and the citizen; the nomadic and the civilised tribes' (Morris 1994: 17). This is because having recognised that economic/structural conditions were causing insecurity and poverty, he wanted to identify a group who were responsible for inflicting poverty upon themselves. In trying to identify such a group Mayhew listed their defining physical and social traits, such as 'high cheek bones and protruding jaws', 'slang language', 'repugnance to continuous labour' and 'love of cruelty' (Mayhew in Himmelfarb, cited in Morris 1994: 17).

Similarly, discussion in the late nineteenth century talked of a 'residuum'. Here poverty arose from 'demoralisation', meaning that charity and public relief had led to people choosing not to work. People who were previously industrious workers had become corrupted. Further, those who remained industrious workers – the respectable poor – were in danger of being corrupted by the residuum. Consequently one proposed solution was to remove the residuum from working-class areas, setting them to compulsory work in industrial regiments (Morris 1994: 20 discussing Steadman-Jones 1984). Such attitudes towards the residuum existed alongside the attempt to understand poverty in 'structural' terms, although, as with Mayhew's views on the substratum, such views used a distinction between the material conditions of the respectable poor, and the biological causes of poverty with the demoralised residuum, who choose crime and welfare over work. So, for example, Booth carried out a survey of London in the late 1880s, finding that one-third of the population lived in poverty, including members of the labouring poor (Morris 1994: 21).

> Potentially, says Himmelfarb (1984), this finding 're-moralized' the poor, and challenged any clear cut division between the respectable poor and the residuum. The corrupting influence and moral failure of Booth's lowest class, however, remain: 'Occasional labourers, street-sellers, loafers, criminals and semi-criminals [...] They degrade whatever they touch and as individuals are *incapable of improvement*'.
> (Keating 1976: 114; cited in Morris 1994: 21–2; emphasis added)

Despite recognising that material – or structural – conditions may lead to a situation of economic distress for the working class, the belief in a group of deviants, whose behaviour was biologically caused, led to a division between workers and the residuum.

In inter-war years of the twentieth century, the concept of an underclass persisted in the form of the 'social problem group' (Macnicol 1987: 297). Here an hereditary cause was sought for 'a variety of conditions, ranging from mental deficiency through alcoholism, criminality and unemployment, to "mild social inefficiency"' (Macnicol 1987: 297). Subsequently, the underclass was identified as the 'problem family', following problems concerning anti-social behaviour amongst some urban school children who were evacuated to rural areas in the USA during World War II (Macnicol 1987: 297). Unlike the social problem group, for whom sterilisation and segregation was mooted, members of problem families were deemed to be amenable to reform so that they could conform to the prevailing norms (Macnicol 1987: 297). As regards the social problem group, the 1929 Wood Report advocated sterilisation, providing that there were adequate ways to identify such a group. This report held that although a social problem group definitely existed, there had been little reliable data concerning its identification, and that although the cause for 'social inefficiency' was biological, its identification was to be via social behaviour which was deemed 'inefficient', i.e. 'dysfunctional' (Macnicol 1987: 302). All the attempts by the Eugenics Society (of Britain), though, failed to establish family histories sufficient to prove the case (Macnicol 1987: 306). So, unlike the nineteenth-century studies which did invoke biological explanations despite a lack of empirical evidence, here a biological cause was believed in, although it was not recognised as being 'proved', because no lineage studies were sufficient to identify such a group.

The underclass as a deviant subculture

In the 1960s and 1970s, debate turned upon the notions of a 'culture of poverty' (in the USA), and a 'cycle of deprivation' (in the UK). The argument in both cases was that deprived groups were self-perpetuating because the individuals in such groups shared particular sets of values and forms of behaviour that were antithetical to employment and family stability. Thus Keith Joseph ordered the then Social Science Research Council (later to become the Economic and Social Research Council) to investigate his claim that there was a 'cycle of deprivation'.

> Joseph's central idea was that of the inter-generational transmission of poverty through a 'cycle of deprivation', where inadequate child rearing leads to failure at school, which leads to unemployment and unstable families, which continued the inadequate rearing of children.
>
> (Bagguley and Mann 1992: 121)

The SSRC council found – much to the chagrin of Joseph – that the empirical grounds for such a claim were lacking. Against such a notion of a cycle of deprivation Rutter and Madge argue that

> At least half the children born into a disadvantaged home do not repeat the pattern of disadvantage in the next generation. Over half of all forms of disadvantage arise anew in the next generation. On the one hand, even where continuity is strongest many individuals break out of the cycle and on the other many people become disadvantaged without having been reared by disadvantaged parents.
>
> (1976: 304)

In place of a self-reproducing group there are individuals whose situations change.

Further, we can note that the existence of some (putatively) defining traits may co-exist with other forms of behaviour which are antithetical to the definition of an underclass, and that the interpretation of such behaviour may be open to normative question. For instance, a family which would appear to fit the 'cultural deprivation' stereotype did practise 'deferred gratification', by putting money aside for a life insurance policy, instead of being utterly profligate (Macnicol 1987: 295, discussing Coffield *et al.* 1981). In identifying families which may appear to fit the underclass image, though, it is necessary to remember that the interpretation of behaviour is a normative issue, and that putatively anti-social behaviour may be more accurately understood as functional or adaptive. For example, a father's playfulness was quite aggressive, and this could be interpreted either as causing anti-social behaviour in the children, or equipping them to survive in a 'hard world' (Macnicol 1987: 295, discussing Coffield *et al.* 1981). In short, not only do people move in and out of poverty, making it difficult to sustain the notion of an homogenous underclass cut adrift from 'mainstream' society, but for those that remain in difficult circumstances the interpretation of behaviour cannot simply be read as deviant, as it may be better understood as functional.

The underclass as rational choice utilitarians

Murray (1984 and 1990) develops a New Right definition of the underclass, which emphasises the importance of social bonds and free market incentives to work. This does not mean that, like Joseph, he defines an underclass in terms of a cycle of deprivation, or a culture of poverty. Instead of talking of an homogenous self-reproducing culture, Murray's approach is a form of rational choice behaviourism. His basic argument is that individuals are rational, which means in this context that they respond to positive and negative reinforcement stimuli. Murray does not use such behaviourist terminology, and nor does he espouse rational choice theory as such, but he does talk of individuals responding to the world in which they find themselves, making decisions in the light of the existing 'rewards and penalties'. Specifically, Murray's argument is that individuals respond to the 'rules of the game' as set by government. Murray argues that the features of a black underclass in the USA

> could have been predicted (indeed, in some instances were predicted) from the changes that social policy made in the rewards and penalties, carrots and sticks, that govern human behaviour. All were *rational responses to changes in the rules of the game* of surviving and getting ahead.
>
> (1984: 154–5; emphasis added)

In short, individuals may choose forms of action which produce an underclass, but in doing this, the underclass individuals are not pathological in the sense that they are innately less intelligent, devoid of the ability to work, or innately criminal. They are not misfits or deviants. Rather, they have responded rationally, at least in the short term, given the options put before them. Thus such people are acting in a purely utilitarian way to maximise what they take to be their material self-interest.

This leads us to the issue of Murray's definition of the underclass and the government policies which created it. Murray argues that the liberal response to racism was actually counter-productive in the long term. An unintended consequence of well-meaning intervention since the mid-1960s was a nefarious outcome, which helped create an underclass for poor blacks. Murray holds that the USA underclass is constituted by black single mothers who have never been married, and young black men who are chronically unemployed and who may indulge in criminal activities. The policy changes which helped bring about such an underclass are as follows. As regards single mothers, and unemployed young men, Murray argues that social welfare has now made it more rational for young people to avoid (low paid) work and live on welfare payments. Murray argues that changes to a benefit called AFDC (Aid to Families with Dependent Children) made in the 1960s meant that single mothers received higher benefits than before, single mothers and their partners were now allowed to co-habit (provided that the man was not legally responsible for the child), and that some income from paid employ-ment was permitted without loss of benefit.

To help make his point, Murray discusses a fictional couple – Harold and Phyllis – who are described as being of average intelligence, from poor back-grounds with no skills or qualifications, and who are not stereotypical irre-sponsible poor people (1984: 156–62). Before welfare reforms, Harold could not live with Phyllis, if she received AFDC, and a low-paid job would provide more than welfare. However, it would make sense for Phyllis to marry Harold, rather than receive AFDC, because the benefit is low, and by being married Phyllis could supplement Harold's income with a part-time job, and live with her partner. After the welfare reforms, though, Harold and Phyllis could live together, with one partner having a job, and receive benefits which were higher than those initially given.

Another factor to consider is that any sense of social stigma was removed from receiving welfare, which would influence potential welfare recipients to go on welfare rather than seek low-paid work. Murray describes this as the 'homogenization of the poor' (1984: 179–84). Instead of a distinction being drawn between the deserving and undeserving poor, all poor people were perceived as 'victims' with welfare being a 'right' rather than charity. The belief in self-reliance was replaced therefore with the belief that one had a right to state support. Consequently welfare became a popular option, espe-cially as some work was permitted without loss of benefits. Turning from the issue of welfare and work to the issue of crime, Murray's argument is that sentences have become more lenient and special help programmes are set up for those who do engage in criminal activity, whereas those who struggle without turning to crime get no special attention. The consequence of this is to make it rational for those who are poor to turn to crime. The chances of getting caught have fallen and the penalties faced if caught have been wea-kened. In short, the underclass came into existence because the rules of the game – the positive and negative reinforcement stimuli – were changed, and it was a rational decision to choose not to work, and to engage in criminal activity.

Murray (1990) also discusses the existence of an underclass in Britain. As he puts it, 'Britain does have an underclass, still largely out of sight and still smaller than the one in the United States. But it is growing rapidly' (1990: 3). To make this claim, Murray focuses on three 'early warning signals' which are: illegitimacy, violent crime and drop-out from the labour force (1990: 4). Using data collected by the British government's Statistical Service, Murray argues that all three underclass phenomena are increasing. Illegitimacy is described as 'sky-rocketing' (1990: 5), and this is a problem not simply because of welfare payments, but because 'communities need families [so c]ommunities need fathers' (1990: 7). Illegitimacy is high – and increasing – amongst women in the lowest social class (and class is undefined here), with the result that there are increasing numbers of children who are inadequately socialised. Such children behave like the adults they see around them, and children living in communities full of single mothers will have no fathers to act as role-models, setting the norm as going to work and supporting the family. Instead, they will regard welfare dependency as normal. In addition to this, such children are undisciplined. '[I]n communities without fathers, the kids tend to run wild. The fewer the fathers, the greater the tendency' (Murray 1990: 12).

The reason for the increase in illegitimacy is the attractiveness of benefits, coupled to the decrease in social stigma attached to receiving welfare and having an illegitimate child. Murray points out that he is not saying that women choose to have babies to receive welfare. Rather, his point is that as sex is fun and babies are endearing then the provision of welfare for single mothers allows poor women to do what comes naturally (1990: 30). Similarly, Murray argues that as in the USA, benefits are regarded as a right, and are perceived to have more status than low-paying jobs, and crime has increased due to falling conviction rates. The net result is thus: young people (from underclass families) leave school with no qualifications and barely literate (having had no discipline to work); the young men choose welfare and/or crime over a low-paid job (if they could acquire this, being barely literate), and choose not to support a family (having had no role-model of a responsible father); whilst young women have babies, supported by the state. Murray also goes on to say that with no jobs or family to give life meaning, such young men will turn to drugs which means turning to crime to support this (1990: 31). In this work on Britain, then, Murray is taking more of a culturalist argument as the focus is upon how welfare and changes to norms have created 'dysfunctional' families whereby single mothers bring up undisciplined children who will reproduce the culture of poverty.

The underclass as structural victims of de-industrialisation

Against Murray, Wilson (1987) takes up a 'structuralist' position. He argues that if we accepted Murray's views then the underclass in the USA should be diminishing, as the real value of welfare has decreased since the 1970s. Nevertheless Wilson accepts that there is an underclass, and the reason for this is structural change concerning urban de-industrialisation. Wilson argues that whilst a black middle class and older black working class have managed to leave the run-down inner-city ghettos, the young blacks have suffered from urban de-industrialisation in the 1970s, meaning that they suffer high levels of chronic unemployment, with no prospects for leaving the ghetto. There is also a high level of never-married single mothers, because the levels of unemployment mean that there is a very small pool of marriageable (employed) young men.

Wilson argues that this economic situation undermines the fabric of the local community. He argues that the exodus of middle-class blacks and working-class blacks from the ghetto removes an important 'social buffer' that could deflect the full impact of the kind of prolonged and increasing joblessness that plagued inner-city neighborhoods in the 1970s and early 1980s, joblessness created by uneven economic growth and periodic recessions. This argument is based on the assumption that even if the truly disadvantaged segments of an inner-city area experience a significant increase in long-term spells of joblessness, the basic institutions in that area (churches, schools, stores, recreational facilities, etc.) would remain viable if much of the base of their support comes from more economically stable and secure families. Moreover, the very presence of such families during such periods provides mainstream role models that help keep alive the perception that education is meaningful, that steady employment is a viable alternative to welfare, and that family stability is the norm, not the exception.

(1987: 56)

With economic decline comes a decline in the local institutions of civil society. This decay of institutions which help preserve mainstream values augments a normative alienation of young ghetto blacks from mainstream values. In place of mainstream values new 'pathological' values emerge, which hold that welfare dependency and single-parenthood are the norm.

In underclass areas, characterised by very high levels of single-parent households, there is also a high level of crime, especially violent crime. For example, the Robert Taylor Homes housing project in Chicago houses 0.5 per cent of the city's population, but was host to 11 per cent of the city's murders, 9 per cent of its rapes, and 10 per cent of its aggravated assaults; 93 per cent of the households in the project were headed by a single parent, and unemployment was estimated at 47 per cent in 1980 (Wilson 1987: 25). With the decay of mainstream values and institutions, including the family, come social problems, including high levels of crime.

So, as civil society began to degrade, and without role-model families, mainstream values were undermined. The result was an alienation from the values of education, family life and supporting oneself and one's family by work, and in some cases, a turning to crime, especially violent crime. Wilson denies that he supports the idea of a culture of poverty though, arguing that the right-wing notion of a self-sustaining culture is tautological because it holds that we infer values from behaviour and then use these values to explain behaviour (1987: 15). In place of a 'culture of poverty', Wilson talks of 'social buffers', 'social isolation', and 'concentration effects', which link 'ghetto-specific behaviour' to wider 'problems of societal organization' (1987: 137). His point is that instead of talking of a self-sustaining culture, as an independent entity, we have to realise that economic decay, followed by the decline in mainstream institutions and values, leads to cultural changes. As he puts it,

As the basic institutions declined, the social organization of inner-city neighborhoods (sense of community, positive neighbourhood identification, and explicit norms and sanctions against aberrant behaviour) likewise declined. This process magnified the effects of living in highly concentrated urban poverty areas – effects that are manifested in ghetto-specific culture and behaviour.

(1987: 138)

Consequently, social policy ought not to try to effect a cultural change, but rather, it needs to change the material circumstances in which poor unemployed urban blacks find themselves. *If the material situation improves, civil society will be strengthened and mainstream values will challenge and overcome the 'ghetto culture'.*

Although Wilson thinks it would be dogmatic to say a priori that culture could not develop any autonomy (from economic structures), he is confident in stressing the point that a change in material circumstances leads to a change in outlook and behaviour (1987: 138). Such a view though may still be dogmatic, for it treats cultural factors as epiphenomena of structural factors. As Morris argues, the structure–culture divide is not bridged, because the explanatory force lies with structure (1994: 87; see also 1995: 58). That is, we would have a mono-causal account whereby structure determined culture. Wilson may not be a Marxist, but his argument is similar to (vulgar) Marxist materialist reductionism, because culture is a direct reflection of material circumstances. The 'superstructure' is changed by the economic 'base', or in this case, culture and behaviour are epiphenomena, which will change when the material situation changes. Further, behaviour would be determined by economic structural factors too. This is because behaviour is taken to be identical with culture, in which case the causal chain would run thus: structural change in the economy⇒cultural change leads to mechanical change in behaviour. Behaviour is identical with culture in Wilson's account simply because there is no discussion of how different individuals respond to similar situations in different ways. It is just accepted that a cultural change is identical with behaviour change: as the mainstream mores decline, people act in a new underclass fashion.

In a later work, Wilson (1991) takes a slightly different approach. He replaces the term 'underclass' with the term 'ghetto poor', in order to avoid some of the ideological connotations of the former term. Wilson also reconceptualises the structure–culture relationship. This relationship is analysed using the concepts of 'weak labor force attachment' and 'social context/neighborhood'. Weak labour force attachment refers to structural constraints, meaning limited opportunities for access to employment (1991: 9). There are two sources of weak labour force attachment. The first concerns 'macrostructural' changes in 'broader society', especially in the economy. The second concerns the social milieu (1991: 10).

Focusing on the latter, Wilson argues that social environments with a low opportunity for stable and legitimate employment, and high opportunity for alternative income-generating activities, will create a weak labour force attachment. Specifically, in such neighbourhoods, many people will turn to crime and 'deviant' activities, further alienating them from the labour market. In addition to this, children will be socialised into patterns of behaviour and attitudes which are antithetical to work. Wilson argues that

> the social context has significant implications for the socialization of youth with respect to their future attachment to the labor force. For example, a youngster who grows up in a family with a steady bread-winner and in a neighborhood in which most of the adults are employed will tend to develop some of the disciplined habits associated with stable or steady employment – habits that are reflected in the behaviour of his or her parents and of other neighbourhood adults.

(1991: 10)

This does not mean that all poor communities are understandable in the same terms. Wilson does not think that all poor neighbourhoods will be characterised by the same levels of poverty, because he believes that some poor communities will have a social context which promotes a higher labour force attachment, with better formal and informal networks for job-seeking. Poverty and the ghetto poor are not necessarily the same.

This argument of Wilson's is rather confusing. Weak labour force attachment is a structural concept, concerning structural constraint, such as lack of job-access networks. Some people are more vulnerable to unemployment than others because they face more constraints: their structural situation limits their options. By itself this is tautological: people have poorer job prospects if they have worse access to jobs and if they have worse access to jobs they have poorer job prospects. So, an explanation of this state of affairs is required. Furthermore, as structures are presented as constraints rather than enablements and constraints, determinism may enter into the explanation via a subject–object dualism, unless we can say how agents respond to, and alter, their situations. Wilson's response to the need for an explanation of weak labour force attachment is to turn to another structural factor, viz. economic restructuring. Here a structural cause (economic restructuring) has a structural effect (lack of access to jobs). This may still be tautological, though: economic decline depletes the number of jobs, and the previous access networks may therefore become redundant, and these jobs are depleted because of the economic decline. Apart from this, structural factors remain as external constraints, setting up a subject–object dualism, and this structural explanation by itself does not allow us to distinguish an underclass from other groups of unemployed people. It merely tells us that some people are pushed by structures into unemployment, with poor job prospects stemming from a lack of jobs.

To distinguish an underclass, Wilson introduces the second cause of weak labour force attachment, which concerns the neighbourhood. Now this cannot be a causal factor in its own right, because if it was then Wilson would be advocating a culture-of-poverty theory, whereby the sole cause of long-term unemployment was a deviant anti-work culture. If, though, the character of the neighbourhood is caused by structures, then culture and behaviour are epiphenomena of structures, which gives us a deterministic account. In which case, cultural factors concerning the character of the neighbourhood would not be a cause of weak labour force attachment: joblessness and an anti-work culture would be caused by economic structures. Structures would determine culture which was identical with behaviour, so structures would determine behaviour.

However, Wilson does not want culture to be merely epiphenomenal. Indeed, he relies on culture to distinguish an underclass – or 'ghetto poor' – from other forms of unemployed people. Unlike those poor people who may eventually find work, the ghetto poor have a deviant culture which normalises crime and which socialises children into habits that are antithetical to regular paid employment. Children are socialised into a culture which, lacking in regular employment, leads to an 'incoherent' world, where meaning is derived from the present, and no long-term perspective can be sustained (1991: 10). Here we have a clear-cut culture-of-poverty argument, which maintains that those in chronic unemployment find themselves in such a position because of their socialisation. As Bagguley and Mann (1992: 115–16) argue, Wilson's argument is based on the 'ecological fallacy', whereby generalisations are made about the character of individual people, on the basis of aggregate census data, concerning crime and unemployment. The result is supposition rather than empirical investigation, as evidenced in the argument about dysfunctional socialisation in communities that contained the putative ghetto poor. The upshot is circularity, because as Wilson himself noted, cultural explanations infer values from behaviour and then use these values to explain behaviour.

Wilson may protest that culture is to be linked to structure, but there is a failure to do this. He says that weak labour force attachment has two causes: economic factors and cultural factors. These cannot be independent variables because that would result in a culture-of-poverty argument being co-joined with his earlier structuralist account. So culture must be epiphenomenal, to avoid a culturalist argument which is right wing and in contradiction with the structural argument. Yet in order to distinguish the ghetto poor, the argument turns to a culture which is actively hostile to opportunities should they exist. It is not just that there may be low opportunity for stable employment, but that a high opportunity for crime occurs, and this is because the individuals concerned decide to turn to crime and avoid work, creating a culture of poverty into which children are socialised, to repeat the cycle.

Studying the chronically unemployed as members of the working class

The spurious belief that there is an homogenous underclass culture led neo-Weberians to argue that although there may be a specific *class situation* for those long-term unemployed people who lack the requisite labour-market resources for employment, such a group does not constitute a distinctive *social class*. There may be people different from the mainstream working class but they are not a distinct cultural group, and therefore they are not a social class.

Morris and Irwin (1992a) take up a stance which is opposed to such a neo-Weberian view, as well as the argument that the underclass is a distinct social class. They define class in occupational terms, and argue that instead of talking of a underclass 'class situation', it is better to talk of working-class people who move in and out of working-class occupations.[1] This means studying the life-courses of individuals, rather than trying to define a collective category which will furnish a definitive explanation of a group who are separate from the working class. Drawing on their study of individuals' employment history in Hartlepool, Morris and Irwin focus their attention on three groups: group A (unemployed), group B (stable employment), and group C (recent recruits). They argue that group A is not a qualitatively distinct class from the working class. Rather, group A is constituted by people who are unskilled workers, or people who belong to the Registrar General's class V. The source of their unemployment is to be located in their class position, in which case, it is argued, to call group A an underclass would be to overlook the source of their vulnerability which resides in their class location. As Morris and Irwin put it,

> Since long-term unemployment is bred of a weakness in the labour market by virtue of unskilled status and/or lack of formal craft qualifications, then to separate the unemployed from their class position when in work, is to overlook the source of their vulnerability. This vulnerability is different in nature, however, from that experienced by the insecurely employed, whose composition quite closely approximates that of the secure group, particularly in the preponderance of social class IIIM workers.
>
> (1992a: 418)

Group C is mainly constituted by young workers (under thirty) who belong to the Registrar General's class 3m (or IIIM: skilled manual). This group experiences fragmented work histories, not because the individuals concerned choose constantly to change employer, but because economic restructuring (i.e. industrial decline) has prevented secure employment. This means that instead of slowly moving up the 'job ladder', individuals may well experience 'downward mobility', as well as (limited) 'upward mobility'. It also means that the individuals within this group experience bouts of unemployment. In studying how individuals in group C move out of unemployment, Morris and Irwin study the informal networks for job access. This leads them to take issue with Murray, arguing that those who are insecurely employed do have a will to work, despite frequent unemployment, and this will to work, as manifest in the use of job-seeking networks, forms a collective experience contrary to a culture of poverty.

Doing 'fiddly jobs': an ethnographic understanding of coping strategies to deal with structural unemployment

MacDonald (1994) also deals with social networks in relation to employment. Unlike Morris and Irwin, though, MacDonald's study on industrial decline in Cleveland deals with 'fiddly jobs'; which is local argot for jobs which are undertaken whilst claiming welfare benefits. MacDonald describes how those experiencing long-term unemployment fall into one of two groups. One group, which is the majority, suffers social isolation and struggles to survive on welfare payments. The other minority group has, by being members of the appropriate social networks, access to fiddly jobs. By knowing the 'right' people, and the 'right' pubs, it is possible to get short-term employment with 'no questions asked' and payment in cash.

Fiddly jobs could be jobs such as taxi driving or household repairs, although in Cleveland there were some jobs available in industry. In order to try and stay competitive, the remaining industry sought labour market 'flexibility' in terms of both numerical and functional flexibility, meaning that it wanted a periphery of workers who could be employed on a casual 'as-and-when-needed' basis, and a core of workers that could be reskilled, respectively. This meant that there were sub-contractors who could undercut legitimate competition by providing peripheral workers who were paid less because they were on the 'dole' ('Unemployment Benefit', now 'Jobseekers' Allowance'; or 'Income Support'). The type of work procured was poorly paid, short-term, and involved working long shifts; which often meant double shifts and sometimes triple shifts. MacDonald gives the example of 'Stephen', a twenty-five-year-old man with a wife and two children, who worked twelve hours a day, seven days a week, doing cleaning and maintenance jobs in a steel works, for sixty pounds a week (1994: 514–15). The sub-contractors were paid 'tax' by the workers, who were uninsured against industrial accidents. Fewer women were employed in fiddly jobs, and those who were worked in the service sector, earning even lower wages. For instance, one interviewee ('Muriel') earned thirty-five pounds a week for a full week's work in a private nursing home (which brought her total weekly income to just under seventy pounds).

MacDonald argues that those who engage in such activities regard themselves as adhering to mainstream values about employment and self-reliance, rather than self-consciously adhering to a criminal culture which valued fraud. The attitudes expressed by the men he studied were that fiddly jobs were an acceptable supplement to meagre welfare payments, and were a necessary method of supporting their families. The women expressed similar views, saying that fiddly jobs were justified to support a family or, if single, to supplement a meagre income in the short term ('Muriel' only worked for six weeks). In order for the men to continue receiving fiddly jobs, they had to have a reputation as a reliable hard worker, who would not let the sub-contractor down. They had to be 'good workers', not 'shirkers', or 'trouble makers' who complained about pay and conditions. Claiming benefits whilst having a normal wage, or engaging in large-scale organised benefit fraud, were regarded as wrong by those engaged in fiddly jobs. Those who were unemployed and not engaged in fiddly jobs usually shared such views, saying that fear of being caught, or lack of opportunity, prevented them doing fiddly jobs. It was also stated that the cumbersome bureaucracy, and wait for money, involved in re-starting a claim if one 'signed-off' benefits to work legitimately for a short while, led to people claiming benefits whilst working on short-term jobs.

So, although the act of claiming was fraudulent, the attitudes expressed conformed to mainstream values about self-reliance through work, instead of welfare-dependency which would be antithetical to any work ethic. Indeed, MacDonald argues that

> fiddly work could, ironically, be understood better as representing a culture of enterprise, rather than as one of dependency. If the political Right is worried that the work ethic is under threat, this study should help allay their fears. Because 'proper jobs' were not available some showed high degrees of personal motivation, initiative, local knowledge and risk-taking.
>
> (1994: 528)[2]

In place of a culture of dependency some people are able to work, and although this is illegal, the values expressed about such activity conform to mainstream values, concerning self-reliance and hostility to fraud for the sake of profit alone. Further, such activity shows a high attachment to the work ethic associated with the New Right's economic and normative individualism. MacDonald does not discuss the concept of an underclass *per se*, but he does reject the cultural explanations advocated by such New Right ideologues as Peter Lilley, arguing that there is no culture of dependency, or 'something for nothing society', to use Lilley's polemical locution.

The role of gender

Men, public space and control

As we have seen, for those who hold to the culturalist explanation about the formation and continuity of an underclass, the focus is on how single mothers fail to socialise their children into mainstream norms concerning work, responsibility and discipline. The single mothers are held to be bad role-models because they rely on welfare and, without a father, the children will not be disciplined. The result is that the female children grow up expecting welfare payments to support them; and male children grow up expecting welfare and, as they are male, they will turn to crime as well, because males are held to be more aggressive than females. All of which is held to be in contrast with 'normal' families whereby a breadwinner is seen to take responsibility for himself and his family by submitting himself to the discipline of work, and by submitting his children to the discipline that will ensure their ability to work at school and in paid employment.

Beatrix Campbell takes issue with this in her (1993) book *Goliath: Britain's dangerous places*, where she explores the attitudes of men and women living in the depressed communities that experienced rioting in the 1980s and 1990s. She argues that whilst the manifestation of masculinity is different in these areas from the manifestation of masculinity in areas that are not chronically depressed, the underlying masculinity is the same. Basically, patriarchy may be expressed in different ways in different contexts, but the underlying system of norms is the same. So, whereas a working man will define himself in a public (work) role that separates him from direct involvement with the family, and which often means working with men not women, a man who is subject to chronic unemployment will also distance himself from direct involvement with his family, by leaving the home to get involved in the 'black economy' of stolen goods, or by simply staying at home without relating effectively with his partner and children. In neither case would the man define himself in terms of domestic involvement. At its minimum, then, masculinity is definable simply as 'not-femininity', and more extensively, it is definable in terms of men's location in secure normative space as breadwinners who have a clear 'respectable' role that carries with it economic control over 'their family'. When this role disappears the men have a crisis of identity that is more acute than the financial crisis, and so rather than redefine themselves in domestic roles they actively or passively continue to absent themselves from their families.

The young men who grew up in such communities are not, Campbell argues, to be thought of as being cut off from masculine gender norms, as the culturalist right wing arguments hold. Rather the reverse is the case. She argues that the 'lads' 'were soaked in globally transmitted images and ideologies of butch and brutal solutions to life's difficulties' (1993: 323). From an early age boys would soak up images of war and violence where the message was that 'real men' sorted problems out by forcing a solution upon others. Problems were when a man could not assert his will over others and problems were resolved when his will prevailed or, collectively, when states forced their will over other states. Public space was space to be conquered and the domestic sphere was to be held in disdain.

When the boys became old enough they got their partners pregnant and then abandoned them. The lads had no inclination to start a family of their own from which to flee. The lads would live with their mother, and would go out to be with their 'mates'. Being out with their mates could mean drinking or taking drugs, stealing from people's houses, 'joyriding', or intimidating people. Theft of goods from houses might be a means to an end (to buy drugs) but car theft was an end in itself – joyriding was a joy. In an era when citizenship was redefined in terms of consumerism, so that to be a member of the wider political community all one had to do was be a 'respectable spender', the lads consumed fast powerful cars and, having had their fun, they would destroy the cars. No-one actually wanted to own a car. No-one wanted to have the responsibilities involved with owning a car, such as working to pay for it and looking after it. What was wanted was pure consumerism, where the object consumed existed only for as long as it gave pleasure. This does not mean the event was consumed and destroyed in the way the car was, for some joyriders took to video-recording the stolen cars racing around the estates.

Whilst many residents of the hard-pressed estates may have resented the nuisance of speeding cars doing 'handbrake turns' and stolen cars being burnt out, few (if any) residents would complain because there was a fear of being labelled as a 'grass' (informer) and singled out for retribution. The lads did not simply intimidate 'grasses', though. They used intimidation to show their power over their community – it was their space for them to exert their will over. So, when single mothers were moved onto estates, the lads would either assume the space as theirs to be used as they wished (with the lads depositing stolen goods in the young mother's house, or using it as an escape from home for drug taking, and so on), or they would simply demonstrate their power by trying to force the mother out of the house and out of their space. They read the arrival of young mothers as the feminisation of the estate *qua* the lads' space, and if they did not try to colonise this space, they would try to eject the woman.

Campbell also discusses masculinity in relation to the police. She argues that the police force was dominated by an aggressive masculine 'canteen culture' that not only led to high-flying women officers with new ideas being discriminated against. It also led to an adversarial approach to the existence of crime and a failure to take seriously the complaints of some residents (who were seen as less important than people in richer areas). Although Campbell does not develop the point in great detail, the claim is made that creative multi-agency work might have gone some way to reducing the problems of crime, but that this could not happen given the culture of the police, which was based on the police trying to reclaim the estates (occasionally), to exercise their control over public space.

Women, responsibility and the community

After denying that the 1991 riots in Ely had any racist element, despite physical and verbal abuse being directed towards Asian families, the Reverend

Bob Morgan (who saw himself as connected to the 'common man') commented, with the confidence conferred by prejudice, that 'the decline of the estates was commensurate with the rise of the lone mother' (Campbell 1993: 252). Against this stereotyping of single mothers Campbell goes on to note that '[n]o political commentators alluded to the resilience and ingenuity of single parents, or to the capricious and often cruel culture created by the men who abandoned and harassed them' (1993: 252). Against the stereotype of irresponsibility, young single mothers were having to cope not just with poverty, but with the lads.

Managing to support oneself and a child (or two) on welfare would be no mean feat, as Pilger indicates in a chapter in his (1998) book *Hidden agendas*. In this book Pilger describes how two young single mothers – who are 'unpeople', denied a voice by the media and politicians, which prefer negatively to stereotype the powerless, as this blames the victim and masks how the rich get richer – are the model of prudence, contrary to the stereotype about young mothers being 'feckless'. Whilst he was interviewing Trisha (nineteen) and Amy (twenty), the television (which is about twenty years old) had a Labour party conference showing, and the chancellor-to-be Gordon Brown, talked of prudence and discipline being the hallmarks of Labour policy (Pilger 1998: 103). Whilst Brown wagged a finger at the audience, Trish and Amy each described their experience of being single mothers on welfare. Amy described how she hunted round to find a freezer store a few pence cheaper than the one she was using and how she mainly ate baked beans, whilst Trisha, who could not always afford to wash her clothes, described how she sought out caring work, but was unable to take up such work because the wage was too low for childcare (Pilger 1998: 101-3). All this is set against a backdrop where welfare has decreased (Campbell 1993: 241; Pilger 1998: 104).

In her study of the depressed estates, Campbell notes how, according to a community worker, the responsibility for looking after the child by-passes the young father and goes to his mother, who will help the young single mother, by giving her clothes (1993: 201). The older woman will also, according to the same community worker, continue the family relationship with her son's ex-partner, inviting her round for Sunday lunch, for example (1993: 201), which indicates how the women deal with caring and coping, whilst the men reject any domestic responsibility that would impinge on their desire to control the space outside the family and ignore the family space. Indeed, drawing upon the Scarman Report, Campbell argues that extended black families have strong family bonds, which are sustained by women, and where male absence does not result in any weakening of the institution of the family (1993: 107). In which case the loss, or negligible role, of the 'man of the house' will not, contrary to the culturalist arguments, produce a collapse in family values and the sense of responsibility.

The older women on the depressed estates may also seek a public role: they set up community action groups and self-help groups. In extending their role beyond the home, though, such women sometimes encounter male abuse. Campbell describes how a community centre ended up becoming a drinking club when the female members left the centre's committee following verbal abuse from a misogynist (1993: 248). Similarly when the Meadowell Action Group, a successful tenants' group for the Tyneside Meadowell estate, rented a building from the council, to be used by young and old, it ended in disaster. The lads continually broke into the building and vandalised the building, so eventually it was closed. At one point, before it was closed, a pensioner had a heart attack when the building was stoned, and the ambulance that came was also stoned (Campbell 1993: 242–3). The young men did not want to share *their* public space. This is not to imply though that all such schemes were failures. Many succeeded, but required much resilience. For example, the Cedarwood Wellbeing women's group prevented their exercise and office equipment being stolen by having volunteers sleep in the centre (1993: 244).

Campbell also describes female involvement in crime, but whereas men saw crime as a confirmation of their identity, the women often saw it as a 'necessary evil'; with the exception of some young lesbians who mixed with the lads as equals (although Campbell really only notes this point rather than pursuing how and why this occurred). Such crime entailed either stealing goods for their own use, or becoming involved with crime groups led by men, which included such activities as using stolen cheque books to buy goods that are then sold on. Fear was used by the men to prevent information getting to the police so that, in one case, a woman who was caught issuing cheques from a stolen cheque book was beaten by three men to ensure she did not give the police any names (Campbell 1993: 223).

The underclass and the sociological logic of immediacy

Reading underclass behaviour off from a master-ontology

With the sociological logic of immediacy we have a definitive master-ontology that is definitive in the sense that the ontology is held to list all the factors that determine behaviour. Thus to know the ontology is to know all the causes of human behaviour, in which case empirical research would be redundant as one may read-off behaviour from the master-ontology. The structuralist sociological logic of immediacy underpinned the arguments about the putative underclass being constituted by a sub-race or deviant subculture. Here knowledge of the 'race' or subculture would enable commentators to make claims about the putative underclass, with such claims being 'known' as correct independently of any empirical research. As all members of the putative underclass were definable in terms of the same set of causal factors, it followed that the group would be defined as having an homogenous identity. Or, to put it another way, commentators construct negative stereotypes, and hold that all members of the group they have constructed are definable in terms of a particular set of negative traits.

It may be pointed out that practising immanent critique on such views is not possible because they work in the way that they are meant to work. That is to say, as items of political rhetoric designed to blame the poor for being poor, such views may be said to 'work', or at least work insofar as people accept such views as legitimisations for policies that support 'markets' over welfare, and 'stronger' policing tactics. Whilst one cannot practise immanent critique on a group who want to accept a prejudiced view simply because they want to construct and reinforce a negative stereotype, one can practise immanent critique when rhetorical constructions are presented as truth claims in the hope of winning other people over to a political cause. Thus when stereotypes about homogenous deviant groups are wheeled out by the political right and people are invited to accept these stereotypes as 'obvious truths' that the 'politically correct' (whoever that refers to) try to hide, the obvious objections about determinism, and constructing a priori notions of homogenous groups that do conceptual violence to the complexity of social reality, may be turned to as a form of immanent critique. Here one would be exposing how the terms of reference predicated upon the structuralist socio-logical logic of immediacy, in either a biological or culturalist form, failed to account for the cause of poverty and long-term unemployment, together with failing to account for the diverse experiences of the chronically unemployed.

A possible rejoinder to this is to put forward some form of Baudrillardian line and either say that the social has 'imploded' leaving us with the passive 'masses' that just absorb ephemeral images, or agree with commentators like Chomsky that important truths are effectively hidden from most people, because the media tacitly accept an 'establishment' world-view. Now the former may be rejected simply by noting the current anti-globalisation acti-vism, together with more 'grass-roots' green activism against road-building. Here there is no passive mass but an active people.

As regards the latter, we may say that this is true to a large extent. This is not to embrace some form of conspiracy theory, but it is to accept the point that media coverage, as regards both quantitative and qualitative coverage (i.e. the amount of coverage and the style of presentation of issues covered), does tend to reflect values that accord with the status quo. Thus for every investigative documentary, or programme such as *The Mark Thomas Product* (as broadcast by Channel Four on British television) that seeks to expose corruption and abuses of power, etc., there are endless items of news coverage that exclude certain events and people, and present issues in biased and simplified ways. We, in Britain, knew what 'our lads' were doing to the 'Argies' during the Falklands War, and what 'we' were doing to 'liberate' Kuwait in the Gulf War, but most people had no knowledge of the sale of weapons and other items of equipment to authoritarian regimes, and the number of children who have died in Iraq as a result of sanctions. Similarly the British 'popular' press are having, to use a clichéd term, a 'field day' with the issue of asylum seekers 'flooding' the country to rely on 'our' welfare, or even 'stealing' 'our' jobs (and ignoring the demographic need for more immigrants if the economy is to grow with an ageing work-force, and excluding reference to oppressive regimes).

To pursue this further one would need to draw upon the extensive socio-logical literature on the media. However there is not the space to do this, and my point was simply to note that even though there is bias in the media, when a view moves from being a 'received wisdom' or, more accurately, a received false prejudice held by one group, to being articulated as a truth claim for others to absorb, its terms of reference may be criticised. The attempt to stigmatise people with notions of the undeserving poor, using assumptions woven into some master-ontology, may be subjected to immanent critique the moment it tries to serve its real purpose, which is to legitimise a turn to the right (i.e. increased economic liberalism with politically illiberal attitudes to social 'order'). A master ontology that homogenises people into a stereotyped group simply does violence to social reality: its terms of reference and the reality of those concerned are utterly divergent.

Reading the master-ontology into empirical research

Of course there are attempts to apply the master-ontology empirically, rather than assuming it to be true a priori, and trying to get others to accept its a priori claims. As argued before though, if the ontology is taken to be a definitive master-ontology, any attempt to apply it will result in arbitrary verificationism of prior verities. This is most clear in the case of Murray's argument. Murray draws upon the individualist sociological logic of imme-diacy with his utilitarian ontology of human being, and seeks to verify this by turning to the decision making of an hypothetical couple. As this couple exemplify the reasoning of *homo economicus* we may extrapolate from their (hypothetical) decision making, to all the decisions and actions made by actual individuals receiving welfare. Once this is accepted as legitimate, it follows that one can supplement this by making inferences about the rise in recorded crime and the number of people in long-term receipt of welfare being caused by naive reformers misunderstanding 'human nature', and giv-ing positive reinforcement stimuli to such activity. If one does not accept the master-ontology of human being, though, one will not see quantitative data as an immediate vindication of the thesis that an underclass has been created by foolish 'do-gooders' who misunderstand how selfish human nature is. If one does not accept Murray's master-ontology of human being, then one must seek other reasons to explain chronic unemployment (other than turn-ing to a culturalist argument, as Murray does in his work on the British underclass).

Wilson's argument initially seems more plausible than Murray's, as chronic unemployment is linked to the decline of the urban manufacturing base, but the result is, as we have seen, the same as the culturalist arguments, for Wilson ends up talking about a self-sustaining culture. In making his argu-ments Wilson ends up reading these assumptions about the self-sustaining culture into empirical data and the result is, as Bagguley and Mann argued (1992), the ecological fallacy. That is, as noted above, Wilson (according to Bagguley and Mann) generalises about individuals' characteristics using quantitative data. This results in a circular argument because the alleged deviant actions are taken as both the cause and the effect: crime is one cause of an underclass culture, defined in terms of criminal activity and welfare-dependency, and crime is also an indication that an underclass exists.

Circularity affects all the arguments about an underclass that turn on the sociological logic of immediacy. This is because whether views are read-off from the master-ontology, or read-into research, the point is that the master-ontology is self-justifying. One holds that ontology is *known to be* true (i.e. accepted as true) either because it is *known to be true* (i.e. *just* accepted as true), or because its assumptions are proved by reading data and interpreting actions in a way that will conform to the assumptions (which includes committing the ecological fallacy), meaning the assumptions are 'correct' because one has established their correctness by assuming their correctness.

Realism as an underlabourer

Most practicing empirical researchers take their work to be a fallible interpretation of social reality, rather than a collection of 'facts' or a mapping of a manifest truth. Such interpretations, though, need to have their assumptions and implicit precepts made explicit because, as Archer (1995) argues, all research is influenced by some ontological assumptions, whether implicit or explicit, and unless the assumptions are explicit there is the risk of arbitrariness (as discussed in relation to methodological collectivism in Chapter 2, and Giddens' structuration theory as discussed in Chapter 4) or, at the very least, an incoherent account of being.

In making explicit the precepts that inform research, a distinction needs to be made between a general meta-theory, a domain-specific meta-theory and specific theories (See Figure 6.1). The general meta-theory supplied the general precepts about being. A social realist meta-theory, as we have seen, would therefore supply the precepts of emergent properties existing in open systems. These precepts, or first principles, concerning social ontology, were derived via an immanent critique of alternative accounts of social being (with regard to the structure–agency problem).

The general meta-theory cannot be applied directly to empirical research because that might result in social realism ending up being predicated upon the sociological logic of immediacy. If one thought that the method of immanent critique was to be practised only at the general level, concerning the general definition of being (in the form of the structure–agency problematic), and that the social realist precepts could then be used prescriptively, with empirical facts being classified as CEPs, SEPs and PEPs, then there is the danger that the precepts would become a definitive ontology, and that these precepts were simply read-into empirical 'facts'. There would be the very real

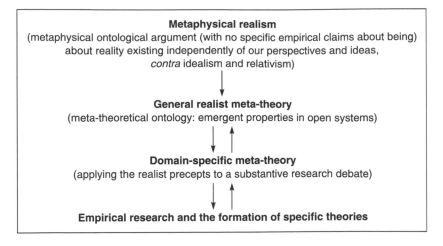

Figure 6.1 Levels of realist theorising.

danger that social realism verified itself by classifying data according to its
ontology and then verifying the ontology by saying that the (putative)
research 'facts' mirrored the ontology. That is, there would be the danger
of saying that one saw CEPs and SEPs and so on, and then verifying the
ontology by saying that it is a correct reflection of manifest facts. Any notion
of the general meta-theory being a fallible theory in the transitive domain
would be lost as the underlabourer became a master-builder. The reason for
this is that the notion of general emergent properties is too general to be used
in a way that is non-elastic or circular.

To avoid this possible outcome it is necessary to construct a domain-specific
meta-theory. A domain-specific meta-theory would use the method of immanent critique to examine the existing terms of reference that had been used to
analyse a particular research topic. In constructing the domain-specific meta-
theory one would therefore have to examine how the existing terms of reference failed to account fully for the reality that the said terms of reference were
supposed to explain. One would then begin to develop an alternative framework by trying to overcome the noted shortcomings and, in doing this, one
would draw upon the general meta-theory. This would not entail a dogmatic
application/verification of the ontological precepts from the general meta-
theory because those precepts about social being were derived from an immanent critique of alternative general social ontologies and, more importantly in
the context of constructing a domain-specific meta-theory, the general precepts would be interpreted to fit the research problematic. It would not be a
question of reading some general ontological precepts into putatively manifest
empirical 'facts', but of internally criticising the prevailing paradigms and
then constructing some realist terms of reference using the general precepts.

In short, the precepts from the general ontology would inform the construction of new terms of reference, and this construction of new terms of reference would be sensitive to the existing verisimilitude of the pre-existing terms of reference. The precepts from the general meta-theory would not therefore be used as the new terms of reference without any translation. The domain-specific meta-theory would not simply be a reflection of the general meta-theory, but instead it would develop the general precepts in accordance with the specific empirical and conceptual issues raised in the immanent critique of the pre-existing paradigms.

The domain-specific meta-theory could not be applied directly to empirical research (whether quantitative, qualitative or both) because as a meta-theory it would still be too general to provide specific terms of reference and, if it were assumed that research must fit the meta-level terms of reference, we might be returned to the problem of reading a general ontology into putatively manifest facts. Instead it needs to be recognised that the domain-specific theory will supply the conceptual resources for the development of specific theories, that are developed in relation with the on-going empirical research.

This is not to imply a top-down model whereby theory legislates upon the terms of reference used prior to any empirical research. After all, meta-theories are fallible aspects of the transitive realm, and the conceptual content of the meta-level frameworks may be changed in the light of future empirical research. Thus not only may specific theories and empirical research lead to changes in the conceptual resources of the domain-specific meta-theory, but the general meta-theory may change too in the light of reconsidered analysis of social (or natural) being. Whilst different domain-specific meta-theories may be developed by different researchers, and whilst the domain-specific meta-theories in, say, sociology, economics, history, law, etc., will vary in content, and may be open to frequent revision, as the meta-theories are developed in relation to on-going debates within the disciplines, the general meta-theory will probably remain unchanged. However it may well change in the future because it may be that, from an analysis of the way that domain-specific meta-theories are developed in relation to on-going debates and empirical research, a better general ontology of emergent properties in open systems may be developed. A realist meta-theory is not an ahistorical, unrevisable and definitive claim about being.

Notes for the construction of a domain-specific meta-theory for researching the chronically unemployed in Britain

Immanent critique

Engaging in a detailed discussion of the underclass debate that drew upon a thorough analysis of the empirical data used by social scientists, politicians, policy analysts and ideologues would require (at least) a book-length study.

My task here in this chapter then is more modest: my task is just to sketch out some ideas for the construction of a domain-specific meta-theory for the study of chronic unemployment. This will entail drawing upon the studies described above, that provide a sample of the range of arguments.

So far, we have seen that arguments predicated upon the sociological logic of immediacy are to be rejected because they entail a spurious deterministic homogenised conception of the putative underclass. In other words, the terms of reference of these positions do not deal adequately with the reality of chronic unemployment. What though of the work of Morris and Irwin, MacDonald, and Campbell?

Morris and Irwin use quantitative data in a way that avoids the ecological fallacy. However, Morris and Irwin's reliance on quantitative data turns upon an extant empiricism, where measured frequencies or correlations are taken to be indicative of causal processes. The problem then is that whilst we have a subtle *description*, this is not sufficient by itself to be an *explanation*. We have a statistical mapping of what is happening, and whilst this may not be false, it does not tell us as much as we could know. That is, the study can be used to criticise the notion of a deviant underclass, but it does not tell us how the unskilled may be a section of society that have a lesser access to skills training, for whatever reason, or how people deal in different ways with long-term unemployment, and so on.

To be sure, in a different study (1992b) Morris and Irwin do analyse the forms of support network people have access to, and discuss financial support plus 'help in kind', in relation to employed and unemployed households. In this study, which also relies on survey data, they argue that

> The level of unemployment in kinship and friendship networks will be class related; the unskilled being most likely to have contact with others of their kind, and so to suffer particularly from unemployment. It is thus in explaining the employment sources of aid, rather than in structuring flows, that social class seems to have a bearing.
>
> (1992b: 206)

However, the problem, as before, is that we just have a description rather than an explanation. We know that the forms of support differ according to social class (and, slightly according to gender as well), but we do not have an explanation of the context that does shape who acts in what way.

MacDonald offers a useful qualitative analysis of unemployed people's coping strategies in Cleveland. The argument is built up from discussions with individuals and from this generalisations are made about norms and agency. Whilst this provides a useful insight into how the 'right people' get 'fiddly jobs', and how this is seen as a legitimate way to be a 'breadwinner', there is the problem that the terms of reference are based on an implicit individualist ontology. The social world presented to us is one of individuals, their actions, and their justifications for their actions. So, if we wanted to say why an individual failed to get a fiddly job, it would be in terms of the individual being regarded as the 'wrong sort of person' by other individuals.

While such an account may not be descriptively false, it does soon begin to run out of explanatory content, because we do not have the conceptual resources to explain notions about the 'right face'. That is, whilst informal networks play an important role in MacDonald's analysis, we cannot explain these networks in terms other than the dispositions that certain individuals have. All of which returns us to the problems mentioned in the discussion of methodological individualism and dispositions in Chapter 2. As we cannot say where dispositions 'come from' because we cannot link dispositions to the socio-historical context (understood as being non-reducible to individuals), and as there is no social reality beyond individuals, we are left in the position of holding, ultimately, that social networks (read: individuals' actions) are a reflection of dispositions. Actions would be direct expressions of dispositions, unless frustrated by the disposition-cum-action of another individual, so functioning networks would be an expression of dispositions that individuals happened to hold in common. This would not only be ontologically false because individuals' agency is constrained (as well as enabled) through social factors, but it could also lead to the political conclusion that individuals 'made their own circumstances' and that poor people were less able or criminal. That is, one could argue that if some individuals could get illegal work then others could, and that those who had the practical ability to seek out illegal work ought to have the practical ability to seek out legitimate work, unless they held to deviant dispositions that inclined them toward criminal acts such as working and claiming welfare.

There is also a gender-blindness in MacDonald's work. Women are mentioned but there is no discussion of how women get access to care-sector jobs without using the 'right face in the right pub' network, whilst men rely on the said macho network. Most of the discussion is on how the men get access to industrial 'men's jobs', and how men see themselves as 'breadwinners'. From the disposition to be a breadwinner we have the action of men working in illegal industrial employment and, *ex hypothesi*, most women have a disposition to be 'homemakers' confined to the private sphere.

Whilst gender norms about being a breadwinner are important, although unanalysed in MacDonald's work, Campbell makes gender the centre of her study. With Campbell we have the argument that criminal and violent men who are unemployed are not socialised into a deviant set of norms, but rather, that they are acting on patriarchal norms about power, domination, and the exclusion of women from public space to the private sphere. Whereas normal forms of power and exclusion may be perceived as normal ways of going on, the actions of the unemployed men were not masked by social convention, and so they could be seen for what they were, viz. a destructive obsession with power to 'prove oneself' against others. The problem with this is that it may move toward the structuralist sociological logic of immediacy, with all men behaving according to the norms of patriarchal culture, whether this was in the context of 'normal' patriarchal expression or the expression of patriarchal norms by the unemployed men. Certainly, from reading the accounts of men's behaviour, whether the men were unemployed or serving in the police for instance, we are left with the impression that most – if not all – men are determined by norms about 'pride' and control of public space.

Whilst the women were presented as being concerned with the well-being of their family and the community (contrary to stereotypes about feckless underclass women on 'sink estates'), thus drawing upon gender norms about women being 'carers', there was a disjunction between the norm of feminine roles and lived reality of life in deprived areas. Although Campbell does not talk explicitly of 'standpoint epistemology' (Harding 1996), we may say that Campbell is advancing a similar view, which is that women are 'outsiders within', and that this affords them epistemic advantage. The prevailing norms concern women being passive homemakers (or at least homemakers with a 'job on the side'; even if many women have 'breadwinner' jobs) and the men being active breadwinners, but in order to cope, the women have to be extremely active, whilst the men are only being active in a destructive way. The (masculine) institutions (such as the police) have a culture whereby poor people from distressed areas are regarded as underclass individuals who bring problems upon themselves, and the men are not helpful, so the women struggle to exist in a world where there is little help, much hostility, and a culture that defines women as housewives divorced from worldly cares. From her presentation of the way women saw themselves, Campbell suggests that these women are aware of the injustice and inequality that affects them as a collectivity (of poor women), whilst the men individualise the problems, focusing more on their 'macho' identity than on broader factors, concerning class and gender inequality.

So, economic-structural factors put women into a position whereby class and gender inequality, and the discrepancy between life as they lived it and the norms of family life, led to a more critical world-view. In which case women's epistemic advantage is a result of structural factors, rather than being due to (some) women simply taking a critical attitude. Therefore women would not seem to escape determinism either, as they were caused by structural factors to change their perspective. However, against this it may be argued that women were not determined, but that the difficulties they faced simply led to a more questioning attitude. In which case we have a double set of ontological books: men are determined by patriarchal norms, whilst women have the ability to question and critique those norms and inequalities.

Of course Campbell's book was written as a piece of political literature rather than social science as such, in which case (as with Pilger's work) it may be judged on its rhetorical ability to persuade us to see things differently, rather than claiming epistemic virtue by following a qualitative sociological research method. Such a neat distinction ought to be questioned, though. For social science cannot gain truth by assuming that some formal methodological principles will unlock a reality that is assumed to fit the methodological key, and literature needs to be more than rhetoric if its ability to persuade is to go beyond ideological caricatures for those who already accept a given position.

Whilst there will be differences obviously, we still ought to retain the notion that, with works such as Campbell's (that seek to be serious explorations of social and political issues), the precepts of the argument are to be judged in the way that they affect the claims made about the socio-political realm. It is therefore appropriate that the text be judged with the criteria that one would use for judging social science work in mind. This is not to say that the work must conform to some methodological principles concerning, say, how ethnographic field work may be *the* method, but it will have to be judged by some consideration of how it frames its truth claims. That is, we need to examine how its assumptions – as well as its style – affect the claims made, and the coherence of those claims. Such a consideration would lead to the recognition that the double set of ontological books was linked to a prior concern to establish that men were cultural dopes, whose constructed 'nature' was unreflexively to reproduce patriarchy, whilst women were able reflexively to 'see beyond' the constraining norms. The 'double book' starting assumptions are complemented by a rhetorical style (or 'method') that invites the reader to generalise from anecdotal data; which is also an hallmark of Murray's culturalist arguments where he generalises from individuals' comments about their experience of 'bad families'.

The domain-specific meta-theory: CEPs, SEPs, agents and networks

Given what has been argued we may conclude that a domain-specific meta-theory is required that can define social being without falling into individualism and avoiding the structuralist sociological logic of immediacy, and do so in a way that includes reference to economic and cultural factors. To do this we may draw upon the work of Archer (1995) and use the notion of SEPs (structural emergent properties) and CEPs (cultural emergent properties). The SEPs would refer to the material-economic conditions, such as the decline of manufacturing and state policy on welfare, in Britain.[3] The CEPs would concern patriarchal gender norms and, specifically, the way that men's and women's responsibilities towards others were 'exclusive' and 'inclusive', that is, concerned with control and excluding people from areas of control (especially excluding women) and including people in a sense of community responsibility, respectively. These emergent properties may be referred to as the 'generic SEPs and CEPs'.

The meta-theory would also have the notions of primary and corporate agents (Archer 1995). A primary agent would be a group of individuals in a similar economic position with shared norms who did not organise collectively to advance their interests. A corporate agent would be a collectivity that did organise and mobilise. Relations within and between agents may be described in terms of networks that are constituted by network-specific CEPs and SEPs, that are derived from, but also different from, the generic CEPs and SEPs. Network-specific emergent properties may be of two kinds: intra-agent CEPs and SEPs for networks internal to agents, and inter-agent CEPs and SEPs for networks that link actors in different agents (see Figure 6.2).

At this stage two corporate agents may be postulated, viz. community groups and organised crime gangs. In the former case the intra-agent network-specific CEPs may be 'feminine' (in Campbell's terms of reference), and there may be no SEPs, as questions of resources would be a matter of individuals providing what they could as individuals. If a community group became more formalised by, for instance, having relatively institutionalised connections with a local authority, then actors might find themselves in a new inter-agent network, based on more formalised CEPs and where there were SEPs in the form of policy-linked decision-making relations. As regards organised crime gangs, we may speak of masculine intra-agent network CEPs and intra-agent network SEPs concerning the allocation of material resources according to the hierarchy within the agent (see Figures 6.3 and 6.4).

Whilst some individuals experiencing chronic unemployment will lead rather atomistic lives, disconnected from the actions of other individuals and groups, it is still the case that individuals in some groups will be very active, even though the group they are in has not mobilised as a collectivity to further its ends. Whereas the primary group with individuals who are quite inactive will not have networks as such (but rather loose connections between individuals), primary agents with more active individuals will have networks. The primary agents I have in mind here are fiddly job seekers and joyriders, and the networks of these primary agents will be characterised by network-specific renderings of the generic patriarchal CEP and, in the case of the fiddly job seekers, a network-specific SEP concerning the material power of the subcontractor (see Figure 6.4). No reference is made to inter-agent emergent properties as there can be no such relations between actors in different primary agents (hence Figure 6.2 only makes reference to corporate agents with regard to inter-agent networks). This is because there can only be more formalised, or more substantial, linkages between groups over time if the agents exist as self-conscious collectivities with a shared purpose and goal(s).

Intra-agent network	Inter-agent network
Relations within a primary or corporate agent, enabled and constrained by CEPs, or CEPs and SEPs unique to the agent	Relations between actors in different corporate agents affected by CEPs, or CEPs and SEPs, unique to the relationship between the actors from the different agents

Figure 6.2 Network-specific CEPs and SEPs.

Corporate agent	Intra-agent network	Inter-agent network
Community groups	CEPs (inclusive attitude applied to the community) (possibly SEPs if personal relations move to being more formalised)	SEPs (policy related) CEPs (more formalised relations)
Crime gangs	CEPs (exclusive attitude in the context of criminal power) SEPs (concerning material power over lesser members, with a clear hierarchy)	N/A

Figure 6.3 Corporate agents and networks.

Using a domain-specific meta-theory

The contents of this meta-theory are meant to serve as an underlabourer and so, in the course of empirical research, not only would specific theories be developed to interpret the data and guide actual research but, as importantly, the precepts of the domain-specific meta-theory would be open to

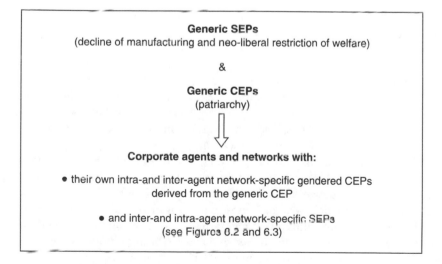

Generic SEPs
(decline of manufacturing and neo-liberal restriction of welfare)

&

Generic CEPs
(patriarchy)

Corporate agents and networks with:

• their own intra-and inter-agent network-specific gendered CEPs derived from the generic CEP

• and inter-and intra-agent network-specific SEPs
(see Figures 0.2 and 6.3)

Figure 6.4 Contexts and corporate agents.

Primary agent	Generic SEP	Intra-agent network CEP	Intra-agent network SEP
Fiddly job seekers	Patriarchy	Breadwinner and having the 'right face' (controlling private space)	Material power of sub-contractors
Joyriders	Patriarchy	Displays of power (controlling public space)	N/A

Figure 6.5 Primary agents and networks

revision. The realist ontology ought to be used in a rather Lakatosian (1993) fashion: the 'core' precepts (concerning the general ontology) will remain in place (for some time) whilst the 'outer-belt' (of precepts supplied by the domain-specific meta-theory) are revised in the course of research.

I say revised rather than falsified because whilst the (domain-specific) meta-theory is scientific in the Popperian sense of being empirically falsifiable, it is not the case that empirical testing takes complete priority over the formulation of a theory (with the testing continuing until the theory 'breaks down' and is falsified). The whole point of theoretical development is to improve the terms of reference of past theories, and whilst Popper's notion of knowledge as a searchlight, constantly being refocused to take account of past falsifications, would not be wholly antithetical to this, there is the problem that Popper places the emphasis not on building theories to take account of past failed theories (or partially true theories), but instead almost entirely on empirical testing (which is in some tension with the post-Kantian aspect of Popper's philosophy, as the emphasis swings to reality-in-itself). All of which is problematic because theories are not *ex nihilo* constructs, but are perspectives developed to take account of 'blind spots' in past theories. As we cannot step outside perspectives we need to develop perspectives via immanent critique of past theories, and via the revision of domain-specific meta-theories in the process of empirical research.

The empirical research in this case would entail using the morphogenetic cycle methodology (Archer 1995). Here we may postulate the existence of various agents and networks, and then use empirical research to study the socio-cultural interaction of actors whose agency is mediated – but not determined – by these prevailing emergent properties. The outcome would be assessed not so much in terms of morphogenesis or morphostasis, because the very act of *interpreting* the generic CEPs into network-specific CEPs, together with the *formation* of network-specific SEPs would entail morphogenesis. Further, the way in which individual actors personalised their actor-roles would entail an act of morphogenesis, and this would be on-going as actors would have to reinterpret their roles within networks in the face of changing events. (This ubiquity of change is emphasised in Archer 2000, where Archer uses the notion of an inner dialogue to explain how individuals are continually adapting themselves in the face of changed circumstances and/or reflection of continuing relations). In studying such socio-cultural morphogenesis we could ascertain to what extent the gender-specific CEPs were drawn upon by people of both sexes, and how, possibly, people from different sexes interpreted the gender CEP associated with the other sex to fit their circumstances.

There is no sense in which the mapping exercise undertaken above would be premised upon, or lead to, the sociological logic of immediacy. This is because the claims about being are constructed as starting points and not end points: the underlabourer prevents empiricist empirical research whilst avoiding the presumption of acting as a master-builder ontology. Given what has been argued above it is the case that the domain-specific meta-theory could be a useful starting point for social science research into the agency of the chronically unemployed. This research could be used to challenge the ideological 'certainties' that rest upon a spurious master-ontology, such as that cherished by ideologues.

Notes

Introduction

1 On the issue of relativism, postmodernism and social science see Callinicos 1991, Harvey 1992, Nicholson and Seidman 1996, Norris 1990, 1993, and 1997, and Sayer 2000.

1. The philosophical logic of immediacy: the epistemic fallacy and the genetic fallacy

1 Popper (1975) refers to the philosophy of mind as 'subjectivism', and against it, he argues for 'objective knowledge', which does not mean knowledge based on verified certainty, but knowledge that exists as theories. Popper argues that there are three ontologically distinct sub-worlds, which are the physical world (first world), the world of mental states (second world), and the world of theories and the possible objects of thought (third world) (1975: 154). Science concerns the third world, and scientific knowledge cannot be based on the second world. The mind cannot define the world.

2 This notion of making bold conjectures which may then be refuted *in toto* has been subject to extensive critical debate, with one argument being that it is unnecessary to reject an entire theory if part of it is falsified. Hence Lakatos (1993) draws a distinction between the 'hard core' of a research programme, and a 'protective belt', arguing that falsification of the latter does not imply falsification of the former.

3 Such theories are therefore authoritarian because if one disagrees one *must necessarily be in the wrong*. Popper does not restrict the charge of epistemic authoritarianism to Marxism and psycho-analysis though. He also argues that Bacon and Descartes put forward doctrines which set up experience and reason, respectively, as authorities (1972b: 15–17). So if every individual has the capacity for knowledge then every individual is morally guilty for ignorance and error and in need of an authority to impose 'the truth'.

4 Note that Popper does accept that scientific theories may have some metaphysical elements within them (1996: 179), and that a metaphysical theory may be developed into a falsifiable (scientific) theory (1996: 191). This does not contradict the above, because there is a major difference between having some untestable elements within a theory, and having an untestable theory. Where Popper does contradict himself, though, is where he says that methodology 'can be or, I think, even has to be, to a great extent based on realism' (1974: 966). A more ambivalent passage exists in 1996: 81, where Popper argues that whilst realism is not a presumption, it is a 'background that gives point to our search for the truth', which 'permeates' his work the *Logic of Scientific Discovery* (1972a).

5 Popper (1974; 1996) refers to the view that he is a naive falsificationist as 'the Popper Legend'; and this legend underpins most reactions to Popper's methodological writing in the critical literature.

6 Contrary to the epistemic individualism of empiricism, Popper does accept that individuals' perceptions are influenced by the prevailing norms and concepts. As regards Kuhn's list of similarities between himself and Popper, see Kuhn 1993a; 1993b. His point is that both reject positivism for an emphasis on theories and traditions, although Popper is criticised for believing that we can change framework easily, and for downplaying the way theories influence perception.

7 On the subject of paradigm change, Kuhn argued that a change would be rational during a revolution when an old paradigm was being superseded, as anomalies were recognised. It is not clear though how 'anomalies' may be recognised within a paradigm, without a stronger reference to an external reality.

8 In this book I am focusing only on Putnam's arguments about 'internal realism'. For Putnam's more recent work see Putnam 1994; 1995b; 1996. Basically, Putnam adopts a far more Wittgensteinian position, moving away from defending philosophical propositions as such. Whilst the work of Putnam which I discuss is influenced by the work of the later Wittgenstein, the later work of Putnam is more Wittgensteinian, because it seeks to eschew 'philosophical problems' altogether.

9 For an attempt to defend the God's-eye view, see Williams' (1978) discussion of Descartes. For Putnam's response to this book, see Putnam 1992b.

10 Putnam argues that there may be an implicit pluralism, as regards concepts, in Kant's work, and links the ideas on practical reason to Wittgenstein. The specifics of this argument have been avoided because the point is to describe Putnam's views on conceptual relativity and realism, rather than become side-tracked into detailed exegesis concerning Kant and Wittgenstein. For Putnam's arguments on this topic see 1991: 41–4 and 1995a: 27–52; and on Wittgenstein specifically see 1995b: 158–79.

11 As Putnam (1981: 63) notes, Kant did not explicitly say he was rejecting the correspondence theory of truth, let alone advocate a coherence theory of truth. However, Kant's epistemology is opposed to correspondence by being opposed to the similitude theory of reference.

12 This is an example of fallibilism, rather than contingency as such, because in the context of the other points, it means that we get better perspectives – we learn from our mistakes. Or in Popperian language, we learn by trial and error, making conjectures and moving on, in the light of refutations.

2. The influence of empiricism on social ontology: methodological individualism and methodological collectivism

1 Note the anti-Keynesian/interventionist flavour of his example.

2 Note that Mandelbaum (1992b) also holds that it is possible to refer to some forms of socio-historic laws without entailing reification or determinism. Such laws are referred to as 'functional' and 'abstractive'. What this means is that, taking a synchronic rather than diachronic approach, one may refer to specific elements, rather than 'global laws', saying that in certain situations, the outcome will necessarily reflect the constituent aspects of the situation. This is against holism and historicism because it is not discussing fixed general laws or temporal laws. Instead it is saying that certain specific situations will have certain specific outcomes.

3 As we will see in Chapter 5, Archer argues that social structures *qua* emergent properties are activity-dependent in the past tense.

3 Post-Wittgensteinian pragmatism: Rorty, anti-representationlism and politics

1　The term 'methodolatry' comes from Rorty 1999: xxi.
2　This critique of epistemology is similar to Putnam's arguments, and although Rorty regards Putnam as a fellow post-Wittgensteinian pragmatist, Putnam rejects the link, arguing that Rorty is a relativist. The 'debate' between them occurs mainly in scattered references in various works, although Rorty does address the issues specifically at one point: see Rorty 1993 (reprinted in 1998a: 43–62). For a defence of Putnam's view see Hartz 1991. For a reading of Putnam which agrees with me that he is a relativist, see Trigg 1989; 1993: 116–121; 1997.
3　This was pointed out to me in conversation by Professor Roger Trigg.
4　Gellner (1993: 51) criticises Popper for putting the emphasis on the difference between liberal and Stalinist states, arguing that there was no 'Big Ditch', or discontinuity, in scientific method (viz. trial and error) from ancient times to modern, except when authoritarian states perverted this tried and tested method. For Gellner this is too politically driven, and amounts to an ideological linkage of free enquiry, and scientific success, with commercial interests, or the 'free' market.
5　Here I am referring to the metaphysical realism described and defended in Chapter 1, rather than Rorty's definition of realism as an epistemic thesis.
6　For slightly different accounts of Rorty's positivism, see Bhaskar 1991: 5–23, and Harré and Krausz 1996: 204–5.
7　Note though that positivism would be opposed to determinism because determinism is a metaphysical thesis.
8　See also Hollis 1990: 247 for a similar argument.
9　The argument about truth and justice is also published in the *New Left Review* 209, cited as Geras 1995b in my bibliography.
10　On the subject of nationalism note that Rorty has often been read, by both friendly and hostile critics, as advocating an American nationalism. For an example of the former see Rée 1988a: 20, and for an example of the latter, see Billig 1993. See also Wagner 1994: 152–3, who argues that a recommendation for practising political liberalism, based on reference to contingencies which are not grounded in any substantive socio-historical explanation, is empty and amounts to Whiggish historiography.
11　Reé (1998a: 19) argues that whereas realism would base political action on fixed certainties, which cannot be attained, pragmatism would allow for intervention based upon immediate sentimentality. This however could have very illiberal results, as Reé (1998b: 10) accepts, when he says that Rorty's prioritising of politics (i.e. action) over theorising could justify the actions of a Leninist 'vanguard party' manoeuvring for power. In other words, politics without truth can lead in any direction, and to be 'pragmatic' could support the activities of those opposed to the existence of liberalism.
12　For Wittgenstein's argument against the possibility of private languages, see Wittgenstein 1995: ¶241–346.
13　On this issue see Critchley 1996: 26; Dews 1990: 112; and Geras 1995a: 47–70.
14　Whereas Critchley links this conception of harm and human nature to Rousseau's notion of *pitié*, Warren (1990) argues that by basing solidarity upon fear of harm, Rorty's argument is similar to Hobbes' conception of the reasons behind setting up the social contract.
15　On this issue see Ball 1990: 103; Bhaskar 1991: 90, 103; Laclau 1996: 64; and Warren 1990: 119–21.
16　This work of Rorty's is referred to in my text as Rorty 1992.
17　Also published in *Radical Philosophy* 59, cited as Rorty 1991 in the bibliography. This article received a critical rejoinder in *Radical Philosophy* 62, from Wilson

(1992) and Skillen (1992), who both argue that feminism necessarily implies a commitment to truth claims.

18 Cited here from Rorty 1994a: 197–202.

19 This is not to say either that God exists or does not exist, but as far as anti-representationalism is concerned, there could be no metanarrative about a non-/ superhuman moving-force.

20 The term 'text' here pertains to philosophical and political arguments as well as literary texts.

21 Mouffe (1996b: 3) notes that Rorty has a piecemeal social engineering approach to policy, but she fails to bring out the positivistic implications of this.

22 See Bell 1960 for the classical statement of the end-of-ideology position.

23 For a classical statement of pluralism, or plural elite theory, see Dahl 1956 and 1961.

4 Post-Wittgensteinian sociology: Giddens' ontology of practices

1 Marx, K. (1990) 'The Eighteenth Brumaire of Louis Bonaparte' in D. McLellan (ed.) 1990.

2 An example would be the concept of inflation. Note though that this point is rather weak, as most social science concepts are not used, even in simplified ways under different names, in lay discourse. Unless that is, one holds that the structure-agency problem is being discussed when lay agents talk of problems in getting better employment, etc., in which case the social science concepts are evacuated of meaning.

3 According to Sayer 1990, Giddens' structuration theory is very similar to the key points made by Marx, except that Marx emphasised history, whereas Giddens evacuates any historical context, producing concepts which are too abstract. Against this, Giddens (1990) replies that (a) Marx can be anything to anyone, and (b) Marxism places too much emphasis on allocative resources, meaning that it is economically reductionist and determinist. See also Giddens 1982 where, in an interview with Bleicher and Featherstone, Giddens argues that Marx's evolution-ism (like all evolutionary and teleological theories) is untenable, and that we need to 'deconstruct' historical materialism, rather than trying to reinterpret it. Such a deconstruction would mean putting the emphasis on praxis (i.e. agents' practices) rather than moving forces of history, such as necessary class struggle.

4 I am not arguing that Wittgenstein argued for a formal definition of meaning as deriving from use, as Wittgenstein would be opposed to such formal philosophical propositions, and especially such a meta-argument about the definition of meaning *per se*.

5 For more on this issue, see Giddens 1993a: 34, where he discusses the different conceptions concerning the limits of language, in the early and later works of Wittgenstein. See also Giddens 1993a: 9–48; 1993b: 59–65, where Wittgenstein's emphasis on language and practices is contrasted with structuralist and post-structuralist emphasis on linguistic signs which are divorced from agents' practices.

6 One could also argue that Winch deviated from Wittgenstein, by offering a phi-losophy/sociology that turned on formal propositions, concerning the definition of agency in terms of ideas and practices. An alternative and, arguably, more faithful rendering of Wittgenstein may be found in Pleasants' (1999) argument that in place of formal propositions we ought to shift to 'ways of seeing the world differ-ently'. One of the examples used by Pleasants is Baumans' work on the holocaust which helps us see post-Enlightenment Western European civilisation in a new way. This work then is not to be judged in epistemological terms, as providing

propositions which unlock 'the truth', but as a way of helping us see ourselves and the world in a unique way. One problem with such a view is that social and political discourse may become aestheticised, with purely subjective arguments about the beautiful people/good people being argued for in terms of rhetorical force rather than epistemic force. The sophists would replace the philosophers, when what is needed are philosophers who realise the fallibility of knowledge, rather than sophists who (ab)use the power of rhetoric.

7 As many have pointed out, it was naive for Durkheim to accept suicide statistics as a valid and reliable indicator given the difficulty of ascertaining the individuals' intention, the different national criteria for defining a death as suicide, and the impact of religion, influencing some to make a suicide look like accidental death. More importantly though, Durkheim could not avoid reference to individuals. He discussed how a suicidogenic current, such as lack of integration (or 'egoism') may result in suicide amongst educated Protestants, but the only way to explain why not all members of a group affected by a suicidogenic current committed suicide was to say that some individuals were 'suicide prone'. Which, as Lukes (1992: 214–15) argues, introduces a social psychology, connecting individuals' mental states to a broader social context.

8 In other words, Giddens is making the same criticisms of methodological individualism that were discussed in Chapter 3.

9 See also Archer 1982; 1990; 1993; 1996a; 1996b.

10 Layder (1994: 141) has a similar point, arguing that Giddens' attempt to resolve the structure-agency problematic ends up 'resolving' his own agency-based problematic which prioritises agency over structure, by changing the meaning of structure.

11 This is simplifying Archer's discussion slightly, but the point is to say that informal practices can be objective constraints, rather than pre-empting a full discussion of Archer's ontology.

12 Problems similar to those discussed in this section on rules also arise when considering resources. One follower of Giddens, Sewell (1992), realises the problem in arguing that resources are virtual until instantiated. His response is to argue that resources, quite simply, are not virtual until instantiated, and, further, he admits that formal rules have such a 'real' existence too, which leads him to reclassify formal rules as resources. Archer (1995: 109) criticises this, pointing out that resources, unlike formal rules, can be procured in different amounts by different individuals. She also argues that Sewell cannot sustain an argument for the duality of structure because his argument that the actual and the virtual are mutually dependent fails to say how this is so, without making one side of the equation epiphenomenal (Archer 1995: 110–14). For a defence of Lockwood, which argues that he, unlike more contemporary thinkers such as Giddens, does adequately connect structure and agency, see Mouzelis 1997.

13 So to use a micro–macro dichotomy would result in a subject–object dualism, whereby the social object was divorced from the individual subject, which is not to say that defining structure and agency as emergent properties – and therefore *not* as a duality results in a subject–object divide, because an emergent properties ontology can link structure and agency. It is misleading therefore, as Archer (1995: 7) points out, to claim, as Layder (1994: 3) does, that the micro–macro, agency-structure, and individual–society distinctions are the same.

14 See also New 1994, who regards Giddens and Bhaskar as holding very similar ontologies.

15 Baert (1998) holds that Bhaskar's ontology is very similar to Giddens', but he says that they differ as regards the definition of structure (1998: 196–7). This, as Archer (1995) argues, though, is the key point: realists such as Archer and Bhaskar define structures as emergent properties, whilst Giddens eschews any notion of emergence.

5 Social realism: overcoming the sociological logic of immediacy

1 This is not to say that only Archer has developed the work of critical – or social – realism's founding figure, Roy Bhaskar, but Margaret Archer is the person who has done the most to develop a social ontology based upon Bhaskar's works which, vitally, includes showing how Bhaskar's realism is different from Giddens' structuration theory.

2 Given that my concern is primarily with social realism the following section, on Bhaskar's philosophy of natural science, will be rather schematic. My purpose is simply to note the contours of his realist philosophy rather than get drawn into technical debates in the philosophy of science; which lack of space precludes anyway.

3 See also Bhaskar 1986: 28–33; 1993: 16; 1998: 9.

4 Note that positivism and post-Kantianism are treated as 'ideal-types' by Bhaskar, who argues that elements of both exist in many philosophies (1997: 26).

5 This is an ideal-typical example of deductivism. Variations on this model go under the following rubrics: the covering-law model, the deductive-nominological model, and the hypothico-deductive model.

6 I take this example from Sayer 1992: 170.

7 See also 1998: 6.

8 Realism has been known as 'critical naturalism' and 'critical realism', with the latter being a popular current term. I prefer 'social realism' because the 'critical' in critical realism has two meanings and, in this book, I am only concerned with the first. The first meaning pertains to the fallibilism of knowledge, and stresses the need to always seek better knowledge claims. The second meaning of critical pertains to the fact–value argument, and the view espoused by Bhaskar, and others, that value conclusions can be derived from factual premises. These two meanings may be mutually exclusive, given that in order to derive value judgements from factual premises one needs some form of epistemic certainty about the facts, to prevent a plurality of necessary but potentially mutually exclusive value commitments. In other words, one would have gone from the transitive realm to the intransitive realm to ground one's values. On the issue of the fact–value argument in relation to realism, see part 3 in Archer *et al.* (eds) 1998; Collier 1999; Dandeker 1983; Lacey 1997; Sayer 1998 and 2000 (part 4); and for a pragmatist argument against drawing normative conclusions from factual premises see Rorty 1999.

9 This 'dialectical position' is similar to some aspects of Giddens' social ontology, which manages to over-emphasise both individuals' agency, and the social object against the agent / subject.

10 For a similar critique of Berger and Luckmann, see Layder 1994: 88–9.

11 As Sayer (1992: 122–3) notes, we can distinguish intrinsic and extrinsic conditions of closure. The former pertains to the internal coherence of, say, a group or institution (with all the people involved pursuing the same goal, or working consistently towards a single end). The latter pertains to relations between a group and other groups together with the prevailing structural context. Although regularity may occur, the existence of free will, together with unintended consequences, we may note, means that closure will be, at best, ephemeral. That is, there will be no closed social systems even if regularity does obtain in some areas for a short while. Social continuity may by definition involve regular patterns of action, but we are to understand this in terms of a contingent correlation, caused by a particular combination of decisions, actions and structural constraints and enablements. Causality is understandable in terms of unobserved structural factors conditioning agency, which will have contingent outcomes, rather than in terms of putatively indefinitely occurring correlations *per se*.

12 On this see Durkheim 1994.

13 As regards the third ontological limitation, concerning the point that social structures are only relatively enduring, Benton (1981: 18) argues that the same is true for natural structures. Bhaskar's reply accepts this in a qualified way. He argues that '[t]he relevant difference is that [historicity, i.e. change] is far faster and (e.g. in cities) denser than is normally the case in nature' (1998: 175).

14 First edition originally published in 1979 by Harvester Wheatsheaf (Brighton).

15 Originally published in 1989.

16 1997: 157.

17 Fay is responding to an article by Isaac (1990), but the points made are of general relevance.

18 A similar critique which deals with the ontology of human being, specifically, the notion of agency being essentialist, is made by Pleasants (1997). For a detailed account and defence of agency and human being, see Archer 2000.

6 Social realism and the study of chronic unemployment

1 As Crompton (1993: 50–3) argues, though, identifying class in terms of occupations can be problematic. Crompton argues that occupational class schemes fail to grasp inequality, and fail to comprehend the nature of class relations. A list of occupations tells one very little about capitalism and the way it results in social stratification, and thus one is told virtually nothing about the formation of class and the relationship between classes.

2 See also MacDonald 1996, where he argues that those who are self-employed in economically depressed areas are not the entrepreneurial stereotype described by the New Right, who create jobs and wealth by 'working harder' than others. They are people who use state assistance to become self-employed to escape long-term unemployment, and most of these new businesses will fold in the short-term. There was no long-term boost to the local economy. Rather, some people took an alternative to fiddly jobs, using some form of state assistance to try and survive on the economic margins.

3 See Becker 1997 for a discussion of policy-related issues on this topic.

Bibliography

Alexander, J. (1987) 'Action and its environments' in J. Alexander, B. Giesen, R. Munch and N. J. Smelser (eds) *The micro-macro link*. Berkeley: University of California.

Ansell-Pearson, K. (1994) *An introduction to Nietzsche as political thinker: the perfect nihilist*. Cambridge: Cambridge University Press.

Archer, M. (1982) 'Morphogenesis versus structuration: on combining structure and action'. *The British Journal of Sociology* 33, 4: 455–79.

Archer, M. (1990a) 'Human agency and social structure: a critique of Giddens' in J. Clark, C. Modgil and S. Modgil (eds) 1990, 73–84. See also Outhwaite's reply to Archer, ibid., 85–6.

Archer, M. (1990b) 'Archer replies to Outhwaite' in J. Clark, C. Modgil and S. Modgil (eds) 1990, 85–6.

Archer, M. (1993) 'Taking time to link structure and agency' in H. Martins (ed.), *Knowledge and passion: essays in honour of John Rex*. London: Routledge.

Archer, M. (1995) *Realist social theory: the morphogenetic approach*. Cambridge: Cambridge University Press.

Archer, M. (1996a) *Culture and agency: the place of culture in social theory*. Revised ed. Cambridge: Cambridge University Press.

Archer, M. (1996b) 'Social integration and system integration: developing the distinction'. *Sociology* 30, 4: 679–99.

Archer, M., Bhaskar, R., Collier, A., Lawson, T. and Norrie, A. (eds) (1998) *Critical realism: essential readings*. London: Routledge.

Archer, M. (2000) *Being human: the problem of agency*. Cambridge: Cambridge University Press.

Baert, P. (1998) *Social theory in the twentieth century*. Cambridge: Polity Press.

Bagguley, P. and Mann, K. (1992) 'Idle, thieving bastards? Scholarly representations of the "underclass"'. *Work, Employment and Society* 6, 1: 113–26.

Ball, T. (1990) 'Review symposium on Richard Rorty'. *History of the Human Sciences* 3, 1: 101–4.

Baudrillard, J. (1983) *Simulations*. P. Foss, P. Patton and P. Beitchman trans. New York: Semiotext(e).

Becker, S. (1997) *Responding to poverty: the politics of cash and care*. London: Longman.

Bell, D. (1960) *The end of ideology*. New York: Collins.

Benton, T. (1981) 'Realism and social science: some comments on Roy Bhaskar's "The Possibility of Naturalism"'. *Radical Philosophy* 27: 13–21.

Berger, P. and Luckmann, T. (1991) *The social construction of reality: a treatise in the sociology of knowledge*. London: Penguin.

Berkeley, G. (1929) *Essay, principles, dialogues, with selections from other writings*. M. W. Calkins ed. New York: Scribners.

Bhaskar, R. (1983) 'Beef, structure and place: notes from a critical naturalist perspective'. *Journal for the Theory of Social Behaviour* 13: 81–95.

Bhaskar, R. (1986) *Scientific realism and human emancipation*. London: Verso.

Bhaskar, R. (1991) *Philosophy and the idea of freedom*. Oxford: Basil Blackwell.

Bhaskar, R. (1993) *Reclaiming reality: a critical introduction to contemporary philosophy*. London: Verso.

Bhaskar, R. (1997) *A realist theory of science*. 2nd ed. London: Verso.

Bhaskar, R. (1998) *The possibility of naturalism: a philosophical critique of the contemporary human sciences*. 3rd ed. London: Routledge.

Billig, M. (1993) 'Nationalism and Richard Rorty: the text as a flag for *pax Americana*'. *New Left Review* 202: 69–83.

Bonefeld, W. Gunn, R. and Psychopedis, K. (eds) (1992) *Open Marxism. Vol. 1. Dialectics and history*. London: Pluto.

Brodbeck, M. (ed.) (1969) *Readings in the philosophy of the social sciences*. London: Macmillan.

Bryant, C. G. A. and Jary, D. (eds) (1991a) *Giddens' theory of structuration: a critical appreciation*. London: Routledge.

Bryant, C. G. A. and Jary, D. (1991b) 'Introduction: coming to terms with Anthony Giddens' in C. G. A. Bryant and D. Jary (eds) 1991a, 1–31.

Callinicos, A. (1991) *Against postmodernism: a Marxist critique*. Cambridge: Polity.

Campbell, B. (1993) *Goliath: Britain's dangerous places*. London: Methuen.

Chomsky, N. (1989) *Necessary illusions: thought control in democratic society*. London: Pluto.

Clark, J. Modgil, C. and Modgil, S. (eds) (1990) *Anthony Giddens: consensus and controversy*. London: Falmer.

Cohen. I. (1989) *Structuration theory: Anthony Giddens and the constitution of social life*. Basingstoke: Macmillan.

Cohen, I. (1990) 'Structuration theory and social order: five issues in brief' in J. Clark, C. Modgil and S. Modgil (eds) 1990, 33–45.

Collier, A. (1994) *Critical realism: an introduction to Roy Bhaskar's philosophy*. London: Verso.

Collier, A. (1999) *Being and worth*. London: Routledge.

Connolly, W. E. (1990) 'Review symposium on Richard Rorty'. *History of the Human Sciences* 3, 1: 104–8.

Corvi, R. (1997) *An introduction to the thought of Karl Popper*. P. Camiller trans. London: Routledge.

Craib. I. (1992a) *Modern social theory: from Parsons to Habermas*. 2nd ed. London: Harvester Wheatsheaf.

Craib, I. (1992b) *Anthony Giddens*. London: Routledge.

Critchley, S. (1996) 'Deconstruction and pragmatism – is Derrida a private ironist or a public liberal?' in C. Mouffe (ed.) 1996a, 19–40.

Crompton, R. (1993) *Class and stratification: an introduction to contemporay debates*. Cambridge: Polity.

Dahl, R. (1956) *A preface to democratic theory*. Chicago: Chicago University Press.

Dahl, R. (1961) *Who governs?* New Haven: Yale University Press.

Dahrendorf, R. (1987) 'The erosion of citizenship'. *New Statesman* 12 June: 12–15.

Dandeker, C. (1983) 'Theory and practice in sociology: the critical imperatives of realism'. *Journal for the Theory of Social Behaviour* 13, 2: 195–210.

Descartes, R. (1986) *Discourse on method and the meditations*. F. E. Sutcliffe trans. and intro. Harmondsworth: Penguin.

Dews, P., in T. Ball, W. E. Connolly and P. Dews (1990) 'Review Symposium on Richard Rorty'. *History of the Human Sciences* 3, 1: 101–22.

Durkheim, E. (1993a) *The rules of sociological method and selected texts on sociology and its method*. W. D. Halls trans. S. Lukes Ed. and intro. Basingstoke: Macmillan.

Durkheim, E. (1993b) *Suicide: a study in sociology*. J. A. Spaulding trans. G. Simpson trans. and intro. London: Routledge.

Durkheim, E. (1994) *The division of labour in society*. W. D. Halls trans. L. Coser intro. London: Macmillan.

Durkheim, E. (1995) *The elementary forms of religious life*. K. E. Field trans. and intro. New York: Free Press.

Fay, B. (1990) 'Critical realism?' *Journal for the Theory of Social Behaviour* 20, 1: 33–41.

Featherstone, M. (1982) 'Symposium on Giddens'. Theory, Culture and Society 1, 2: 63–106.

Fraser, N. (1990) 'Solidarity or singularity? Richard Rorty between romanticism and technocracy' in A. R. Malachowski (ed.) 1990, 303–21.

Gans, H. J. (1993) 'From "underclass" to "undercaste": some observations about the future of the postindustrial economy and its major victims'. *International Journal of Urban and Regional Research* 17: 327–35.

Gellner, E. (1969) 'Holism versus individualism' in M. Brodbeck (ed.) 1969, 254–68.

Gellner, E. (1993) *Postmodernism, reason and religion*. London: Routledge.

Geras, N. (1995a) *Solidarity in the conversation of humankind: the ungroundable liberalism of Richard Rorty* London: Verso.

Geras, N. (1995b) 'Language, truth and justice'. *New Left Review* 209: 110–35.

Giddens, A. (1973) *The class structure of the advanced societies*. London: Hutchinson.

Giddens, A. (1976) *New rules of sociological method: a positive critique of interpretative sociologies*. London: Hutchinson.

Giddens, A. (1982) 'Historical materialism today: an interview with Anthony Giddens'. *Theory, Culture and Society* 1, 2: 107–13 (Interview with J. Bleicher and M. Featherstone.)

Giddens, A. (1990) 'Structuration theory and sociological analysis' in J. Clark, C. Modgil and S. Modgil (eds) 1990, 297–315.

Giddens, A. (1991a) 'Structuration theory: past, present and future' in C. G. A. Bryant and D. Jary (eds) 1991a, 201–21.

Giddens, A. (1991b) 'A reply to my critics' in D. Held and J. B. Thompson (eds) 1991, 249–301.

Giddens, A. (1993a) *Central problems in social theory: action, structure and contradiction in social analysis*. London: Macmillan.

Giddens, A. (1993b) *Social theory and modern sociology*. Cambridge: Polity.

Giddens, A. (1995a) *The constitution of society: outline of the theory of structuration*. Cambridge: Polity.

Giddens, A. (1995b) *The consequences of modernity*. Cambridge: Polity.

Giddens, A. (1995c) *Politics, sociology and social theory: encounters with classical and contemporary social thought*. Cambridge: Polity

Goldstein, L. J. (1992) 'Two theses of methodological individualism' in J. O'Neill (ed.) 1992, 277–86.

Gunn, R. (1988) 'Marxism and philosophy: a critique of critical realism'. *Capital and Class* 37: 87–116.

Harding, S. (1996) 'Standpoint epistemology (a feminist version): how social disadvantage creates epistemic advantage' in S. P. Turner (ed.) *Social theory and sociology: the classics and beyond*. Oxford: Blackwell.

Harre, R. and Krausz, M. (1996) *Varieties of relativism*. Oxford: Basil Blackwell.

Hartz, C. G. (1991) 'What Putnam should have said: an alternative reply to Rorty'. *Erkenntnis* 34: 287–95.

Harvey, D. (1992) *The condition of postmodernity: an enquiry into the origins of cultural change*. Oxford: Blackwell.

Held, D. and Thompson, J. B. (eds) (1991) *Social theory of modern societies: Anthony Giddens and his critics*. Cambridge: Cambridge University Press.

Hollis, M. (1990) 'The poetics of personhood' in A. R. Malachowski (ed.) 1990, 244–56.

Hume, D. (1963) *Enquiries concerning the human understanding and concerning the principles of morals*. 2nd ed. L. A. Selby-Bigge ed. and intro. Oxford: Clarendon.

Isaac, J. C. (1990) 'Realism and reality: some realistic reconsiderations'. *Journal for the Theory of Social Behaviour* 20, 1: 1–31.

Kant, I. (1965) *Critique of pure reason*. N. K. Smith trans. New York: St. Martin's Press.

Kant, I. (1992) *Political writings*. H. Reiss ed. Cambridge: Cambridge University Press.

Kuhn, T. (1970) *The structure of scientific revolutions*. 2nd ed. London: University of Chicago.

Kuhn, T. (1993a). 'Logic of discovery or psychology of research?' in I. Lakatos and A. Musgrave (eds) 1993, 1–23.

Kuhn, T. (1993b). 'Reflections on my critics' in I. Lakatos and A. Musgrave (eds) 1993, 231–78.

Lacey, H. (1997) 'Neutrality in the social sciences: on Bhaskar's argument for an essential emancipatory impulse in social science'. *Journal for the Theory of Social Behaviour* 27, 2: 213–41.

Laclau, E. (1996) 'Deconstruction, pragmatism, and hegemony' in C. Mouffe (ed.) 1996a, 47–67.

Lakatos, I. (1993) 'Falsificationism and the methodology of scientific research programmes' in I. Lakatos and A. Musgrave (eds) 1993, 91–196.

Lakatos, I. and Musgrave, A. (ed.) (1993) *Criticism and the growth of knowledge*. Cambridge: Cambridge University Press.

Layder, D. (1985) 'Beyond empiricism? The promise of realism'. *Philosophy of the Social Sciences* 15, 3: 255–74.

Layder, D. (1994) *Understanding social theory*. London: Sage.

Locke, J. (1988) *An essay concerning human understanding*. J. W. Yolton ed. and intro. London: Everyman.

Lukes, S. (1968) 'Methodological individualism reconsidered'. *British Journal of Sociology* 19, 2: 119–29.

Lukes, S. (1992) *Emile Durkheim, his life and work: a historical and critical study*. London: Penguin.

MacDonald, R. (1994) 'Fiddly jobs, undeclared working and the something for nothing society'. *Work, Employment and Society* 8, 4: 507–30.

MacDonald, R. (1996) 'Welfare dependency, the enterprise culture and self-employed survival'. *Work, Employment and Society* 10, 4: 431–47.

Macnicol, J. (1987) 'In pursuit of the underclass'. *Journal of Social Policy* 16, 3: 293–318.

Magil, K. (1994) 'Against critical realism'. *Capital and Class* 54: 113–36.

Malachowski, A. R. (1990) (ed.) *Reading Rorty: critical responses to philosophy and the mirror of nature (and beyond)*. Oxford: Blackwell.

Mandelbaum, M. (1992a) 'Societal facts' in J. O'Neill (ed.) 1992, 221–34.

Mandelbaum, M. (1992b) 'Societal laws' in J. O'Neill (ed.) 1992, 235–47.

May, T. (1998) *Social research: issues, methods and process*. 2nd ed. Buckingham: Open University Press.

McLellan, D. (1990) ed. and intro. *Karl Marx: selected writings*.

Mills, C. W. (1967) *The sociological imagination*. Oxford: Oxford University Press.

Morris, L. (1994) *Dangerous classes: the underclass and social citizenship*. London: Routledge.

Morris, L. (1995) *Social divisions: economic decline and social structural change*. London: UCL Press.

Morris, L. and Irwin, S. (1992a) 'Employment histories and the concept of the underclass'. *Sociology* 26, 3: 401–20.

Morris, L. and Irwin, S. (1992b). 'Unemployment and informal support: dependency, exclusion, or participation?' *Work, Employment and Society* 6, 2: 185–207.

Mouffe, C. (1996a) (ed.) *Deconstruction and pragmatism*. London: Routledge.

Mouffe, C. (1996b) 'Deconstruction, pragmatism and the politics of democracy' in C. Mouffe (ed.). 1996a, 1–12.

Mouzelis, N. (1989). 'Restructuring structuration theory'. *Sociological Review* 37, 4. 617–635.

Mouzelis, N. (1995) *Sociological theory: what went wrong?* London: Routledge.

Mouzelis, N. (1997) 'Social and system integration: Lockwood, Habermas, Giddens'. *Sociology* 31, 1: 111–19.

Murray, C. (1984) *Losing ground: American social policy 1950–1980*. New York: Basic Books.

Murray, C. (1990) *The emerging British underclass* (Choice in Welfare Series No. 2). London: Health and Welfare Unit, Institute of Economic Affairs.

New, C. (1994) 'Structure, agency and social transformation'. *Journal for the Theory of Social Behaviour* 24, 3: 187–205.

New, C. (1995) 'Sociology and the case for realism'. *Sociological Review* 43, 4: 808–27.

Nicholson, L. and Seidman, S. (eds) (1996) *Social postmodernism: beyond identity politics*. Cambridge: Cambridge University Press.

Norris, C. (1990) *What's wrong with postmodernism: critical theory and the ends of philosophy*. London: Harvester Wheatsheaf.

Norris, C. (1993) 'Old themes for New Times: Basildon revisited'. *Socialist Register* 29 ('Real problems false solutions'). London: Merlin.

Norris, C. (1997) *Against relativism: philosophy of science, deconstruction and critical theory*. Oxford: Blackwells.

O'Neill, J. (ed.) (1992) *Modes of individualism and collectivism*. Aldershot: Gregg Revivals.

Outhwaite, W. (1987) *New philosophies of social science: realism, hermeneutics and critical theory*. London: Macmillan.

Outhwaite, W. (1990) 'Agency and structure' in J. Clark, C. Modgil and S. Modgil (eds) 1990, 63–72. See also Archer's reply, ibid., 86–8.

Pilger, J. (1998) *Hidden agendas*. London: Vintage.

Pleasants, N. (1997) 'Free to act otherwise? A Wittgensteinian deconstruction of the concept of agency in contemporary social and political theory'. *History of the Human Sciences* 10, 4: 1–28.

Pleasants, N. (1999) *Wittgenstein and the idea of a critical social theory: a critique of Giddens, Habermas and Bhaskar*. London: Routledge.

Popper, K. (1962) *The open society and its enemies volume two. The high tide of prophecy: Hegel, Marx, and the aftermath*. London: Routledge and Kegan Paul.

Popper, K. (1972a) *The logic of scientific discovery*. London: Hutchinson.

Popper, K. (1972b) *Conjectures and refutations: the growth of scientific knowledge*. 4th ed. London: Routledge.

Popper, K. (1974) 'Replies to my critics' in *The philosophy of Karl Popper*. P. A. Schilpp ed. La Salle, IL: Open Court.

Popper, K. (1975) *Objective knowledge: an evolutionary approach*. Oxford: Oxford University Press.

Popper, K. (1989) *The poverty of historicism*. London: Routledge.

Popper, K. (1993) 'Normal science and its dangers' in I. Lakatos and A. Musgrave (eds) 1993, 51–8.

Popper, K. (1996) *Realism and the aim of science (postscript to the logic of scientific discovery vol. 1)*. W. W. Bartley ed. London: Routledge.

Putnam, H. (1981) *Reason, truth and history*. Cambridge: Cambridge University Press.

Putnam, H. (1991) *The many faces of realism*. La Salle, IL: Open Court.

Putnam, H. (1992a) *Realism with a human face*. J. Conant ed. and intro. London: Harvard University Press.

Putnam, H. (1992b) *Renewing philosophy*. London: Harvard University Press.

Putnam, H. (1994) Dewey lectures. 'Sense, nonsense and the senses: an enquiry into the powers of the human mind'. *The Journal of Philosophy* 91, 9: 445–517.

Putnam, H. (1995a). *Pragmatism: an open question*. Oxford: Blackwell.

Putnam, H. (1995b) *Words and life*. J. Conant ed. and intro. London: Harvard University Press.

Putnam, H. (1996) 'On Wittgenstein's philosophy of mathematics'. *Proceedings of the Aristotelian Society* 70: 243–64.

Rée, J. (1998a) 'Rorty's nation'. *Radical Philosophy* 87: 18–21.

Rée, J. (1998b) 'Strenuous unbelief' [review of R. T. Rorty (1998) *Achieving our country* and *Truth and progress*]. *London Review of Books* 20, 20: 7–11.

Rorty, R. (1982) *Consequences of pragmatism: essays 1972–1980*. Brighton: Harvester.

Rorty, R. (1987) 'Thugs and theorists: a reply to Bernstein'. *Political Theory* 15, 4: 564–80.

Rorty, R. (1991) 'Feminism and pragmatism'. *Radical Philosophy* 59: 3–14.

Rorty, R. (1992) *Contingency, irony and solidarity*. Cambridge: Cambridge University Press.

Rorty, R. (1993) 'Putnam and the relativist menace'. *The Journal of Philosophy* 90, 9: 443–61.

Rorty, R. (1994a) *Objectivity, relativism and truth: philosophical papers vol. 1*. Cambridge: Cambridge University Press.

Rorty, R. (1994b) *Philosophy and the mirror of nature*. Oxford: Blackwell.

Rorty, R. (1996a) 'Remarks on deconstruction and pragmatism' in C. Mouffe (ed.) 1996a, 13–18.

Rorty, R. (1996b) 'Response to Simon Critchley' in C. Mouffe (ed.) 1996a, 41–6.

Rorty, R. (1998a) *Truth and progress: philosophical papers vol. 3*. Cambridge: Cambridge University Press.

Rorty, R. (1998b) *Achieving our country: leftist thought in the twentieth century*. London: Harvard University.

Rorty, R. (1999) *Philosophy and social hope*. London: Penguin.

Rutter, M. and Madge, N. (1976) *Cycles of disadvantage*. London: Heinemann.

Sayer, D. (1990) 'Reinventing the wheel: Anthony Giddens, Karl Marx and social change' in J. Clark, C. Modgil and S. Modgil (eds) 1990, 235–50.

Sayer, A. (1992) *Method in social science: a realist approach*. 2nd ed. London: Routledge.

Sayer, A. (1997) 'Essentialism, social constructionism, and beyond'. *The Sociological Review* 45, 3: 453–87.

Sayer, A. (1998) 'Critical realism and the limits to critical social science'. *Journal for the Theory of Social Behaviour* 27, 4: 473–88.

Sayer, A. (2000) *Realism and social science*. London: Sage.

Searle, J. R. (1995) *The social construction of reality*. London: Allen Lane.

Sewell, W. H. (1992) 'A theory of structure: duality, agency, and transformation'. *American Journal of Sociology* 98, 1: 1–29.

Shotter, J. (1992) 'Is Bhaskar's critical realism only a theoretical realism?' [review of R. Bhaskar (1991) *Philosophy and the idea of freedom*]. *History of the Human Sciences* 5, 3: 157–73.

Shusterman, R. (1988) 'Postmodern aestheticism: a new moral philosophy'. *Theory, Culture and Society* (special issue on postmodernism) 5, 2–3: 337–55.

Skillen, T. (1992) 'Richard Rorty: knight errant'. *Radical Philosophy* 62: 24–6.

Stanley, L. and Wise, S. (1983) *Breaking out: feminist consciousness and feminist research*. London: Routledge.

Thompson, J. B. (1991) 'The theory of structuration' in D. Held and J. B. Thompson (eds) 1991, 56–76.

Trigg, R. (1989) *Reality at risk: a defence of realism in philosophy and the sciences*. 2nd ed. Hemel Hempstead: Harvester.

Trigg, R. (1993) *Rationality and science: can science explain everything?* Oxford: Basil Blackwell.

Trigg, R. (1997) 'The grounding of reason'. Inaugural address for the Aristotelian society at the University of Warwick (July 1997). *Proceedings of the Aristotelian Society* 71: 1–17.

Wagner, H. (1964) 'Displacement of scope: a problem of the relationship between small-scale and large-scale sociological theories'. *American Journal of Sociology* 69, 6: 571–84.

Wagner, P. (1994) *A sociology of modernity: liberty and discipline*. London: Routledge.

Warren, M. E. (1990) 'Review symposium on Richard Rorty'. *History of the Human Sciences* 3, 1: 118–22.

Watkins, J. W. N. (1992a) 'Historical explanation in the social sciences' in J. O'Neill (ed.) 1992, 166–178. (Originally published as 'Methodological individualism and social tendencies' in M. Brodbeck (ed.) 1969, 269–80).

Watkins, J. W. N. (1992b) 'Ideal types and historical explanation' in J. O'Neill (ed.) 1992, 143–65.

Watkins, J. W. N. (1992c) 'Methodological individualism: a reply' in J. O'Neill (ed.) 1992, 179–84.

Williams, B. (1978) *Descartes: the project of pure enquiry*. Hassocks: Harvester.

Willis, P. (1977) *Learning to labour*. Farnborough: Saxon House.

Wilson, C. (1992) 'How did the dinosaurs die out? How did the poets survive?' *Radical Philosophy* 62: 20–4.

Wilson, W. J. (1987) *The truly disadvantaged: the inner city, the underclass, and public policy*. London: Chicago University Press.

Wilson, W. J. (1991) 'Studying inner-city social dislocations: the challenge of public agenda research. 1990 presidential address. *American Sociological Review* 56: 1–14.

Winch, P. (1990) *The idea of a social science and its relation to philosophy.* 2nd ed. London: Routledge.

Wisdom, J. O. (1974) 'The nature of "normal" science' in P. A. Schlipp (ed.) *The philosophy of Karl Popper*, vol. 2. La Salle, IL: Open Court.

Wittgenstein, L. (1995) *Philosophical investigations.* 3rd ed. G. E. M. Anscombe trans. Oxford: Basil Blackwell.

Index